STUDIES IN ETHNOME
AND CONVERSATION ANALYSIS
No. 4

STEPHEN HESTER and PETER EGLIN

CULTURE
IN ACTION

Studies in Membership
Categorization Analysis

1997

University Press of America

Washington, D.C.

Copyright © 1997 by
International Institute for Ethnomethodology
and
University Press of America,® Inc.
4720 Boston Way
Lanham, Maryland 20706

3 Henrietta Street
London, WC2E 8LU England

Co-published by arrangement with the International Institute for
Ethnomethodology and Conversation Analysis

Library of Congress Cataloging-in-Publication Data

Culture in action : studies in membership categorization analysis /
edited by Stephen Hester and Peter Eglin.
p.   cm.--(Studies in ethnomethodology and conversation analysis ; no.
4)
Includes bibliographical references and index.
l. Conversation analysis. I. Hester, Stephen. II. Eglin, Peter III.
Series.
P95.45.C85 1997   302.3'46--dc20   96-46051 CIP

ISBN 0-7618-0583-4 (cloth: alk. ppr.)
ISBN 0-7618-0584-2 (pbk: alk. ppr.)

Studies in Ethnomethodology and
Conversation Analysis

is co-published by the

International Institute for Ethnomethodology
and
Conversation Analysis

&

University Press of America, Inc.

iii

Acknowledgments

Special thanks are due to George Psathas for his encouragement and support of this project. We are also grateful to Claire Davis for her expert assistance in preparing the manuscript for publication.

Stephen Hester & Peter Eglin, June 1996

Authors

Stephen Hester received his BA and PhD in Sociology from the University of Kent, Canterbury. Formerly Associate Professor at Wilfrid Laurier University, he is currently Senior Lecturer in Sociology at the University of Wales, Bangor. His research interests are in ethnomethodology and conversation analysis, deviance and education. His publications include *Deviance in Classrooms* (1975, with David Hargreaves and Frank Mellor), *A Sociology of Crime* (1992, with Peter Eglin) and *Referral Talk: The Local Order of Deviance in School* (forthcoming).

Peter Eglin received his BA from University College London and PhD from the University of British Columbia. Since 1976 he has taught at Wilfrid Laurier University where he is currently Associate Professor in Sociology. In his research he combines interests in ethnomethodology with critical inquiry into human rights. His publications include *Talk and Taxonomy* (1980) and *A Sociology of Crime* (1992, with Stephen Hester).

Rod Watson received his BA and MA in Sociology from the University of Leicester and his PhD from the University of Warwick. He has published extensively in English and French in the spheres of ethnomethodology, conversation analysis, ethnography and sociological theory. He is currently Francqui Inter-University Professor in the Human Sciences, Belgium (1995-96), and has recently held visiting professorships for shorter periods at the École des Hautes Études en Sciences Sociales, Marseille, France and at the University of Montana, USA. On his return to the Victoria University of Manchester he resumes his Readership in Sociology.

Carolyn D Baker received her BA, MA and PhD from the University of Toronto. She is currently Reader in the Graduate School of Education at The University of Queensland, Brisbane, Australia. In her research she has applied ethnomethodological and conversation analytic approaches to the analysis of texts and talk, primarily in the field of education. She has published extensively on early literacy materials and methods, including co-authorship with Peter Freebody of *Children's First School Books: Introductions to the Culture of Literacy,* (1989), and co-editorship with Allan Luke of *Towards a Critical sociology of Reading Pedagogy.*

Michael Lynch received his BS at Cornell University and his PhD from the University of California at Irvine. He is currently Professor of Sociology in the Department of Human Sciences at Brunel University, West London. His ethnomethodological research focuses on discourse and practical actions in the natural sciences and other specialised settings. His books include *Art and Artifact in Laboratory Science* (1985), *Representations in Scientific Practice* (1990, with Steve Woolgar), *Scientific Practice and Ordinary Action: Ethnomethodology and Social Studies of Science* (1993), and, with David Bogen, *The Spectacle of History: Speech, Text, and Memory at the Iran-Contra Hearings* (1996).

David Bogen is Assistant Professor of Sociology at Emerson College in Boston, Massachusetts. He received his MA and PhD from Boston University. He is the author (with Michael Lynch) of *The Spectacle of History: Speech, Text, and Memory at the Iran-Contra Hearings* (1996) and of *Order Without Rules: Critical Theory and the Logic of Conversation* (forthcoming). His current research focuses on the relationship between ethnomethodology and technology design.

David Francis obtained his BEd and his PhD at the University of Manchester. he has taught at Manchester Metropolitan University (formerly Manchester Polytechnic) since 1976 where he is currently Senior Lecturer in Sociology. His research interests are in the field of ethnomethodology, conversation analysis, work and organizations and social interaction in educational settings. he is co-author, with Ted Cuff and Wes Sharrock, of *Perspectives in Sociology* (1990).

Christopher Hart gained his BA and his PhD at Manchester Metropolitan University. He is currently Senior Lecturer and Research Director in the School of Information Studies at the University of Central England. His research interests are in ethnomethodological studies of the media and the social construction of images.

Contents

Chapter One

Membership Categorization Analysis: An Introduction

Stephen Hester and Peter Eglin

Our aims in this introduction are firstly to outline the key concepts and methods in membership categorization analysis as established by Harvey Sacks. Secondly we review the development of the field since Sacks through its principal studies. Thirdly we seek to specify the *ethnomethodological* character of membership categorization analysis and thereby to differentiate it from ostensibly cognate modes of inquiry outside of ethnomethodology. These include cognitive anthropology and linguistics. Fourthly we introduce the studies contained in this collection.

The Conceptual Framework of Membership Categorization Analysis

Ethnomethodology (EM) is, above all else, a policy towards inquiry, an analytic mentality, that insists on (1) doing studies, by (2) working on materials to see what can be discovered in and from them, rather than selecting problems and data on the basis of some theoretically-specified agenda (Sharrock and Watson 1989: 434-435). In this way it is homologous with its own subject matter, namely social order as the ongoing achievement of members of society conceived as practical actors who are themselves (1) practical analysts of, and inquirers into, the world, (2) using whatever materials there are to hand to get done the tasks and business they are engaged in. Insofar as members' tasks, business and inquiries are overwhelmingly, inescapably and irremediably carried out in language, especially talk, EM's own inquiries find themselves unavoidably taken up with the analysis of language as a condition of inquiring into the social. Furthermore, insofar as all talk is a constitutive feature of the circumstances in which it occurs EM inevitably treats members' inquiries as *locally* occasioned, managed and accomplished, within and with reference to the 'here-and-now' circumstances of their production.

Since the classic studies of Garfinkel (1956, 1963, 1967) and of his 'student' and collaborator, Sacks (Garfinkel and Sacks 1970; Sacks 1963, 1989, 1992a, 1992b), ethnomethodology has developed into a discipline characterized by a diversity of forms and directions of inquiry (Maynard and Clayman 1991). Without wishing to contrive arbitrary distinctions, we might say that there now exists a family of overlapping strands of inquiry among which resemblances and differences obtain. Several exercises in ordering this diversity in terms of these similarities and differences are now available, notably those of Benson and Hughes (1983), Coulter (1990), Cuff, Sharrock and Francis (1990), Heritage (1984), Livingston (1987), Maynard and Clayman (1991) and Sharrock and Anderson (1986). What we are calling 'membership categorization analysis' (MCA) comprises one such strand.[1]

Whilst both 'conversation analysis' (CA) and membership categorization analysis have their origins in the work of Sacks (1992a, 1992b; see Button 1977), these two forms of inquiry have developed to a large degree independently of each other, with differing attention on the part of each to the salience of the other, and with conversation analysis having been the most widely practised. Conversation analysis has focused its analytical attention on the sequential features of conversational interaction; there is an overwhelming preoccupation with the positioning of utterances as units of speech relative to one another (Atkinson and Heritage 1984; Button and Lee 1987; Sacks, Schegloff and Jefferson 1974; Schenkein 1978; etc.). This focus has, we suggest, been at the expense of the categorical aspects of conversation, although there is a small class of studies which have combined to varying degrees both forms of analysis.[2] We would suggest that both the sequential and categorizational aspects of social interaction inform each other. Thus, the production of particular types of sequential items is informed by an orientation to the membership categories of the speakers, just as these items contribute to the categorization of the speakers. Social identity provides for a sense of the (sequentially organized) talk, just as the talk provides for a sense of social identity. Teachers, for example, establish their credentials as incumbents of such a category through the production of particular sorts of sequentially positioned utterances, just as their utterances trade off a presumed social identity (as teachers) for their accountable production and recognition. Further, we would suggest that in practice these aspects (the sequential and the categorizational) are so closely intertwined as to be separable only for the purposes of analysis.

The focus of MCA (Membership Categorization Analysis) is on the use of membership categories, membership categorization devices and category predicates by members, conceptualised as lay and professional social analysts, in accomplishing (the sociology of) 'naturally occurring ordinary activities.' MCA directs attention to the locally used, invoked and organized 'presumed common-sense knowledge of social structures' which members are oriented to in the conduct of their everyday affairs, including professional sociological inquiry itself. This presumed common sense knowledge or culture is made available through a method by which the ordinary sense of talk and action is made problematic (for the purpose of analysis) and is conceptualised as the accomplishment of local instances of categorial ordering work. The aim of such analysis is to produce formal descriptions of the procedures which persons employ in particular, singular occurrences of talk and action (cf. Sacks 1984: 21)

Membership categories, as defined by Sacks, are classifications or social types that may be used to describe persons. By way of illustration an occasioned list of such categories might include 'politician,' 'gravedigger,' 'pimp,' 'nerd,' 'astronaut,' 'skinhead,' 'boozer,' 'former boy scout leader' and 'grandmother.' Since Sacks, it has been suggested that 'collectivities' and non-personal objects (Eglin and Hester 1992; Hester 1992; Jayyusi 1984; McHoul and Watson 1984;) can be seen in similar ways to those of (personal) membership categories, a conceptual development which was indeed anticipated by Sacks in his discussions of 'classes' in relation to the organization of topic in ordinary conversation (Sacks 1992a). Collectivities or 'collectivity [membership] categorizations' (Coulter 1982: 37; Jayyusi 1984: 47-56, 122-150; Sharrock 1974) range from 'concretely located,' named institutions usually linked to architectural structures (X bank), through more abstract designators such as 'the legal system,' 'state bureaucracy,' 'the health-care system,' etc., to holistic constructs such as 'the middle class,' 'feudal society' and 'free enterprise system" (Coulter 1982: 36). Examples of categories used to describe non-personal (including abstract) objects might include 'delphinium,' 'fencepost,' 'traffic light,' 'bebop,' 'foot,' 'beaujolais' and 'house.' The ways in which the use of such categories displays organizational features similar to those in relation to personal membership categories are not to be presumed *a priori*; they are a matter for empirical investigation.

Membership categories may be interactionally linked together to form classes, collections or 'membership categorization devices' (MCDs) which Sacks (1974a: 218) defines as 'any collection of membership categories, containing at least a category, which may be applied to some population containing at least a member, so as to provide, by the use of some rules of application, for the pairing of at least a population member and a categorization device member. A device is then a collection plus rules of application.'[3]

The idea that membership categories form collections refers to the fact that, in the locally occasioned settings of their occurrence, some membership categories can be used and heard commonsensically as 'going together,' whilst others cannot be so used and heard. For example, the collection or MCD 'family' may be so heard to include such membership categories as 'mother,' 'father,' 'son,' 'daughter,' 'uncle,' 'aunt,' etc., and to exclude 'trumpet player', 'dog,' 'marxist feminist' and 'Caucasian.' One particular type of membership categorization device is the 'standardized relational pair.' Sacks developed this concept in relation to his study of calls to a suicide prevention center helpline. These were calls made in the course of a 'search for help' by the caller. According to Sacks, the search was organized in terms of such paired categories as 'husband-wife,' 'parent-child,' 'friend-friend,' 'cousin-cousin,' 'neighbour-neighbour' and 'stranger-stranger.' One regularly communicated topic of such calls was that the suicidal person 'had no one to turn to,' a conclusion produced and recognized as the outcome of a search through the relevant subset of such category pairs. Besides 'intimates' such as husband-wife the concept of standardized relational pairs has been extended to such occupationally based category pairings as 'doctor-patient,' 'lawyer-client,' 'teacher-pupil/student,' and 'police-officer-suspect.' We shall return to the issue of what may be included and excluded in a collection, that is, to how 'going together' may best be understood, below.

There are two rules, according to Sacks, for applying membership categories. The first of these is the *economy rule* which provides for the adequacy of using a single membership category to describe a member of some population. This does not mean that more than one category cannot be used, but that in describing persons and to be recognized as having described them, a single category will suffice. This means, for example, that when a person is, say, introducing a new friend to his or her family it would be interactionally redundant to provide on the occasion of the introduction an extended list of the membership categories with which the friend might be described; one, such as 'a student at Laurier,' will do. The second rule of application, the *consistency rule*, holds 'if some population of persons is being categorized, and if a category from some device's collection has been used to categorize a first member of the population, then that category or other categories of the same collection may be used to categorize further members of the population' (Sacks 1974a: 219). This means, for example, that if a person has been categorized as 'first violin' then further persons may be referred to in terms of other membership categories comprising the collection 'members of the orchestra.' Sacks also identified a corollary or 'hearer's maxim' with respect to the consistency rule. This maxim holds that 'if two or more categories are used to categorize two or more members of some population, and those categories can be heard as categories from the same collection, then: hear them that way' (Sacks 1974a: 219-220). The now famous example in Sacks's work is the child's story, 'The baby cried. The mommy picked it up.' Here, with reference to the hearer's maxim, the two categories, 'baby' and 'mommy,' may be and are routinely and commonsensically heard as both belonging to the collection 'family.'

Another aspect of Sacks's conceptual framework which needs introduction is that of 'category boundedness.' Sacks speaks in particular of 'category bound activities' which are those activities that are expectably and properly done by persons who are the incumbents of particular categories. He notes that categories selected to categorize some member performing a category-bound activity and categories selected to categorize that activity are *co-selected*. Thus, although it is possibly correct to say of a baby crying that it is a male shedding tears, it is not possibly recognizable as a correct or appropriate description of the scene. The 'preference' for category co-selection is a strong and generative one and helps us to understand some of the organizational and selectional features of such utterances as the one with which Sacks began: 'The baby cried, the mommy picked it up.'

Subsequent researchers have extended Sacks's thinking on this matter. Jayyusi (1984), Payne (1976), Sharrock (1974), and Watson (1976, 1978, 1983) for example, have all observed that category-bound activities are just one class of *predicates* which 'can conventionally be imputed on the basis of a given membership category' (Watson 1978: 106). Other predicates include rights, entitlements, obligations, knowledge, attributes and competencies. We provide further details of these studies in the following section of this introduction.

A second 'hearer's maxim' is introduced with respect to category predicates. Thus, Sacks (1974a: 224) points out:

> If a category-bound activity is asserted to have been done by a member of some category where, if that category is ambiguous (i.e. is a member of at least two different devices) but where, at least for one of those devices, the asserted activity is category

> bound to the given category, then hear that *at least* the category
> from the device to which it is bound is being asserted to hold.

Thus in the case of the category-bound activity 'crying' it is asserted that this is done by a member of the category 'baby.' This is an ambiguous category: it may be heard, that is, as a member of the device 'family' and the device 'stage of life.' However, following this maxim, if for one of these devices the asserted activity 'crying' is category-bound to the given category 'baby,' then hear that the category is one which belongs to the device for which the category-bound activity holds. In other words, if one can hear the activity as bound to a category then hear the activity as being done by an incumbent of that category. In the case of 'the baby cried, the mommy picked it up,' then, the category 'baby' is heard as one belonging to the device 'stage of life' since crying is bound to the category 'baby' which is a member of that device; crying is not bound to the category 'baby' as a member of the device 'family,' though incumbents of that category *may* cry. This hearer's maxim, then, provides for a minimal hearing: the 'baby cried' refers 'at least' to 'baby from the stage of life device.' This maxim is not used by itself. Hearings are the result of the use of more than one maxim. The maxim above is used *in combination* with the consistency rule corollary. The latter gives 'baby' as a member of 'family,' whilst the former gives 'baby' as a member of the 'stage of life' device. Combining these hearings provides us with the result that the 'baby' is not only the baby of the mommy but also a baby for whom crying is category-bound.

Sacks (1974a: 225) also identifies two *viewer's maxims*. The first is as follows:

> If a member sees a category-bound activity being done, then, if
> one can see it being done by a member of a category to which the
> activity is bound, then: See it that way.

This means that the category to which the activity observed is bound has a special relevance for the identification of the doer; it permits inferences as to the identity of the doer. The second viewer's maxim states that:

> If one sees a pair of actions which can be related via the
> operation of a norm that provides for the second given the first,
> where the doers can be seen as members of the categories the
> norm provides as proper for that pair of actions, then: (a) See
> that the doers are such-members and (b) see the second as done
> in conformity with the norm.

This maxim provides for inferences about the identity of persons through assumptions about the relation of norms to activities and to the categories to which they are bound.

The Tradition of Studies in Membership Categorization Analysis[4]

Following the dissemination of dittoed copies of Sacks's unpublished lectures in the late sixties and early seventies, and a visit there by his student, Jim Schenkein, in 1971 and by himself in April 1973, Manchester in England became the engine-room of developments in categorization analysis, and ethnographic CA more generally (Sharrock 1989). For reasons that future historians may wish to discover, the divergence or simply division of (the considerable) labour of sequential CA and MCA did not proceed to the same degree in the UK as among American ethnomethodologists. The former is more readily characterized in terms of the 'ethnographic conversational [sic] analysis' formulated by Hustler and Payne (1985: 267) to refer to 'a form of conversational analysis which remains sensitive to the orientations people are working with in particular settings.' This sensitivity has meant an attention to the contribution made to the 'discourse identities' of co-conversationists of those setting-, activity-, task- or topic-relevant identifications they make (cf. Schegloff 1987 with Sharrock and Watson 1988, 1989). 'Ethnographic' conversation analysts have found the 'apparatus' of MCA useful in this regard, notably Atkinson (1980); Atkinson, Cuff and Lee (1978); Atkinson and Drew (1979); Baker (1982, 1984; Baker and Freebody 1987), Benson and Drew (1978), Cuff (1994; Cuff and Francis 1978; Cuff and Sharrock 1985), Drew (1978), Eglin and Hester (1992), Francis (1989), Hester (1992; Hester and Francis 1994), Hustler and Payne (1983, 1985), Jalbert (1989), Jayyusi (1984, 1988, 1991a, 1991b), Lee (1984), Lee and Watson (1993); McHoul and Watson 1984; Payne (1976; Payne and Hustler 1980), Watson (1974, 1976, 1978, 1983, 1986, 1987, 1990, 1992, 1994; Watson and Weinberg 1982), Wowk (1984). Through his teaching and research Wes Sharrock was particularly influential in bringing CA (and EM) to receptive colleagues and students. Though not explicitly employing the language of MCDs his 'On owning knowledge' (1974) nicely details the relationship of (particular) membership categories and the knowledge that they may requiredly possess, thus making intelligible a notion such as 'Baka medicine.' We will simply note here the 'developments' in the field made by these Manchester School and allied practitioners. Much of this work was done in the early 1970's, but not published till later as would-be anthologies, for a variety of reasons, failed to materialise.

An early classical example of the work done in the 1970s is Lee's analysis of the headline 'Girl guide aged 14 raped at Hell's Angels convention' (Lee 1984). Lee examines the use of category-bound activities and attributes of 'girl guide' and 'Hell's Angel' which provide for the intelligibility of this headline, namely that the girl guide was raped *by* Hell's Angels at a Hell's Angels' convention. Subsequently, in studies of the beginning of a school lesson (Payne 1976; see also Payne and Hustler 1980) and the re-commencement of a meeting (Atkinson *et al.* 1978) the analysts cogently reveal the interactants' reliance on the practice of treating the relevant membership categories and action-descriptions as *co-selected* and *mutually constitutive* in meaning. They propose new candidate SRPs, namely 'teacher-pupil' and 'chairman-member,' and demonstrate the interactional utility of indexicals such as 'no one,' 'we,' 'now,' 'last time' and 'again' for accomplishing the recognizability of action, identity and setting (after Sacks 1976; see also Watson 1987). The 'stage-of-life' MCD is elaborated in Atkinson's 'Some practical uses of a 'natural lifetime',' which is notable for discussing the category-sensitivity of identifications of action. Thus, 'can you play the guitar any better?' asked by a *child* of a person who is tuning a violin stands to be heard as innocent fault; said by one who is *not a child* it comes off as possible sarcasm, leg-pulling or joking.

In a series of publications Watson (1974, 1976, 1978, 1983, 1986, 1987, 1990, 1992, 1994; Watson and Weinberg 1982) has worked with the Sacksian apparatus in efforts to explicate the intelligibility and interactional organization of counsellor-client talk on the telephone, police-suspect interrogation, sociological interviews and categorial order in public space. For example, in the 1983 study on the presentation of victim and motive in discourse he proposes new SRPs such as the 'racial' categories 'black-white' and the sexual orientation categories 'heterosexual-homosexual' (see also Watson (1987: 278-279) for 'member of the congregation-vicar'). He discusses the matter of mapping identifications onto other categories, such as mapping 'nigger' onto 'victim', and proposes that a category may have several labels which may be ranked and thus afford interactional possibilities of up- and down-grading those to whom the labels are applied (cf. Speier 1973: 184-190). He also extends the range of features tied to categories beyond the domain of (Sacksian) 'activities,' using the term 'predicates' to name them (as we note above on p. 7). Of possible predicates 'motives' come in for particular attention. Categorizations have motivational implications. Depending on the category of the user ('white', for example), the categorization 'nigger' may be said to carry the motive 'racial hatred'. Insofar as motive imputation is further tied to the identifiability of action (seeing *why* that' is to see *what* 'that' is), the category-related features of motives become available to interactants for the moral work of justifying and excusing actions - all this being done through the use of categories for describing persons. A murder suspect may argue 'victim-precipitated homicide' if he can sustain the description of his victim as a 'tramp' (Wowk 1984: 77).

Similarly, Drew (1978: 1) wants 'to examine how a practical interactional task - an accusation - may be achieved through the production of descriptions.' But the descriptions are extended to include not only person identifications but 'scenes,' that is location formulations. He shows how speakers may map the former ('Protestants') onto the latter ('Shankill Road'). Like Watson, he mentions other characteristics conventionally tied to membership categories. Most important is his claim that the boundedness of an activity to a category is not only device-sensitive but *occasioned*, an issue we address below.

There is a discernible consistency between Drew's discussion of members' uses of location formulations and 'religious geography' and Schegloff's earlier study of members' practices of 'formulating place' through the use of 'locational formulations' and a more general reliance on a 'common-sense geography which many North Americans (at least) share' (Schegloff 1972: 85). In one of the very few studies to examine the interrelatedness of sequential organization (Schegloff examines 'insertion sequences') and categorization work ('selecting formulations') - Drew's itself being another (see also Watson 1986) - Schegloff separates the orders of interactional organization bearing on the problem of selecting and hearing locational formulations. These orders refer to the 'location analysis,' 'membership analysis' and 'topic or activity analysis' a member may be said to (have to) engage in to produce or recognize a right or competent location formulation (rather than a merely referentially 'correct' one). While space considerations preclude an adequate summary of this work, several signal points may be mentioned. He suggests place formulations may form *collections* such as 'G' for 'geographical' ('2903 Main Street' ...) and 'Rm' for 'relation to members' ('John's place,' 'Al's home,' 'home,' 'the store' ...). Depending on topic or activity a formulation may be subjected to a *transformation*. There may be a *preference* for Rm terms over G terms. The *consistency rule* becomes relevant as a basis for selection. But consistency is extended to 'consistency for a topic or activity', and to the matter of *co-selection* of membership categorization and location formulation. Finally, Schegloff (1972: 105) postulates an order of '*unspoken primary categorizations*' that may be said to underpin the efforts of Lee, Watson and Drew to map one set of categories onto another.

In a study by Cuff (1994 [1980]) reservations are made about (i) the tightness of the link between category and activity in Sacks's idea of 'category-bound activities', and (ii) 'the apparatus surrounding membership categories ... [being] too abstract to provide for members a

practically-adequate specification of identities in particular settings'
(Watson 1986: 99, 103). Jayyusi's (1984) work and that of Watson (1986)
and McHoul and Watson (1984) can be seen as, in part, attempts to remedy
this and related problems of the genre.

Jayyusi sought to elaborate the conceptualization of membership
categorization by, on the one hand, introducing and more tightly specifying
a variety of distinctions pertaining to categories and category-related
features and, on the other hand, loosening up the relation of reference by
invoking such Wittgensteinian notions as family resemblance and open
texture.[5]   Thus, for one example, Jayyusi elaborates the 'logic' of
membership categorization *devices* and their associated rules while showing
that adequate categorial reference may be achieved *without* the use of any
device - categorizations may be simply setting-appropriate or self-
explicating in context or selected via an orientation to a 'relevant category
environment' (Jayyusi 1984: 135). For a second example, the concept of
category-boundedness is supplemented with the notions 'category-
constitutive', 'category-tied', 'category-embedded', 'category-generated' and
'category-relevant', but then is defined to hold only in an occasioned way
(although, as we noted elsewhere (Eglin and Hester 1992), there is some
possible confusion in the use of the terminology here).

Watson (1986) examines telephone calls to a crisis intervention
center ('Lifeliners') for the methods used by the parties to do the 'explicative
work' whereby they come to a mutual determination of just what the
nature of the 'help' is that the organization offers and whether, indeed, it is
what the caller is after.   Such explicative work consists largely of
descriptions, including categorizations applied to the organization and to
the parties to the call. However, the capacity of the categorizations to be
explicative on any occasion of use is not independent of the sequential
organization of the talk in which they occur. Adjacency pairs are a
sequential device by which the parties may secure joint orientation to, and
mutual understanding of, the categorizations they are making. But then
how do the interlocutors make any second pair part come off as hearably
designed for *just this* first pair part *this* time around?

> One resource for establishing the unique adequacy of [say] an
> answer to a question is through the rules for the use of
> membership categories. The most basic technique is the
> preservation of a single category across a question-answer pair
> (Watson 1986: 102).

As we said above, Watson's work is one of the few places where
membership categorization analysis and sequential analysis are combined

in CA/EM (see now his 1994 and Chapter Three below). Here we see him using this combination to address the 'haecceity' issue raised by Cuff (and more generally by Garfinkel).

Similar concerns and considerations motivate a study by McHoul and Watson (1984) of the methods 'by which 'commonsense knowledge' ... is relied upon as a resource ... by teachers and students for the production and acquisition of 'formal' (or 'subject') knowledge' (McHoul and Watson 1984: 281) in a school geography lesson. They supplement membership categorization analysis (applied, innovatively, to place formulations) with analysis of the 'common sense geography' used by parties to organize those same formulations. While this is consonant with Jayyusi's appeal to 'setting-appropriateness,' 'self-explicating contexts' and a 'relevant category environment' as members' criteria for categorization selection (additional to device-based relevance), McHoul and Watson go further to bring out the embeddedness of these criteria in that 'family of interpretive procedures termed the 'documentary method of interpretation". As in Watson (1986) they also develop Schegloff's point about 'consistency for *topic*' as a basis of category co-selection. Again both these points are efforts to counter what some would call that same tendency to 'excessive formality and abstractness' in MCA studies as is claimed to be exhibited in some sequential studies (see, for example, Coulter 1983 and Hester 1981, 1985). The key issue raised here concerns respect for the 'haecceitic' character (and 'unique adequacy') of social actions, or for 'the in situ production of the local visibility of recognizably everyday activities and settings' (Cuff and Sharrock 1985: 149). This issue may be said to be related to, if not grounded in, an ambiguity locatable in Sacks's MCA work itself. Accordingly, we address this problem in the next section.

Membership Categorization Analysis as Ethnomethodology: Culture-in-Action [6]

From an ethnomethodological point of view, membership categories, membership categorization devices and category predicates, like other natural language phenomena, are all examples of indexical expressions. Their sense, in other words, is a situated, contextually embedded sense. Furthermore, in formulating the irreconcilability of interest between ethnomethodology and constructive analysis in sociology with respect to the phenomena of everyday life, Garfinkel and Sacks (1970: 341) observe that 'those differences have one of their foci in indexical expressions.' Thus, ethnomethodological studies 'have shown in demonstrable specifics (1) that the properties of indexical expressions are ordered properties, and (2) *that* they are ordered is an ongoing, practical accomplishment of every actual occasion of commonplace speech and conduct.' Where 'professional sociology', with respect to the 'central task of general theory building' has sought to 'repair' indexical expressions, ethnomethodology's purpose 'is to describe that achievement in specifics in its organizational variety.' Insofar as membership categorization devices, membership categories and predicates are *ordered*, therefore, their orderliness consists in and as the ordering practices used in actual occasions of 'commonplace speech and conduct.'

The ethnomethodological conception of MCA stands in marked contrast to what may be called the *decontextualized* model of membership categorization. This approach treats language use as a resource for uncovering culture, knowledge, meanings, etc. which are treated as independent of such language use and as members' resources in making sense of their environments. In turn, such reified entities are treated by social scientists as explanations of ordinary members' talk and action. The indexical character of referential terms is stripped from them and they are treated as lexemic *symbols* (Eglin 1980: 31). Such a decontextualized approach is exemplified in the work of cognitive anthropology (Eglin 1976, 1980; Frake 1964; Goodenough 1957; Tyler 1969a; Wieder 1970;) and in the semantic theory associated with Chomskyan transformational generative grammar (Chomsky 1968; see Coulter 1973), both of which seek to provide formal accounts of a determinate structure of 'knowledge' which members or speaker-hearers are said to possess for producing meaningful descriptions as a precondition for competent interaction. Ethnographic semantics, for example, deals with collections of terms said to share a common feature of meaning such as kinship terms, colour terms, plant terms and animal terms. Such collections are said to form semantic domains. Componential analysis of such a domain, among other methods, produces an ethnosemantic description, the core of which is a set of rules which specify the necessary and sufficient conditions under which a given term names a given (class of) object (Eglin 1980: 19). Such a 'theory of descriptions' (Tyler 1969b: 5) seeks to explicate 'a society's culture [which] consists of whatever it is one has to know or believe in order to operate in a manner acceptable to its members' (Goodenough 1957: 167). Such cultural knowledge is said to be embedded in the semantic structure of the language, which is in turn said to be stored in a set of cognitive categories in persons' minds (see Eglin 1980: 28-29). While this semantic structure will be subject to pragmatic rules of application to local settings, occasions or circumstances of actual talk, it pre-exists such applications and specifies the parameters in terms of which they occur.

Some commentators have assimilated EM into ethnographic semantics, saying that they 'share a methodological stance in that both give primacy to explicating the competence or knowledge of members of a culture, *the unstated assumptions which determine their interpretations of experience'* (Gumperz and Hymes 1972: 301; cited in Eglin 1980: 27). While, from an ethnomethodological viewpoint the first quoted phrase may be unobjectionable enough, it is the pre-given, objectivist and determinist - that is, decontextualized - model embedded in the emphasised phrase that is problematic here. As Lee (1991: 214) comments:

> Their [cognitive anthropologists'] version of social order is that interactants, in the course of interaction, make correct recognitions of objects or activities to bring them under some appropriate norm. They are seen as doing so 'transituationally'. Consequently, it seems that there must be some shared set of general rules for category application so as to achieve 'transituational' regularity Such rules must be applied to a setting from without. They are seen as being cognitively stored, and as having the kind of ontological status that they have in most social theories of order and regularity.

An ambiguity between a decontextualized model on the one hand, and an ethnomethodological approach on the other hand, can be discerned in Sacks's work. Thus, a careful reading of Sacks's corpus reveals his attention to the local contextual dimensions of categorization. However, there are various points in his writings which might, unadvisedly, lead one to conclude that Sacks was not wholly averse to a decontextualized model of membership categorization. Indeed, in this connection, Livingston observes that attempts to build conversation analysis, whether sequential CA or MCA studies, have run the risk of abandoning ethnomethodology and falling back into constructive analysis. As he puts it (Livingston 1987: 77):

> 'Practical reasoning' referred to a co-conversationist's producing an utterance so that it would be heard in the accountable way that it was, not to a reflective activity The analysability of the 'first sequence' ['The baby cried. The mommy picked it up'] is part of that sequence itself. However, as the category devices and rules began to be developed, the 'machine' being built seemed increasingly similar to linguists' theorised constructions. The utterances, and the lived-work of conversation surrounding and embedded in them that they themselves are, were no longer self-sufficient - as they are for co-conversationists - to win the day.

What Livingston reminds us of here is that the risk resides in a potential affinity between, and in fact a partial historical derivation of, MCA and cognate work in cognitive anthropology and linguistics. One interpretation of MCA studies in the tradition of Sacks is that they simply provide the missing pragmatics, that is they articulate a set of rules, which are culturally pre-given, by which speaker-hearers, for example, link identity and action descriptors to the interactional tasks and settings that form the context of their talk. That is, a possible reading of MCDs is that they comprise pre-existing structures of category-organized knowledge which flesh out, or contextualize, componential-analytic accounts of the semantic structure of language.

We shall identify three expressions of what could be read as the deployment of the decontextualized model of membership categorization in Sacks's work. Whilst these are problematic from our point of view, we will suggest that they are offset, indeed belied, by other aspects of Sacks's work, specifically his focus on co-conversationists' local use of categories, predicates and devices. We shall then, drawing on what is not articulated but nevertheless implicit in Sacks, recast membership categorization analysis in ethnomethodological terms as the study of 'culture in action'.

Three expressions of decontextuality in Sacks

A first expression of the decontextualized model can be discerned in Sacks's method, that is, in how Sacks sets up his analytic task. Thus, a distinction is made between recognizable, commonsense, vernacular descriptions and a machinery or apparatus which accounts for or generates such descriptions. As Schegloff (1992: xl) puts it:

> One of the central tasks which Sacks sets himself in the lectures on 'The baby cried' is providing an account of how recognizable activities are done, and done recognizably. And in particular how the activity of 'describing' is done, and done recognizably. The key starting point here is that descriptions *are* recognizable, *are* recognizable descriptions, and are recognizable descriptions without juxtaposition to their putative objects. Much of Sacks's effort in the early years of this analytic enterprise was given over to building an apparatus that provided recognizable descriptions without reference (by real life co-participants or by professional investigators) to what was putatively being described.

Furthermore (Schegloff 1992: xli):

> The 'membership categorization devices' ... are key elements in such an apparatus ... Sacks begins the discussion of 'The baby

cried' with a number of observations which he makes about the components of this little story, and offers the claim that his audience would have made (perhaps did in fact make) the same observations. But these are not sociological findings, he insists. They are simply the explication of commonsense or vernacular knowledge. Rather than constituting analysis, they serve to pose a research problem, namely the construction of an apparatus that would generate (or that has generated) such observations, that would (in that sense) have produced them. And such an apparatus would constitute findings.

According to Schegloff, 'both parts of this analytic operation are important: making explicit the understandings which common sense provides of the world which members of the society encounter, including the conduct of others; and the provision of something that can account for those understandings.' Accordingly, then, Sacks separates (a) common sense understanding from (b) a pre-existing apparatus which makes that understanding possible. In fact, there are three parts in Sacks's method, not two. Thus, not only are common sense understandings and observations *made*, they are also *made strange* for the purpose of analysis. This *problematization of sense* involves taking the categories 'out of context' (where the categories have their sense) and entertaining the possibility of their having alternate meanings. It is then the task of the machinery or apparatus to resolve the problem or puzzle made available by such 'bracketing' of the ordinary contextually provided sense of the description. In other words, Sacks's method might be characterized as: first, 'decompose' the ordinary sense, and then, second, put it back together again by using the pre-existing device.

Whilst 'making common sense' and the 'problematization of sense' are unobjectionable features of Sacks's method, it is in the third step of this procedure that the devices are reified, the machinery externalised, the apparatus conceived as objective and independent of the actual occasions of interaction being studied. Membership categorization devices are endowed with a thing-like quality, lying behind, pre-existing their use in particular instances of membership categorization. The machinery can be understood as a decontextualized machinery, an apparatus to be taken up and used and which is a pre-formed resource for doing description.

A second expression of Sacks's reification of membership categorization devices and membership categories is evident in certain stipulative statements and definitive comments on *the* categories making up a categorization device. For example, he states (Sacks 1974a: 219):

> An instance of a categorization device is the one called 'sex'; its collection is the two categories (male, female).

Similarly (Sacks 1972: 33):

> While many devices ... are not Pn-adequate ones, it is perfectly obvious that there are at least two Pn-adequate devices that Members do have available to them and do use. For example, there are the devices whose collections are (1) sex (male, female), and (2) age (young, old). There are of course others.

Likewise, with respect to the device 'family,' Sacks (1974a: 219) states:

> ... let me observe that 'baby' and 'mommy' can be seen to be categories from one collection: the collection whose device is called 'family' and which consists of such categories as ('baby,' 'mommy,' 'daddy'...) where by '...' we mean that there are others, but not any others, e.g. 'shortstop.'

In these extracts, it is possible to infer that Sacks is saying that *the* categories making up the *sex* device *are* male and female, and that the device *family* consists of the categories baby, mommy, daddy, etc. Furthermore, Sacks appears to exclude definitively from these collections other possible categories. In this stipulative conception, the meaning of the collections 'sex' and 'family' appear to be offered in some pre-given and decontextualized sense; the constituent categories of these devices appears to have been settled in a once-and-for-all manner.[7]

A third expression of Sacks's deployment of notions consistent with a decontextualized version of membership categorization is observable in a distinction he makes between 'natural' and 'occasioned' collections or classes of categories. Sacks (1992a: April 17, 1968) distinguishes 'natural' and 'topic-occasioned' collections or devices in the following way. 'Natural' devices are those where, once the device is known, persons can name the members whilst 'topic-occasioned' devices are those whose members would be 'puzzling' if one did not know in advance the topic providing for the relevance of the device.

To identify what he means by 'topic-occasioned' devices Sacks uses the following example:

A:	I have a fourteen year old kid.
B:	Well that's all right.
A:	I also have a dog.
B:	Oh, I'm sorry.

As Sacks says, the status of kids and dogs as co-class members may initially be puzzling. It would seem that we would not 'naturally' think of kids and dogs as co-class members. But, in this context they are 'topic-relevant' objects where the topic 'renting an apartment' makes relevant the collection 'possible disqualifiers'.

Sacks's distinction between 'natural' classes or collections on the one hand, and 'occasioned' classes or collections on the other hand implies *some* collections (the 'natural' ones) are pre-given components of common-sense knowledge, whilst *others* have an occasioned quality to them. It is our view that this, together with the notions of definitive members of membership categorization devices and an external machinery for membership categorization, is problematic for an EM sub-discipline for which the radical occasionality of meaning (sense) is a primordial claim.[8]

Whilst there is a sense in which it may reasonably be acknowledged that members of society 'possess knowledge' and that this may be described, in part, as a 'machinery' or 'apparatus' comprising membership categorization devices, membership categories, and so forth, this decontextualized conception of members' knowledge ignores the ways in which the *use* of knowledge is always *situated*. Furthermore, *that* members of society know anything at all is also something that is inferred from their action in particular circumstances. The decontextualized model, then, diverts our attention from the local character of human activities. With regard to Sacks's stipulative and definitive remarks, it does not take much effort to upset the notion of a natural class called 'sex'. That is, according to occasion the relevant collection members might be 'male' and 'female' or 'chromosomal types' or 'types of sex act' (genital, oral, anal, animal, ??) or etc.[9] Therefore, it is necessary to know what it means before one can say what the categories of this 'device' are. 'Sex' can mean different things. That is, what a device collects depends on how it is used *this time*. There is clearly, then, an occasioned quality to 'sex'. Recognition of this brings us to Sacks's distinction between 'natural' and 'occasioned' devices.

With respect to the distinction between 'natural' and 'occasioned' devices or classes, two objections can be made. Firstly, the example Sacks cites of 'topic-occasioned' devices fails the test he proposes for distinguishing them from 'natural' devices, namely a negative answer to the question 'can one name the members of the device's collection, given the collection?' For, just as one *can* provide the categories 'male' and 'female' in answer to the question for the 'natural' collection 'sex', so also can one readily enough provide a list for the 'topic-occasioned' collection of 'possible disqualifiers for renting an apartment'. Secondly, in contrast to the decontextualized conception of membership categorization devices, the ethnomethodological view is that there is always an occasioned element to these collections, including so-called 'natural' ones. That is, *all* collections are occasioned in the sense that it has to be recognized that this is what they mean for this occasion. These collection-names can mean different things, and hence the categories they collect will vary. That is, where one can name the members of a collection, before one can do it, one has to know what the collection means *this time*. This means that one cannot speak definitively, that is in a decontextualized way, of what a device consists of without saying what the device means *this time*. A device can mean different things and hence can collect different categories on different occasions and in different contexts. Membership categorization devices have multiple meanings. Thus, take, for example, the device 'family'. This device can collect other categories beside mother, father, son, daughter, etc. As members of a cultural community we also know that 'family' may be used in other ways (which, incidentally do not exhaust the term's possible meanings). Thus, whilst one might well speak of family in the sense of kinship, one may also speak of 'family' in the sense of 'species' or 'genus', as in a 'family' of roses or other plants. Alternatively, a 'family' might mean a religious organization or community, such as a church. It might also refer to a type of criminal organization or to the 'human family.'

    Doubt, then, can be cast on the distinction between natural and occasioned collections or devices. To reiterate, this is because all categorizations are indexical expressions and their sense is therefore *locally* and *temporally* contingent. There is, to use a phrase of Garfinkel's 'no time out' from the here-and-now character of all sense making, every usage of a category or a collection. It has to be decided in each and every case what the category *means* and this will involve a figuring out of what collection the category belongs to, *for this occasion*. Similarly, in the absence of contextual detail, it is difficult, if not impossible to say what a particular device, say 'family', means and hence what its constituent membership categories are.

Local Categorial Order

    In spite of the reification of membership categorization devices implied by his methodological practices and stipulative remarks, it is also clear that Sacks's studies exhibit a central concern with the local specifics of membership categorization. That is, the decontextualized model of membership categorization is belied elsewhere in the ethnomethodological investigation of MCDs contained in Sacks's corpus. As Lynch and Peyrot (1992: 114) put it:

Consistent with the emphasis in Garfinkel's early work, ethnomethodologists reject the idea that persons make sufficient sense of each others actions by attaching culturally encoded meanings to particular words and gestures. Instead, ethnomethodologists treat meaning *contextually*, which means that they endeavour analytically to unpack relational configurations that enable sense to be made and understood *in situ.*

Sacks's recognition of the local character and embeddedness of membership categorizations is widespread in his lectures. This can be appreciated, for example, in his lecture of 16 February 1996[10] where he considers how an action, namely the utterance 'Ken, why don't you make those arrangements out of here', can be heard as 'disciplining' if and when those present to its production invoke the standardized relational pair 'therapist-patient', assigning 'therapist' to the speaker, 'patient' to its recipient, 'disciplining' as a category-tied action to the utterance, and 'group therapy session' as a category-tied setting to the occasion. Thereby, their category-membership, their co-membership of the device 'therapist-patient', the relevant action-description of the utterance and the formulation of the setting are constituted for that occasion:

> What you get is, there are actions which for them to be effective, need to be formulated via some particular Device. And then those actions invoke that Device (Sacks 1976: G6).

Similarly, Sacks's (1972: 37-39) elaboration of the features of the MCD he calls 'R' (standardized relational pairs) is made as part of the analytic task of accounting for hearable aspects of a particular kind of task conducted in talk, namely the work of searching for help. Likewise, his account (Sacks 1974a) of the MCDs 'family' and 'stage of life' is made in the course of explicating another interactional episode, namely the beginning of a child's storytelling. In neither case does he subscribe to the view that these devices have transcendental relevance. That such devices are made and found relevant by members across a variety of social occasions speaks only to their relevance for members, not to any cultural pre-programming regarding usage.

Whilst the local use of devices and categories is topicalized in Sacks's studies, we wish to draw attention to an implication of this which is not articulated by Sacks. If, as we stated earlier, the constituents of the MCD 'apparatus' are indexical expressions, then their 'orderliness' is to be regarded ethnomethodologically as a practical accomplishment in local settings. Thus, an implication of Sacks's emphasis on the local use of categories and devices is not just that members *use* culture to do things, but that culture is constituted in, and only exists in, action. For membership categorization analysis, this means that the orderliness of cultural resources (categories, devices and the rest) is constituted *in their use* rather than *pre-existing* as a *machinery* for whatever uses members might want to put them to. Our central point is that it is *in* the use of categories that culture is constituted *this time through*. It is in their *use* that the *collect-able* character of membership categories is constituted and membership categorization devices *assembled in situ*: membership categorization devices are *assembled objects*.

This conception of membership categorization *analysis* as a members' activity and of membership categorization devices as assembled objects can be found in at least two places in Sacks's corpus. Firstly, it can be found in relation to his remarks about the 'ambiguities' of membership categories. Thus, Sacks (1974a) makes the point with reference to the 'family' and 'stage of life' devices that 'various membership categorization-device categories can be said to be ambiguous'. By this he means, firstly, that a particular category may have different meanings. That is, the same categorial word is a term occurring in several distinct devices, and can in each have quite a different reference (Sacks 1974a: 220). For example, the categories of 'boy' and 'girl' can be heard to belong to (at least) the stage-of-life device and to the device or the relational pair 'boyfriend-girlfriend.' Such ambiguity clearly applies to other membership categories. The category 'sister', for example, may mean 'sister' in the sense of 'family member,' it may mean a member of a religious community or a hospital organization, or it may be a term applied by feminists to one who shares their politics, amongst other possible meanings. In other words, the membership category 'sister' may belong to various collections of categories or membership categorization devices, depending on the type of 'sister' being talked about. Finally, at the risk of labouring the point, consider the category 'mother'. This category can also be used in a variety of ways. It may, for example, be used to speak of biological relations between persons, to insult someone, to describe someone as fussy, to refer to a member of a rock band, to the head of a religious order, amongst others. Thus, 'mother,' as a membership category, may belong to different devices and hence mean different things in different contexts.

It is also quite clear from Sacks, contrary to the notion that some categories are excluded (Sacks 1974a: 219) from combination with others, that *any* category may be combined with *any other* category in a collection for certain purposes. An appreciation of this is afforded in some of Sacks's remarks on 'topic organization.' Thus, Sacks speaks of 'classes' or 'classes for a topic.' He suggests that 'one basic way that 'topical talk' is exhibited involves the use of' *co-class membership*. As Sacks (1992a: 757) puts it:

> A given part of an utterance can be analysed to find that it has some (actually many) class statuses. Having found some class status for that given item, one may in the next utterance present such a term as stands in co-class membership with a term used in the last. So A talks about cigars, B can talk about pipes.

As Sacks comments, this is a 'perfectly obvious' way to speak of doing 'attention to topic' and as he observes 'it isn't very discriminative to say that, e.g., pipes and cigars are co-class members - *cigars and horses may be co-class members also*' (our emphasis). In other words, *virtually any members can be co-members of a class*. Their co-class membership depends on the topic at hand, the method used to collect some items as co-members of a class 'invented' for this occasion. For example, a 'class' may be the list provided for by the topic 'my favourite things' which, presumably, could include almost anything or could be limited to a specific class of, say, 'kitchen utensils', if that was the referent of 'things' for this particular occasion.

Similarly, whilst it is conventionally or commonsensically known (notwithstanding the occasionality of such knowing) that the membership categorization device 'family' is one which, on the one hand, collects or subsumes membership categories such as 'father,' 'mother,' 'son,' 'daughter,' 'uncle,' 'aunt,' etc., but on the other hand can exclude categories such as 'footballer,' 'police officer,' and 'fascist,' this is not to say that we could not, given further reflection and on some particular occasion of use, arrive at a collection for these 'strange bedfellows.' Furthermore, persons could say 'shortstop' and it could mean family member - it depends on what 'shortstop' means *this time*. It is not difficult to imagine a context in which 'shortstop' belongs to the same collection as 'mommy,' 'daddy,' etc., because 'shortstop' can be used *as an understandable substitute* for, say, a person's brother.

Contrary, then, to the decontextualized conception of membership categorization as pre-existing structures or 'devices', ethnomethodology stresses that membership categorization is an *activity* carried out in particular local circumstances. Membership categorization devices or collections are therefore to be regarded as in situ achievements of members' practical actions and practical reasoning. Categories are 'collected' with others in the course of their being used. In turn, then, this means that the 'collection' to which a category belongs (for this occasion) is constituted through its use in a particular context; it is part and parcel of its use *in that way*. Its recognizability is part of the phenomenon itself. What 'collection' the category belongs to, and what the collection *is*, are constituted in and how it is used *this time*.

The Studies in this Collection

In this chapter two alternative approaches to the study of membership categorization have been drawn. The first is the decontextualized approach, the second the ethnomethodological approach. In contrast to the former, the latter focuses on the local production of categorial order and emphasises that all categorizations are indexical expressions and their sense is therefore *locally* and *temporally* contingent.

Sacks's work, we have suggested, is ambiguous in so far as it exhibits two contrasting approaches to the study of membership categorization devices, membership categories and category predicates. On the one hand, there is evidence of a *reification* of membership categorization devices in his methods and in his stipulative and definitional remarks. On the other hand, there is a clear recognition of the contextual embeddedness of membership categorization activities. To the extent that the former is emphasised the continuity between Sacks and work conducted in cognitive anthropology and other forms of 'cultural analysis' is evident, whereas to the extent that the latter is exhibited then Sacks's work can be seen to be congruent with the concerns of ethnomethodology[11]. We draw attention to the discernible ambiguity in Sacks's work only to underscore the ethnomethodological character of his actual analyses. That such an ambiguity may be discerned in his work does not detract for us from the remarkable scope, depth and brilliance of that work as an exemplary sociological oeuvre.

The studies assembled here are firmly rooted in the ethnomethodological grounding of membership categorization analysis, though this is not to say that they each make the issue topical as we have done above. Rather such grounding is evident in the analytic treatment accorded their various substantive subjects. In Chapter Two Hester and Eglin develop the argument of Chapter One through an analysis of the reflexive ties between category, predicate and context in descriptions of 'problem children' in teacher-psychologist talk, and of those involved in reading newspaper headlines about suicide. In Chapter Three Watson discusses the relations between membership categorization analysis and the conventionally regarded independent field of sequential conversation analysis. In Chapter Four Baker elucidates the methods teachers used in a particular school setting to accomplish justice for students for all practical purposes. For Lynch and Bogen in Chapter Five '(not) remembering' is not a matter of cognition and the salience of information, but of the relationships between recollections of the past, credibility and the ties between actor-categories and actions. They reveal these categorical resources and relationships by examining instances of interrogations in the Iran-Contra Hearings in 1987, and in the O J Simpson murder trial in 1995. In Chapter Six, in their analysis of a television commercial, Francis and Hart focus on the membership categories and devices which provide the narrative with its intelligible coherence. Finally, in Chapter Seven, Hester and Eglin investigate the accomplishment of sociology itself as a professional mode of inquiry through its practitioners' use of methods for formulating social structures. In each chapter 'culture in action' is exhibited as a locally used and constituted 'production and recognition apparatus' (Garfinkel and Sacks 1970).

Chapter Two

The Reflexive Constitution of Category, Predicate and Context in Two Settings

Stephen Hester and Peter Eglin

This chapter seeks to illustrate with empirical case materials the argument about the essentially indexical character of category use developed in Chapter One. The ethnomethodological vision of membership categorization analysis is one which regards categories and devices as indexical expressions, emphasises the local, contextual specificity and use of categorizations, and sees categorial order as a local accomplishment of the use of categories-in-context. This ethnomethodological approach is exemplified with reference to categorizations in two different settings, namely (a) talk between teachers and educational psychologists in the course of whose meetings children referred from schools to the School Psychological Service in England are discussed, and (b) readings of suicide headlines in Canadian newspapers. Our focus in on the reflexive relation between the context, the category membershipping of the participants, and the features predicated of the categories. It is therefore shown that the 'collection' to which a membership category belongs is always a locally accomplished, contextually embedded and reflexively constituted phenomenon. For ethnomethodology, membership categorization devices are not a 'basis' for practical reasoning, as constructivist versions imply. Rather, the device and the category sense are occasioned, mutually elaborated matters of practical reasoning. Both devices and categories are 'in-context'.

Ethnomethodology and 'Social Context'

Before examining some instances of categories-in-context, it is necessary to clarify the nature of ethnomethodological interest in the phenomenon of 'context'. Thus, it might be thought that a possible way to proceed with respect to the relationship between categories and context is to assume that the sense of a category 'varies according to context' and that one way of 'taking context into account' is to conceive of persons 'filling in' the contextual details surrounding category, collection or predicate usages. The problem with this procedure is that it implies a separation between the categorization on the one hand and the context on the other. It therefore resurrects with respect to 'context' the reification of *a priori* structures which were located in the decontextualized model of MCDs which we discussed in Chapter One. Thus, from our point of view, it is necessary to avoid the reification of 'context' just as much as that of 'cultural meanings' or MCDs; we reject the view that categorizations and their contexts are separate, independent phenomena. It is not that the 'context' *determines* the categorial meaning (in the traditional sociological sense) nor that context is *independent,* as if it somehow 'stands outside' the category or device being used, a container which shapes and influences; it is not that persons somehow 'fill in' or 'attach' a context any more than they 'attach a cultural meaning' to some categorization. Rather, from an ethnomethodological point of view, categorizations and their contexts are mutually elaborative, separable only for the sake of analysis; the sense of a description is part and parcel of the context in which the description occurs. Consequently, for ethnomethodology, the phenomenon is not 'categories' in a 'context' but rather 'categories-in-context'. The context is not 'filled in', it is inseparable from the category in the first place. Just as persons do not learn a language apart from the contexts in which it is used, so also are categories learned and known not in isolation but in relation to their contexts of use. So, when people hear a category being used, they don't 'attach' anything, they hear it as a category-in-context (and nowhere else).

In terms of this conception, then, the meaning or sense of a category is constituted through the use of features of the context, and the contextual features are themselves constituted through the sense of the category. As Lynch and Peyrot (1992: 114) put it:

'Context' 'is not some fixed set of social, cultural, environmental or cognitive 'factors' impinging upon specific instances of conduct as through from outside'. Rather, it refers to 'a reflexively' constituted relationship between singular actions and the relevant specifications of identity, place, time, and meaning implicated by the intelligibility of those actions'.

In saying, then, that 'meanings are arrived at *contextually*', we mean 'that analysts and ordinary members are oriented to the 'relational configurations that enable sense to be made and understood *in situ*' (Lynch and Peyrot, 1992: 114). Furthermore, 'it is the task of ethnomethodology to 'unpack' those configurations'. Such 'relational configurations' comprise such elements-in-relation as actions, topics, identities, places, times, etc. It is to this recognition of the relationally configured character of category and context that Livingston (1987: 77) points when he states, in speaking of 'The baby cried. The mommy picked it up' that the analysability of this 'story' is part of the sequence itself. It does not refer to reflective activity through which some 'context' or 'meaning' is attached 'after the event'.[1]

Contrary, then, to the decontextualized conception of membership categorization as pre-existing structures or `devices', ethnomethodology stresses that membership categorization is an *activity* carried out in particular local circumstances. Membership categorization devices or collections are therefore to be regarded as *in situ* achievements of members' practical actions and practical reasoning. Categories are 'collected' with others in the course of their being used. In turn, then, this means that the 'collection' to which a category belongs (for this occasion) is constituted through its use in a particular context; it is part and parcel of its use *in that way*. Its recognizability is part of the phenomenon itself. What `collection' the category belongs to, and what the collection *is*, are constituted in and how it is used *this time*.

It follows from the foregoing that, with respect to membership categorization, ethnomethodology's interest is in the 'occasioned corpus' rather than the 'decontextualized corpus'. Thus, as Zimmerman and Pollner (1971: 94) put it:

By use of the term *occasioned* corpus, we wish to emphasize that the features of socially organized activities are particular contingent accomplishments of the production and recognition work of parties to the activity. We underscore the occasioned character of the corpus in

contrast to a corpus of member's knowledge, skill, and belief
standing prior to and independent of any actual occasion in
which such knowledge, skill, and belief is displayed or
recognized. The latter conception is usually referred to by
the term culture.

By use of the conception of an occasioned corpus, we mean
to transform any social setting and its features for the
purposes of analysis by bringing them under the constituent
recommendations comprising this notion, that is, to examine
a setting and its features as temporally situated
accomplishments of parties to the setting.

This, of course, implies a rather different conception of 'culture'
as situated or 'occasioned' activities or, as we would put it, 'culture in
action'.

Given the irremedial indexicality of devices and categories, the
ordered properties of these indexical expressions are to be seen as
locally occasioned productions of members' practical action and
practical reasoning. Accordingly, it is to some methods of 'assembling
a sense' of their constitutive 'relational configurations' that we shall
now turn. The point is to examine the reflexively constitutive relations
between category and context. The 'resources' used to produce a sense
of the category are endogenous to the categorization itself (category-in-
context). Furthermore, in the relational configurations so constituted,
the 'collection' to which a category belongs can be seen to be
constituted through its use in context, that is, it is part and parcel of its
use *in that way*.

Categorial Order in Referral Talk

The membership categories of the participants in the referral
meetings are *teacher* and *educational psychologist* respectively. Together,
they comprise the collection 'parties to a referral meeting' which is an
example of a standardized relational pair of categories. These 'parties
to the referral meeting' constitute the event or setting for what it
recognizably is through their activity. The category predicates or
category bound activities of 'teacher' and 'educational psychologist' in
this setting center around 'problem talk'. It is talk about the kinds of
problems for which children are referred from school to the
educational psychologist. Such talk includes describing the problem,
finding out what the problem is, discussing what to do next, making
recommendations, etc.[2] A characteristic distribution of turn types also
constitutes the context and is constituted by it, with the educational
psychologist asking questions, for example, and the teacher providing

answers. The participants are also expected to know and display an orientation to such knowledge as to how to talk and talk understandably and be so recognized as having talked. It is observable that the parties do not, say, discuss or make recommendations about whether or not to send a referral to prison. That type of discussion is tied to other categories of person (judge) and to other types of setting (trials). It would be an 'odd', accountable matter, if the teacher began talking about sending a referral to jail. It would be beyond the scope of category entitlements of the educational psychologist to make such a recommendation so there is little point in the teacher making such a request. Were it made, it would be made in the manner of an 'aside' ('by the way', 'in my opinion', 'but that's by the by'), that is, not a matter for this occasion and the category incumbents who are present.

The reflexive constitution of membership categories, category predicates and social context in referral meetings can be appreciated firstly through consideration of the *meaning* of a particular categorization, namely 'thief' as used to describe a particular referral.

Thief? What kind of thief?

> (1)   MP/51
> TI: Now, the other side which I see of him is that (0.7)
>   he's a thief (0.7) you know, hgh he'll pick up
>   anything (-) y'know errgh (1.3)

In this extract the teacher categorizes the referral as 'a thief' and as one who will 'pick up anything'. Our question is what is meant by such categorizations. Does the category 'thief' refer to bank robbery, jewel theft, or industrial espionage? Is the teacher talking about fraud, picking pockets or white collar crime? Does 'picking up anything' refer to picking up litter, boys or girls? We take it that none of these 'understandings' seem appropriate, but rather that the kind of theft to which the teacher refers is 'petty theft', probably committed around the school (other pupils' property, for example) and that the reference to 'picking up' refers to his proclivity for theft and not for sexual encounters.

The *contextual resources* used in making sense of this categorization include the category membership of the subject (referred pupil), the setting (referral meeting), the category membership of the participants (teacher and psychologist) and the immediate context of the co-selected descriptions. These, together with the categorization in question, stand in a reflexively constitutive relationship or configuration. They comprise a 'category-in-context'.

As far as knowledge of the subject is concerned, it is known that he is a child, a referred child, a pupil in school, in his early teens (as it happens). Now, whilst it has been the case, and may be the case, that schoolboys might engage in all manner of thievery, there is no indication that the theft refers to bank robbery or other 'serious' forms of theft. Such forms of theft are not, so to speak, predicates of teenage or schoolboy thieves. We do not readily associate such forms of theft with schoolboys, although we would not conventionally speaking, entirely rule out their possibility.

Furthermore, the occasioned device ('parties to a referral meeting'), its constituent categories (teacher and psychologist) and their category bound activities (talking about referral problems) all provide for the reasonable inference that the 'thieving' is not only petty but is a description of a problem for which the child has been referred to the psychologist and not to the police. Hearably, then, this is *what* the category means; *this* is how it is *ordered*.

It may also be observed that following the use of the membership category 'thief', the teacher mentions that 'he'll pick up anything'. This is recognizable as an elaboration of the category 'thief'. Clearly, the sense of 'picking up' also may vary, depending on topic. A person may 'pick up litter', 'pick up girls' or 'pick up boys', they may 'pick up' in the sense of 'recover'. In this context, however, 'picking up anything' is heard as a description of what the person in his capacity of a thief does, namely he opportunistically steals or takes objects which do not belong to him. This sense, then, is one which derives from the category 'thief'; it is heard as a predicate of that category. Such a hearing indicates the use of the 'thief' and 'pick up anything' as co-selected descriptions with regard to which a consistency rule corollary (or hearer's maxim) operates, namely that if consecutive categorizations can be heard as belonging to the same device or collection then hear them that way. There is a presumed consistency between these consecutive categorizations.

The production of the sense of the category and its predicate reflexively constitutes the various contextual features used as resource in producing that sense. Thus, it contributes to the sense of the category membership of the participants, to their co-membership of the device 'parties to a referral meeting', and to the character of the context as a 'referral meeting'. This is because 'talking about problems like this one' is a category predicate of the parties to the referral meeting.

The orderly features, then, of the indexical expression 'thief' are reflexively constituted *in situ*. The meaning of the category and hence the collection to which it belongs are context embedded and context constitutive. The contextual features constitute the orderliness of the expression, whilst that orderliness contributes to the sense of the contextual features. Category and context comprise a reflexively constituted relational configuration. The categorial order so produced - this person is a 'thief', where 'thief', as a membership category can be heard to belong to the collection 'referral problems' - is therefore a local organized, relationally configured, reflexively constituted phenomenon.

Shy Boys and Drama Lessons

Our second data extract not only displays the mutual intelligibility of category and context, it also comprises an instance of what can be heard as an 'account'. Such a property, like the intelligibility of descriptions considered in the previous section, is also a locally organized, relationally configured, reflexively constituted feature.[3]

> (2)   MP/184
> TI: Nobody's s-s:poken of this lad as a discipline
>   problem as such: if anything he's rather introverted
>   (0.5) err (1.5) there have been comments which
>   were made to me when I first became involved
>   which said e-is-his mathematics are atrocious.....
>   ....
>
> EP: Well in-in seventy eight errm he was referred to us
>   err being sort of shy and withdrawn but I should
>   think poor mathematics an an so on err didn't mix
>   well.....
>   ......
>
> T2:   The only subject that he's been in sort of any trouble
>   in is drama where it says he's always making
>   excuses not to do any work that's the only one
>   where he's actually (0.8) actively lazy I suppose .hh
>   (0.8) just sits there quietly and doesn't say
>
> TI: [He]would have to expose himself there, wouldn't
>   he?

In the first fragment of this extract, the first teacher (TI) describes the referred pupil as 'rather introverted'. The educational psychologist (EP) then reports that the child was referred previously because he was 'shy' and 'withdrawn'. The second teacher (T2) then reports that the child is 'in trouble' in drama, he 'makes excuses not to do any work', is 'actively lazy' and 'just sits there quietly and doesn't say...'. Finally, TI says that the child 'would have to expose himself there, wouldn't he'? What follows concentrates on the last of these utterances, namely 'he would have to expose himself there, wouldn't he?'

A first issue here is the intelligibility of 'expose himself'. To what 'collection' does this activity belong? Although one culturally available sense of the phrase 'expose himself' might refer to the child revealing some or all the parts of his anatomy for the benefit of his fellow drama students, in the contextual circumstances this is *not* the 'obvious' intelligible interpretation of this utterance. Rather, it is hearable as, and is heard as, referring to a requirement of participation in a drama lesson, namely that one has to 'act' (or, at least, 'express himself') in front of an audience, in this case other children in the referred pupil's class. Furthermore, the description is recognizable as an account of the various forms of behaviour which have just been reported, namely that the child sits quietly, 'makes excuses', and is 'actively lazy'. All of these are accounted for as ways of *avoiding exposure*.

The sense of 'exposure' as reluctance to act or express himself in front of an audience is reflexively constituted through knowing that the context is a drama lesson and that the person in question is a shy (or introverted) boy. Thus, in the drama lesson, the relevant membership category is 'actor' and the category bound activity is 'acting'. This means that the 'parties to the drama lesson' are obliged to perform in front of an audience. 'Exposing oneself' in this sense is a category predicate of 'actor'. However, the meaning of the predicate is also bound to the category 'shy boy' as well as 'actor', but in a different way. Thus, where actors are obliged to expose themselves, shy boys are reluctant to do so. It is, in other words, a category predicate of shy boys that they are reluctant to expose themselves in front of others, and a drama lesson with its requirement of such exposure would seem to be a particularly problematic, even threatening, environment for the incumbents of such a membership category.

In sum, then, the sense of 'expose' is organized *in situ* with reference to the knowledge that (a) the context is a drama lesson, (b) the occasioned membership category is 'actor', and (c) the pupil in question is a 'shy boy'. In turn, this sense is a constituent reflexive feature of the relational configuration which informs it. Thus, once again, this 'problem talk' constitutes their category membership and the character of the occasion, and these are used as resources to make sense of the talk as 'problem talk' (about referrals). The particular sense of 'exposure' is constituted by this context just as it contributes to the intelligibility of that context. The collection to which 'exposing' belongs, then, is one which is occasioned by this context (it is a 'fear of exposure'). That is, its sense is relative to this context and is occasioned by it.

A second issue is the recognizability of 'he would have to expose himself' as an account. This is heard as an account because of what is known about this context, the device 'parties to a drama lesson' which it occasions, the category predicates of these parties and the category membership and predicates of 'shy boy'. Thus, given these contextual features, the shy boy can be seen to have a 'problem': how can he avoid having to expose himself. The solution is he can avoid participation. He can 'make excuses', 'sit quietly', 'say nothing', 'be lazy'. *This is what shy boys do in this context.* Such activities make sense in the present circumstances, in the context of the drama lesson. Given the context, his actions are reasonable. That is to say, then, a possible category predicate of 'shy boy' is 'avoiding exposure' which, in this case, may be constituted by the reported behaviour. The sense of 'he would have to expose himself there, wouldn't he' as an account trades off, and reflexively constitutes, these motivational predicates which are imputed to this particular shy boy in this context.

Battered and bruised: victim or offender?

Our third extract, from a referral meeting between a Head teacher (or Principal) and an educational psychologist, not only exhibits the reflexivity of category and context, it also contains an example of a moral judgement grounded in membership categorization.

(3)   RMSJ/197
HT.   I mean I did have a message oh:: about two or three weeks ago from mother that he had been badly beaten up outside of school
EP·   Yeah
HT.   By some of the boys in this school (1 5) uhmm certainly he came the next day with quite a bruise on his cheek
EP·   Mm
HT.   I I tried to find out what had happened though really and legally I can't do anything about what happens outside school but I do
EP·   Mm

> HT:　　Uhmm and you know I when I got down to brass
> 　　　　tacks it was as usual Robert deliberately tormenting
> 　　　　boys, calling them names, using bad language,
> 　　　　spoiling their game.
> EP:　　Mm
> HT:　　Uhmm they knew they didn't dare touch him in
> 　　　　school so they waited　(-)　till they got him=
> EP:　　　　　　　　　　　　　　　　　[mm hm]
> HT.　　=outside uhmm (the) boys concerned were
> 　　　　punished but really it's a bit like the (...) case
> 　　　　which you weren't involved in I find that I'm
> 　　　　punishing children for something that I partially
> 　　　　sympathise that they are going to react to this child
> EP·　　Yeah

The membership categorization device which is occasioned by the events reported in this extract is 'parties to a beating'. Its constituent membership categories are 'victim' and 'offender' (or attacker). In the course of the extract, the teacher (HT), can be heard to transform the category membership of the child who is 'beaten up' from, initially, a possible 'victim' to, subsequently, an 'offender'. Thus, she describes him at first as having been 'beaten up' outside the school. A possible hearing of this is that the child is therefore a 'victim'. This is achieved via the use of the viewer's maxim:

> If a member sees a category bound activity being done, then,
> if one can see it being done by a member of a category to
> which the activity is bound, then: See it that way　(Sacks
> 1974a).

Thus, the predicates 'badly beaten up outside of school' and 'quite a bruise on his cheek' *can* be heard as predicated of *victim*; therefore the child *is* a victim.

The category transformation into 'offender' is achieved by her reporting what she found out when she got down to 'brass tacks'. She reports various acts perpetrated by the child in question: he 'tormented' those who subsequently beat him up, he 'used bad language', he 'called them names' and he 'spoiled their games'. Furthermore, these acts are described as 'usual' as far as this particular child is concerned. Using the viewers maxim once again, since such predicates can be seen (or heard) as predicates of the category 'offender' then they *are* seen (or heard) that way.

Such 'offensive' acts, it may be noted, are intelligible as acts bound to *this* offender (who also happens to be a child). Thus, when the teacher speaks of 'torment' this is hearable as 'teasing' rather than 'torture', the games are 'in the playground' rather than 'teamgames' or 'sexgames' or 'wargames', the names are 'childish' and 'abusive' rather than complimentary or honorific, and the 'bad language' as 'swearing' rather than 'poor grammar'. The collections, in other words, to which these categories of activity belong are constituted in the ways in which they are used here, where that includes the category membership of the speakers, the context and, of course, the category membership or identity of the referred child.

With this transformation of the category membership of the child, the meaning of the 'beating' is likewise transformed. It is transformed from a possible 'unprovoked attack' to 'revenge' or 'retaliation'. That is, then, just as the 'victim' is transformed into an offender, so the 'attackers' are transformed into victims themselves who then became retaliators who took their revenge.

The category transformation which is achieved through the report of these contextual features involves also a shift in the moral meaning of the beating. Thus, the teacher can be heard to offer approbation of this event - as she puts it, she 'sympathises' with the boys concerned. The 'offender' got the punishment he 'deserved'. The boys were therefore justified in their actions. Such a moral judgement is grounded in the category relations of the 'parties to the beating'. She sympathises with those who are transformed from offenders to victims; she regards the child who is transformed from victim to offender as justly deserving his treatment.

In this extract, then, as in the previous two, the sense of a membership category is to be understood in relation to its context. For the speakers the orderliness of categories and the collections to which they belong is organized is exhibited and constituted, *as they speak*. The relational configuration of category and context is used by the teacher to provide for the 'good sense' of her remarks, just as that 'good sense' contributes to the configuring of those relations. In turn, in speaking this way the parties to the referral meeting can be heard to reflexively constitute their own category relations in this context.

Categorial Order in the Reading of News Headlines About Suicide

Our analysis of the three cases above explicates the reflexive constitution of (a) the meaning of category ('thief'), (b) the meaning of a motivational account ('He would have to expose himself there, wouldn't he?'), and (c) the intelligibility of a moral assessment ('I find that I'm punishing children for something that I partially sympathise [with]'). In the following examination of two newspaper headlines the reflexive constitution of category and context will again be evident. In each case the recognizability of the meaning of categories and of motives or reasons for action will again be the central empirical phenomenon. Neither headline, however, presents a moral assessment, as such, of the state of affairs each reports. This feature, then, of the educational-psychological materials is not repeated. However, what we *will* bring out in the following analysis is the particular part played in meaning constitution by the sort of *task* or *activity* that reading-the-newspaper-for-the-news is.

In the previous section of the chapter the interactional context for the 'problems' talk was partly constituted by the presupposed (and thereby achieved) identities of the parties to a referral meeting, namely 'teacher' and 'psychologist.' The membership categories of the parties to a newspaper reading may be referred to as 'newspaper' and 'news reader' respectively, where 'newspaper' is understood as a collectivity category (an organization), conventionally referred by its name ('The New York Times', 'The Globe and Mail', 'The Guardian'). They are recognizable as comprising the collection 'parties to a newspaper reading' which is a further example of a standardized relational pair of categories. These 'parties to a newspaper reading,' as well as the activity of 'reading the newspaper,' are constituted as what they recognizably are through the news reader's activity alone. But, oddly, part of the news reader's activity is to constitute the other party, namely the newspaper, as an actor, a participant in the interaction. Moreover, that constitutive work involves representing the newspaper as the sole active participant in the interaction, the news reader being merely the recipient of, or audience to, the newspaper's telling or reporting of the news. Thus, 'what The Times said today about the strike' is an accountable ('observable-reportable') matter.

For the standardized relational pair comprising 'teacher' and 'psychologist' the relevantly predicated activity is talk about children *as* problems. The category predicates of 'newspaper' and 'news reader' center around the collection of tasks or activities or practices that make up 'reading the paper to see what the paper says.' Such tasks/activities/practices include 'finding out what's in the news,' 'discovering what happened yesterday at the inquest,' 'looking up the hockey scores,' 'seeing what the weather is today,' 'seeing what Salutin's column said,' 'seeing what position The Globe and Mail is taking on the election,' 'finding out what the solution to the crossword is,' 'seeing what's on sale at Sears,' 'finding out what's on at the movies,' 'seeing who died yesterday,' and so on. They are tasks directed towards the kinds of things newspapers say, report or provide. In particular, the activities of newspaper production and newspaper reading predicate a kind of reader who is expected to know, and display an orientation to such knowledge as, how to 'read,' read intelligibly, and appropriately report to others *the news.'*

That knowledge or orientation is procedural. We may say it is embedded in a *particular* task, activity or practice, namely that of 'looking for the news,' that is, reading in such a way as to dis-cover the newsworthy story (Anderson and Sharrock 1979). That is, just as the kinds of problems children pose for teacher and psychologist were seen to be as of the kind that recommend some local therapeutic solution rather than a trip to jail, so news producers and readers may be presumed to be oriented to those properties of events that make them newsworthy rather than of, say, metaphysical or educational or literary note. Looking for the news is itself a complex matter. The competent news reader is one who can: follow narratives across columns and pages of texts, tell apart such objects as news stories, news features, editorials, advice columns and advertisements, relate what is said today to what was said yesterday, and so on. We are particularly interested here in the reader's recognition and understanding of news 'headlines.' Headlines are to be read as *announcing* the contents of the following 'stories.' They tip the reader to the *angle* that the story will have on the events it recounts. Just as one listens to a joke announced as 'dirty' with ears attuned to recognize the obscenity (and thereby the punch line) (Sacks 1974b), so one reads the newspaper headline *for* the tellable story. As Anderson and Sharrock (1979: 380-381) put it:

> [A] headline in a newspaper seeks to interest, to be newsworthy and this is known by most readers. Headlines then may be read to make news. They may attain newsworthiness by announcing that something we need to know is contained in the subsequent text; by announcing a continuation or conclusion to something we are already interested in or by announcing that something extraordinary has happened. There is a sense in which 'Boy, 16, swims the Channel' .. is about the unlikely achievement of a difficult task Formally the newsworthy elements . are the unlikely nature of the actor for the act ... The essence of this particular newsworthiness resides in its outstanding mentionability

Moreover, being abbreviated, a headline cannot say everything that the article will say, but then it need not do so since, after all, the article itself is there to follow. While it must convey something of the sense of the story in order to be intelligible at all, and while both that and some 'interest' are necessary to keep the news reader from passing on to another headline-and-story without reading the article itself, the sense conveyed need not be definitive, since the article is there to settle any ambiguity. Indeed the ideal headline presumably contains some slight features of a puzzle, sufficient to whet the news reader's inquisitive interest for what's new.

Seeing that a Fiancé Committed Suicide Because His Fiancée Broke their Engagement

(4)   Engagement was broken - Temperamental young man gassed himself

We read this newspaper headline to mean that a young man's engagement to be married was broken by his fiancée and that this made him so unhappy (as losing her) that, (perhaps) somewhat impulsively, he committed suicide. (He probably did this by inhaling poisonous gas from his kitchen stove or from the exhaust of his car.)

How do we, as news readers, 'know' this, given that on the basis of (a knowledge of) the syntax and semantics of the language, several other readings are possible? Specifically, how do we know:

(a)   that the engagement was for marriage (not for dinner),

(b)   that the young man was engaged (not someone else),

(c)   that the engaged parties were engaged to each other (and not to others),

(d)   that the broken engagement was the young man's (not another's),

(e)   that the gassing was a suicide (not an accident, and not less than terminal),

(f)   that first the engagement was broken and then the young man gassed himself (not the reverse),

(g)   that the second happened *because* of the first (not independently of it), and

(h)   that it happened because of desperation arising from the 'loss', assisted by the 'temperamental' aspect of the young man's character (rather than from religious ecstasy or moral outrage .)?

(Furthermore, how is it that we think that he probably did this in one of the manners described above (and not, say, by some more exotic method)?)

As with the educational psychology data we take it that the meanings expressed in (a)-(h) are locally ordered, relationally configured and reflexively constituted through the reader's use of available contextual resources, namely categories, category collections, devices and predicates, made available by the text of the headline *for* a reader who is 'looking for the news'.

Category: Using a Standardized Relational Pair to Find an Engaged Couple
In this case the membership category used in the headline is 'young man.' But what sort of young man? Is he a student, an unemployed young man, an angry young man ...? By using as a local contextual resource the concept of engagement from elsewhere in the headline, we as news readers can find that he is a fiancé (or ex-fiancé) (see the next section). The category 'fiancé' then makes relevant a 'paired' category, namely the other partner to the engagement, the young man's 'fiancée.' That is, assuming, for the moment, the relevance of 'fiancé' as a translation of 'young man,' we may say that 'fiancé' 'goes together with' 'fiancée' as a 'standardized relational pair' (like 'husband-wife,' 'parent-child,' 'stranger-stranger' ...) such that to invoke one part of the pair is to have the other programmatically present; furthermore, use of the paired categories entails that incumbents are related to each other, and not to others. Thus (c) above. But by virtue of this pair of identifications being recognizable without either category being mentioned, successful reference to the fiancé can be made with the use of another category, in this case namely 'young man'. And 'young man' is available to do other 'work,' as we shall see below.

Predicate: Using Grammars of Engagement and Suicide to Identify Persons, Actions and Reasons
A constitutive feature of the category pair, 'fiancé-fiancée', is being engaged for marriage. Features conventionally related to the category pair are being in love, making plans for marriage, wearing rings, going about together and the like. Events happening to an incumbent of one part of the pair may be said to happen to both (Drew, 1978: 15). The categories project a future state in which such matters as marriage, commitment, fidelity, children, anniversaries, etc. are conventionally anticipated features. These matters, we might say, are

part of the grammar of the concept of 'engagement' (for marriage), that is, its predicates. Conversely, one might say that for the 'broken engagement' the 'conventionally anticipated features' might include emotional distress, anger, hurt, a sense of grievance on the part of the 'jilted' party, possible desire for revenge and so on.

As an action 'committing suicide' also has its conceptual grammar, its category-tied predicates. It is done for conventional reasons, in certain psychological states, arising out of conventional interactional and structural social circumstances, with conventional methods, and so on. Why would a fiancé(e) commit suicide? Because of the loss of the (other) fiancé(e) (see Watson, 1983: 35). For whom would the loss of a fiancé(e) be a reason for suicide? The (other) fiancé(e). (Thus our assumption above.) What might a fiancé(e) do in the event of a broken engagement and the consequent loss of the fiancé(e)? Clearly there is a range of grammatical possibilities, narrowed by 'temperamental' considerations, of which commiting suicide is one. Thus, possibly, (a)-(h).

Why *this* jilted lover elected suicide (rather than, say, overwork) can be read off the moral-emotional descriptor 'temperamental.' In a contest of a 'readably' broken engagement and a readable suicide this qualifier can be read as indicating just that element of personality, namely a certain impulsiveness, that would provide for suicide as an explainable outcome. At the same time the perceptive reader may find other possible senses of 'temperamental' - cantankerous, difficult - as relevant candidate explanations of the breakdown of the relationship of the engaged parties int he first place. (And the implicaiton is that readers may find other senses of the word relevant in and as other contexts.) Again, coming to a reading of the meaning of 'temperamental' provides reflexively for the identification of this young man as indeed the jilted lover.

We are reminded here of Cuff's (1994) discussion of 'morally qualified identities' in his study of members' accounts of their marriage breakdowns. Thus, in partial critique of Sacks's 'SRP (standardized relational pair) machinery' he argues that for his data 'unqualified, general categories of husband and wife are inadequate for repairing the sense of what is being reported' (by the wife in this case). 'Rather, hearers might require some more specific identity, such as 'bad' or 'dissolute' husband for *them to find out who it is who is engaging in a range of activities* like gambling, lying, refusing to work and support his wife and children in this marriage. The qualified identity 'bad husband' might then serve to collect together these various activities which can be heard as a collection of the sort of things done not simply by 'husbands' but by 'bad' or 'dissolute' husbands (Cuff 1994: 53; emphasis added). The parallel with 'temperamental young man', we take it, is clear.

So far, then, we are saying that in finding plausible identities and relationships for the parties referred to in the headline, as well as a plausible reading of the nature of their actions and the reasons for them, news readers may have recourse to such contextual resources as an available standardized relational pair of categories and the conceptual grammar of actions and reasons-for-action predicable of those categories. Moreover, as we have argued throughout this chapter, such found readings are relationally configured and reflexively constitued. Thus, as readers we may find that the 'young man' is a fiance by reading 'engagement' as 'engagement' for marriage (not dinner). But then we may see 'engagement' as engagement for marriage (not dinner) by reading 'young man' as a relevant substitute descriptor for fiancé, engagement for marriage being a state conventionally entered into by the young. Furthermore, we may find 'engagement' to be for marriage by seeing one such who is temperamental (where a broken engagement for dinner would not conventionally suffice). At the same time, reading 'engagement' as for marriage and its breaking as an adequate reason for suicide permits finding 'gassed himself' to be the action of committing suicide (rather than death by accident or breaking up in laughter). Finding the meaning of these categorizations, action descriptors and other elements of the context is thus an accomplishment of the reader in which the meaning of each element reflexively constitutes, and is constituted by, the meaning of the others. The meanings are read as elements in a gestalt contexture (Maynard 1984: 156-161) where, via the play of the documentary method of interpretation (Garfinkel 1956; 1967), they are seen as co-selected elements in mutual relationship to each other.

Task: Finding a Tragic Story about a Young Man in the News

We have written above of the reader coming up with a possible, plausible reading. But, we might say, what converts a possible story to a definite one is the reader's use of and appeal to that practice uniquely predicated of the category news reader, namely 'looking for and finding the news.' As Anderson and Sharrock have said, one basis of newsworthiness is 'the unlikely nature of the actor for the act.' In terms of the grammar of 'engagement for marriage' the category 'fiancé' anticipates a future *life*, one moreover rich with the promised fruits of marriage, perhaps children, family life and so on. Suicide is an action not just *not* predicated of fiancé, but one that is opposite to its predicates, being life destroying not life enhancing. Furthermore, insofar as events happening to one member of the fiancé-fiancée standardized relational pair can be said to happen to both, then the shocking consequences attending suicide happen not only to the dead (ex-)fiancé but to the live one too. Given, too, that the normative rights and obligations predicated of those paired categories to whom one turns in the course of a search for help when suicidal (Sacks 1972) presume that the fiancée was turned to for help before the fatal action, then she can find herself bearing guilt and responsibility (however unjustly) for his subsequent drastic step. However, what perhaps especially conveys the pathos of this story is that it is about a 'young man.' That is, while we might say it is bad enough that anybody commits suicide, and that it is in some sense worse if that person is engaged to be married, it is *truly* tragic if that engaged person is young. For young people, we say, 'have their whole lives ahead of them.' In short, and without elaborating further, suicide by a young person who was engaged has major elements of tragedy, at least in the sense employed by newspapers. But tragedy is news. Therefore, our reader may reason, that *is* the story being told in this headline. Our reading is the tellable, newsworthy story (among the possible readings), and therefore, for the reader, *is* the story. Thus (a)-(h), definitely.

Again, reflexive constitution of the meaning of contextual elements is evident. Bringing to the reading of the words on the page the supposition that they comprise a headline and that headlines are written to make news by announcing newsworthy stories, provides the news reader with the interpretive warrant to find the particular tragic story of the young fiancé who committed suicide because his betrothed broke off their engagement for marriage. This is not, after all, a story about a young writer breaking up in hysterics because his agent broke an engagement for a business lunch (cf Wong 1966: C1). At the same time, putting the elements of this cryptic 'utterance' together to produce *this* story of suicide permits the reader to see that these words do indeed constitute a news headline. They are not the title of an advertisement, book being reviewed, obituary, section of the paper, and so on. Moreover, the particular story being told by them is not, in the end, merely a *possible* story. Reading the news is not an invitation to engage in a post-modernist game of interpretation where any story is as good a reading as any other. The news reader may not employ a licence to invent possible meanings. The news headline is not a poem awaiting interpretation. The news reader is enjoined to find just the story announced in the headline, and no other, even if it takes reading the report following the headline to settle any doubts. The status of the words *as* a news headline and the identity of the story being told by them are the news reader's locally ordered, relationally configured and reflexively constituted accomplishment.

Seeing that a Police Officer Committed Suicide Because His Girlfriend Died

(5)   Officer's suicide at girlfriend's grave

This headline is readily readable as saying that a police officer (or perhaps a military officer) killed himself intentionally at the grave of is girlfriend because she was dead.[4]   Again, the question is: how does the reader find *this* meaning, *this* story, in the headline? How does the reader see (i) that the girlfriend is the girlfriend of the officer (and not of someone else), and that the officer is thereby male,[5] (ii) that he committed suicide because of something to do with her (not for some other reason), specifically her death, and (iii) that he is definitely a police officer or, possibly, a military officer (not, say, a company officer like a treasurer).

Category: Using a Standardized Relational Pair to Find a Boyfriend

To come to the conclusion that the girlfriend is the girlfriend of the officer and not of somebody else the reader may engage in two operations, both of which produce the desired results.   Firstly, 'girlfriend' may be heard as half of the standardized relational pair in which it is paired with 'boyfriend.'   Notice that since these categories come in pairs successful identification may be achieved by *naming* only one of them.   The other category-position is then left 'free' to do additional 'work'.   The additional work that 'Officer' is doing we will come to below.

Predicate: Using Properties of Relationships to Find a Boyfriend and a Motive

The second operation is one that trades directly on the reader's presumed commonsense knowledge of suicide, particularly on our notions of what are 'good reasons' for committing suicide. By 'good' we do not mean morally acceptable by some standard, but hearably adequate - we might not think he should have done it, but knowing something of the ways the world works we can figure out why he did. The procedure involves the reader in starting with the action 'suicide' and trying to see if the membership categories in the headline stand in some relevant relationship to the action. In that we may read 'suicide' as the sort of action that is done for some reason, and in that certain events happening to one of a pair of 'intimates' can be seen as sufficient reason for the other to commit the act, then given that 'girlfriend' is part of such a pair of intimates, and given that her death is seeable as one of those 'certain events,' then the one who committed suicide was her boyfriend. That is, the death of an intimate is one of those certain events that stand as adequate reason for the other member of the intimate pair to commit suicide.   By virtue of those conceptual-grammatical connections we can identify the parties involved as boyfriend and girlfriend to one another.

The analysis so far has traded on something we have yet to establish, namely that the officer killed himself *because* of his girlfriend's death. Knowing the linguistic grammar of English and the meanings of words does not itself permit us to make that motivational inference. Yet we do make it, and it seems inescapable. How is that so? The answer seems to be a product of the same analysis that yielded 'girlfriend' as girlfriend of 'officer.'   For just as the conventional relationship of intimacy that relates 'girlfriend' and 'boyfriend' is what allows the reader to see that the dead girlfriend could be the girlfriend of the one who committed suicide, namely the officer, so that same invoked relationship is one that says that one member of the pair may act in a certain way because of what has happened to the other (or what the other has done). Given that we *can* see that one member of the pair has done something relevant to the suicide of the other, namely die, then we *do* see it that way (cf. Sacks 1974a: 221). For this will *explain* the suicide; and this seems not only our overriding interest in the topic but, as both Garfinkel and Sacks claim, the way we go about seeing that a death is a suicide at all.

> [I]f the interpretation makes good sense, then that's what happened (Garfinkel 1967· 106)
> Members take it that they may choose among proposed competing facts by deciding that the fact is present for which there is an adequate explanation, and the fact is not present for which there is not an adequate explanation (Sacks 1972: 57)

Still presupposed in the preceding analysis is the inference that the girlfriend is dead. We do not take it that she is indeed alive, and that the grave is a plot she happens to own, having been acquired in anticipation of a parent's death, and as yet unfilled. This line of reasoning will not explain the action of the [boyfriend], whereas to suppose that she is dead and in that grave will do so. Within the context of the preferred explanation 'grave' selects unequivocally just one feature that describes the girlfriend, namely her being dead. Not only for the reader, but for the finders of the body and all others concerned, the occurrence of the suicide at the grave invites the inference that it is the fact of the one to whom the grave belongs being dead and in the grave that is the relevant feature explaining the suicide.

Task: Finding a Tragedy about a Police Officer in the News

In discussing membership categories above we said that one interesting feature of relational pairs is that only one pair-member needs to be mentioned in order to invoke both. The second category-position is then freed to do other work. If the general claim is true, that membership categories are selected to achieve some sort of fit with the action performed in terms of the reasons for it, then the reader may search for a meaning of 'officer' that is relevant to the action and the reason for it. Beyond that, however, we have already said that it is crucial to remember that this is a newspaper headline, and headlines 'may be read to make news.' Again, a characteristic way to make news is to find 'the unlikely nature of the actor for the act.' It is by reading the headline for its announcement of an unusual event that we can find that the officer is a police officer. For suicide is an unexpected action for an occupational category, police officers, for whom dealing with and sometimes resolving trouble of a dirty, dangerous, and life-and-death sort such as suicide is a routine part of their work. Police are those we turn to in trouble; they are not supposed to be persons who themselves have found no one to turn to. In finding a tragic story in the headline we find it is about a police officer.[6]

As members we have ways to find what we find in the world, and to so produce objects that others can find what is there to be found in them. It is not that we could not find that this headline announces an upcoming event, rather than reporting on one in the recent past. It is not that this 'suicide' could not be an act of metaphorical self-killing, some foolish act with deadly consequences for the officer's career. It is not that, after all, the officer's death was not assisted by some precursor of Jack Kevorkian, with all the doubts about the extent of its voluntariness, about the clarity of its intention that such an association may invoke. There is, in short, no given rule of use for the expression 'suicide' prescribing just exactly what the reader is to take this officer did according to this story. For that we have to invoke what sort of event *could* be the subject of a news story, that the everyday reader *could* discover from just those words with just whatever we might unspecially have at hand on just that day like any other, such as knowledge of what kinds of people commit what kinds of suicide for what kinds of reasons, of what being in love is like and what guilt is, of what graves and policemen are for, and finally as at the beginning, what newspapers mean by tragedy.

Once again, in seeing that this officer is the boyfriend of the girlfriend, and in seeing that the girlfriend is dead, the reader may see that this officer committed suicide *because* she was dead. That is, the reader may construe the contextual particulars about the girlfriend's grave as comprising *relevantly* contextual features of the officer's action, that is, as providing a reason or motive for his suicide. In the same socio-logical moment, that practical determination reflexively constitutes the officer and the girlfriend as a relational pair, and the girlfriend as dead. Both readings trade off each other via the grammar of reasons for suicide as category predicates. Let us emphasise, however, that these are found, in the sense of *made*, predications, just as the categorizations are a found, that is *made*, relational pair this time. They further depend on the reader reading this line of words *as* a headline, and its contents therefore as *news*. For that move can provide the 'motivation' to see the reported event as tragic. And for this to be a story of tragedy that 'suicide' has to be a literal, not metaphorical, one this time. Conversely, finding this event to be a tragic suicide reflexively constitutes the words *as* a news headline. Category, collection (standardized relational pair) and predicate provide formal means by which the reader can assemble for these words on this occasion a locally ordered, relationally configured and reflexively constituted sense.

Conclusion

In Chapter One we indicated that, for ethnomethodology, categories and predicates, as indexical expressions, are constituted as members of collections or membership categorization devices *in their use*. Their orderliness, their 'going together', is achieved and is to be found in the local specifics of categorization as an activity; in short, membership categorization devices are *locally assembled objects*. There is, to use a phrase of Garfinkel's, 'no time out' from the here-and-now character of all sense making, every usage of a category or a collection. The orderliness of these indexical expressions is, then, a property which is organized on each and every occasion on which membership categories are used.

In terms of this conception, this chapter has examined the use of a range of membership categories in referral talk and in newspaper headlines. It has been shown how categories, predicates and devices are deployed in, for example, accomplishing the sense of talk and text, in finding motives, and in making moral judgements. It has also been shown how category, predicate and the contexts of their use are reflexively tied to each other, with each 'part' of the relational configurations which they compose, 'informing' the sense of the other(s). Finally, in using categories and predicates in the ways that we have explicated, categories and predicates have been ordered as members of collections. Indeed, it is their membership of a collection which is a constituent feature of their meaning. 'Thief', for example, was used as a member of the collection 'referral problems', 'shy boy' was used as a 'party to a drama lesson', and 'officer' was used as part of a standardized relational pair 'fiancé-fiancée'. Such uses do not exhaust their interactional possibilities; shy boys, thieves and officers may belong to an indefinite variety of collection. Indeed, in the data we have examined they have more than one meaning and have been 'collected' in various ways. How they are ordered, then, is to be discovered in the local specifics of their practical use.

This last point is crucial for distinguishing the ethnomethodological position on the relation between category and context from the decontextualized model of that relation. In Chapter One we argued that the decontextualized model could be discerned in certain of the programmatic statements remarks of Sacks and more definitely in such fields of language study as ethnosemantics and the ethnography of speaking. Thus Hymes (1962: 19; 1964: 97-8) asserted that form (lexeme) and context mutually determine meaning, while Frake (1964: 133) held that act and situation do so. While such formulations are helpful they remain inadequate to the extent that context and situation are left unexplicated (Wieder 1970: 119-20), or are treated as determinate independently of members contextual or situated uses of them (Eglin 1980: 38). Writing at the dissident extreme of cognitive anthroplogy, Tyler (1969c: 75) posed the problem as follows:

> It does not need demonstration to prove that the total physical surroundings or context of any utterance are never exactly the same on two different occasions Thus, contexts cannot be finite This is the paradox of the contextual theory Since the notion of context violates the idea of rule, we cannot properly speak of meaning as a rule of use Yet, since humans do seem to take contextual features into account, they must have some means of establishing equivalencies among non-identical contexts.

Such establishment, we would suggest, consists precisely in the methodical collect-ability revealed in the use of the categories-in-context we have examined in this chapter.

Chapter 3

Some General Reflections on 'Categorization' and 'Sequence' in the Analysis of Conversation

Rod Watson

Studies of membership categorization have occupied an anomalous position with regard both to ethnomethodology and to the general corpus of conversation analysis.

By and large, ethnomethodology has not entered into any engagement with membership categorization analysis. John Heritage's justly influential study of ethnomethodology (Heritage 1984) scarcely mentions membership categorization, even though categorization phenomena figure in a major way in one of the earliest debates concerning ethnomethodology (cf. Hill and Crittenden 1968: 30-51). Nor have most other major texts on ethnomethodology and/or recent conversation(al) analysis accorded any centrality to membership categorizationphenomena or to studies of them (Sharrock and Anderson 1986)..[1]

Contemporary conversation analysis has increasingly focused on aspects of the sequential organization of utterances, to the virtual exclusion of any focal concern with membership categorization. It should be acknowledged that sequential analyses have proved immensely fruitful, not only in the minute analysis of naturally-situated, naturally-organized speech exchange *per se* but also regarding some of the generic issues in sociology. These are issues which were most famously addressed by Weber and critically elaborated by Schütz concerning what Weber sometimes termed the 'meaning component' of social action. This conceptual issue and others were initially addressed by Harvey Sacks in the 1960's (Sacks 1963; see also 1992a,b), but were subsequently taken up in certain respects by Schegloff, Heritage and Roth and others (see Schegloff 1991)..[2] The generic issues of description have frequently been addressed, often somewhat elliptically, through the discussion of the characterizations of social phenomena cast in terms of 'micro' / 'agency' and 'macro' / 'structure'/ 'institution' and increasingly through discussions concerning the applicability of the descriptive resources of other disciplines, such as linguistics, in the analysis of social phenomena.[3] These discussions are notable in that they have often proceeded on the basis of empirical analysis rather than simply comprising the chopping of logic.

Sequential analysis, then, has in many ways revolutionised the analysis of social action, but it has done so at some cost. One of the costs - a needless one, I shall argue - has been the disattending of membership categorization analysis. This is ironic given the fact that the founder of conversation analysis, Harvey Sacks, spent a great deal of time analysing membership categorization activities in conversation.

More recently, there has been a methodological tendency in 'mainstream' conversation analysis to highlight sequential analysis by setting 'categorization relevances' at zero, and to deal with what were hitherto deemed to be categorization phenomena in terms of contextualisation procedures such as 'recipient design'. Thus we get a decentreing of 'categorization phenomena'.

Metaphorically speaking, this tendency has taken on the appearance of a *gestalt* switch. If we have a sequential-analytic 'take' on conversation, then the membership categorization aspects recede from view. If one adopts the membership categorization 'take' on conversation, it makes the sequential aspects of talk recede into the background. It is as if we can cast our analysis according to one 'take' or the other but not both at the same time. By and large, conversation analysts have opted to make membership categorization analysis recede. To the extent that conversation analysts have done this, their researches rest on constructive analytic foundations.

The fact that membership categorization phenomena have been made to recede does not, however, render them *de facto* inert or inoperative. Even if they are not treated as objects of explicitation they still operate 'behind the scenes'. In other words, aspects of many sequential analyses in conversation analysis rely unrelievedly upon membership categorizations as a resource. This reliance may be a tacit and even unrecognized one but is no less real for that. The fact that categorization relevances may often be set at zero for *methodological* purposes does not mean they cease to operate in our lay reading. Even where categorization relevances are retained they are often relegated to minor status, so as to highlight sequential features of talk: in these cases, we may speak of a sequence-categorization ratio, where the degree to which one is emphasised is the degree to which the other is downplayed.

What is the consequence of the bracketing off of membership categorization phenomena and their consequent relegation into the background? One might suggest that the major consequence is to bring to many sequential analyses a background scheme of (categorial) interpretation to bear on that analysis whilst still allowing of the insistence that sequential organization possesses free-standing, or at least focal, status in the analysis of natural conversation. It permits the according of precedence to sequential analysis.

The most perspicuous (but by no means the only) examples come, perhaps, from those sequential analyses that deal with 'formal' or 'institutional' talk, namely talk occurring in bureaucratic or professional settings where participants' locutionary identities are cast in terms of the formal organization. The very transcription procedures for such occasions of speech exchange indicate a background reliance on the provision of membership categories. Observe the designations in the following stretches of talk

> (MacNeil/Lehrer 2/3/92)
> IE: .....hh And this <u>ru</u>:thless cowar:<u>d</u>ly army overthrows
>   ( ) thuh first democracy that this country's ever
>   had. (.) Our ally our <u>fight</u>,er against
>   commun i s m.
> IR: [But the] administration doesn't approve of
>   <u>that</u>?
> IE: .hh <u>NO</u> but uh: we were thuh first and I was <u>proud</u>
>   of the administration to-to fo:rce an embargo,...

> (From Heritage and Roth 1995: 7)

> Log 99638 149
> Dr: Did y'feel s<u>i</u>ck
>   (0 6)

```
Pt:      A little bit //Ye:s]
Dr:      Mmh hmh.] Right  hh Now c'n yih//tell me-
Pt:      An I wz very white.
         (0 3)
Dr:      Pale?
Pt:      Pa:le 4
```

(From Frankel 1990)

What we have, here, immediately adjacent to the line numbers on the left hand column is an index of categorial incumbency: in the first instance, 'IR' for 'Interviewer' and 'IE' for 'Interviewee', and in the second, 'Dr' for 'Doctor' and 'Pt' for 'Patient'.[5] Given the fact that in our culture we read from left to right the categorial incumbencies are furnished for the reader immediately before s/he reads the transcribed utterance on that line. The left to right reading of the line of transcript thus predisposes the reader toward its reading as 'a doctor's utterance', 'a patient's utterance', i.e. as utterance types tied to institutional identities. In a sense, the transcriber is doing the organization's, or its incumbents', work: it is the task of co-participants themselves to display categorial incumbency where relevant.

Whilst these categorial resources are furnished, in minimised form they are seldom if ever seen as worthy of explication *per se*. For instance, they are seldom if ever analysed in terms of 'standardized relational pairs' of categories, as Sacks once analysed the telephone talk between staff members of a suicide prevention center and callers to the center (Sacks 1972). Instead, the categorial-incumbency-as-transcribed of the parties to institutional talk simply has the effect of throwing into sharper relief such distributional phenomena as the 'pre-allocation' of turns and turn-types to incumbents of differing membership categories (institutional identities). This transcription of categorial incumbency is part of the textual practices whereby 'institutional talk' is rendered visible (or readable) as such. Article titles, contextualising comments introducing particular transcribed instances and the overall textual environs of the instance are all, frequently, category-rich, saturated by categorial identifications. Clearly, such transcribed categorial designations are particularly salient whereas in the two examples above the actual talk could quite plausibly be read as casual (non-institutional) talk between, say, acquaintances, or strangers, perhaps, in the case of example 2, of the 'troubles talk' variety as analysed by Jefferson and Lee (1980), or of the operation of the 'chaining rule' for questions and answers in ordinary, natural conversation (Q-A, Q-A, Q-A).[6]

My argument here is not that the explicit analysis of membership categories can be reinstated at the expense of sequential analysis: far from it. It is, instead, to refuse the opposition between these aspects of conversation analysis, to refuse the according of analytic precedence to one aspect or the other, particularly given the fact that one 'side' has been accorded such precedence that it has come to stand on behalf of contemporary 'conversational analysis' *per se.* What I am saying is that the sequential organization/membership categorization dualism in conversation analysis is unhelpful in a variety of respects: for instance, at present the sense of much sequential analysis relies upon an analytically unexplicated resource, namely the categorial order of the conversations under scrutiny through which an utterance is read over its course in terms of categorial relevances where these relevances are used in making sense of the utterance as a sequential object.

In turn, this runs the risk of treating the sense of an utterance as being structurally - (i.e. sequentially -) given to a greater extent than is, in fact, warrantable. It highlights the sequential sense of an utterance at the expense of the categorically given aspects of this sense, whilst at the same time relying upon these categorically given aspects of sense as an unexplicated resource. The disattended nature of such categorial resources does not mean that they have no power in the utterance-by-utterance sense-making process. Indeed I have tried to indicate that our categorial work informs our reading of what an utterance does and how it is formed. The failure to explicate this categorial work leads to our *assuming* (in part) the sense of an utterance and building our structural analysis on the basis of that assumed sense. In this respect we are tacitly building social structure into our analysis of that utterance: or to be more precise, we are building our sense of social structure into our analytic treatment of the utterance - an unexplicated, unexamined sense - in ways that are usually deemed characteristic of constructive analysis.

This results in the treating of the categorial order of conversation as a dualism and to setting the two poles of the dualism in competition with each other, as though a focus upon one were somehow to occlude a focus upon the other. The dualism thus takes on the form of an opposition. The outcome of this is to render analysts of sequence or of conversational format less than fully sensible of the categorial features of utterance production and ordering and to render analysts of membership categories insufficiently sensible of certain sequential concerns in the forming and ordering of utterances and other social actions. It is, therefore, as I have observed, to leave a constructivist element in the analysis.

Instead of the *gestalt*-type alternation or some kind of zero-sum ratio operating between these two poles, we might see the 'structural' (sequential) and categorial aspects of utterances as reflexively tied, as mutually constitutive. Thus, the 'here and now' specificity of sense of a given utterance or sequence may be seen as derived from (at least) both these concerns. Thus the categorization of a current speaker as 'doctor' and the recipient as 'patient' may impart sense to his/her utterance(s) as 'medical enquiry' or whatever, and the design features of an utterance or sequence (how it is formed and placed, what it does) may render it identifiable as 'category-bound', i.e. as conventionally identifiable as a *'doctor's* enquiries' or as a 'doctor'-'patient' diagnostic sequence. The sequential and categorial aspects may be seen as mutually, reciprocally elaborative such that the interlocutor or analyst operates a 'back-and-forth' procedure between the two aspects in imputing sense to the talk. I should argue that this is how a conversation-analytic transcript is read by a lay or professional observer: readers' and speaker-hearers' practices are coterminous at least in this respect. After all, 'going for an appointment with the doctor' surely inclines one toward hearing the questions and other utterances of that person during the appointment under the rubric 'doctor': categorically-based hearing rules are mobilised.

What I am claiming, then, is that interlocutors' sensible production and monitoring of an utterance and of a series of utterances is both categorial and sequential. Interlocutors' conjoint orientation to categorial relevances informs their orientation to the 'structure' of utterance and series which in turn inform the categorial relevances. In Aaron V. Cicourel's apt phrase, there is a 'folding back' effect in the utterance production and monitoring, a darting, back and forth, reflexive consultation of categorial and sequential relevances in order that utterance or series be rendered describable or identifiable as transacting this or that activity, as forming a component of this or that overall course of action and social setting.

Regarding the identifiability of the talk as (say) 'doctor'-'patient' or 'lawyer'-'client' talk, i.e. in terms of a categorially-defined setting, we may cite Cicourel's (1973: 55-6) observation that:

> talk is continuously folded back upon itself . .as a basis for members to successfully describe the arrangement to each other

Part of this folding back process involves interlocutors' ongoing consultation of utterance form and sequencing to indicate to themselves and to others that the talk accords with the 'normal form' (Cicourel 1973: 53-4), where in this case 'normal form' is categorially-given. The awareness and use of such categories form part of 'what anyone routinely knows' as a condition of her/his being accorded competent membership in society, e.g. being accorded the competence to (for instance) identify a 'doctor'-'patient' consultation.

The characterization and analysis of the reciprocal, back-and-forth elaboration of the categorial and sequential aspects of conversational order may, perhaps, be advanced and deepened by reference to Garfinkel's formulation of 'the documentary method of interpretation' (Garfinkel 1967: Ch. 3).

The 'documentary method of interpretation' comprises a 'family' of lay sense-making practices whereby members conjointly assemble coherence to an array of particulars by interpreting them in terms of an underlying pattern. The particulars are, individually and collectively, taken as 'indexing' or 'pointing to' such a pattern and as warranting its imputation: in turn, the pattern is employed to render the particulars identifiable as a related homologous collection. Thus the particulars gain meaning from each other, too. In this way the operating of the documentary method is akin to the working of a hermeneutic circle: the meaning of pattern and particular(s) is reflexively determined and reinforced in a circular 'feedback effect'. Garfinkel's characterization of the documentary method of interpretation highlights the socially-shared, transparent and public (known and used in common and manifested as such) nature of sense-making as opposed to the conception of sense-making in individualistic and even solipsistic terms as private, internal and opaque (psychologically-enclosed) information-processing operations. It also highlights the methodic or procedural organization of lay or common sense knowledge - 'knowledge how' rather than simply 'knowledge that'. Thus, analytic reference to the documentary method renders available a conception of social action as sensible, this sense being culturally-methodic in character. Social actions - including, of course, conversational utterances - can, then, be commonsensically monitored for their methodicity, their culturally-patterned nature.

With regard to, say, 'doctor'-'patient' talk the documentary method helps us analytically elucidate the reflexive relation of the categorial and sequential 'takes' on sensible conversational order. The categorial aspects of the conversation comprise one indexical particular, utterance form and sequence (conversational format) comprise others: these (at least) may all, severally and collectively, be take as pointing to an imputed underlying pattern whose proper gloss is, for instance, 'a medical consultation'. In turn, the 'feedback' from that pattern lends coherence to the categorial and 'structural' aspects of the talk, such that those aspects are individually and as an ensemble informed by the gloss. Reference to the documentary method, then, guarantees that the analyst treat the categorial and 'structural' aspects of talk as non-extractable and interdependent, and that s/he avoids the conversation-analytic equivalent of the fallacy of unwarranted extrapolation, i.e. the decontextualization of, say, the sequential from the categorial. In doing so, it occludes the initial step which leads to the functionalist interpretations of institutional talk as introduced by McHoul and others, where a strong element of teleology is introduced into the analysis (see Heap 1979, McHoul 1978 and Watson 1995).

Instead of treating the categorial as an unexplicated resource that tacitly informs the analysis of an explicit, though abstracted, topic, e.g. utterance form and sequence, our reference to the documentary method ensures that we treat *both* 'categorial' *and* 'structural' aspects as explicit, mutually-inextricable topics to be explored in their own right, as part of our overall analytic concern with sensible conversational order.[7]

Instances drawn from 'formal' settings, such as doctor-patient talk, provide only the clearest example, but talk between incumbents of the 'informal' categories such as 'friends', 'acquaintances', 'strangers' etc. is 'categorially-informed' to just the same extent.

The mutual inextricability inheres in such matters as the following, again with reference to doctor-patient talk: just as utterance form and sequencing may be seen as categorially informed by the 'doctor'-'patient' relational pair, so the form and sequencing of utterances may also be seen as interactional realisations of that categorial order, as 'folding back' upon the categorial order that has informed their production and monitoring. In turn, both these processes occur under the rubric or gloss 'a medical consultation', and reciprocally document that rubric.

In my view, this approach moves toward a possible resolution of problems and misunderstandings concerning ethnomethodology and conversation analysis, particularly with reference to the analysis of membership categorization activities.

These problems extend far beyond any mere assertion that sequential analyses have been (albeit tacitly) parasitic upon an unexplicated categorial phenomenon or that due attention to categorial order has been denied by sequential analysts in conversation analysis.

Rather, the problem is that the analysis of membership categorization has stood in a problematic relation both to ethnomethodology and to conversation analysis.

Indeed, I feel that the marrying of categorial and sequential analysis under the *aegis* of the documentary method of interpretation helps resolve a perceived tension between ethnomethodology and conversation analysis. Granted, a great deal of this perceived tension has been enthusiastically construed (and misconstrued) (Atkinson 1988) by persons who are not practitioners in these particular analytic pursuits: but it must also be said that practitioners of ethnomethodology and conversation analysis have, often through acts of omission, rendered a hostage to fortune in this regard. These acts of omission have frequently involved the disattending of one major social-organizational aspect of a phenomenon in order to focus attention on another. This has amounted to an 'isolation' of one aspect by relegating one or more others to virtual obscurity, especially if the promotion of the currently disattended aspect would involve some perceived concession to the methodology of one 'wing' or the other, i.e. that of ethnomethodology or conversation analysis.

This deployment of methodological preferences or emphases has allowed 'external' commentators to reify the differences in ethnomethodological and conversation analytic work and then to predicate the imposition of their own external standards on the basis of that reification (see, for example, P. Atkinson, *ibid.*, and others). I hope to have at least indicated above that reference to membership categorization relevances, as explicated by reference to the documentary method of interpretation, works towards the reinstatement of a more inclusive methodological rubric, and as such can show how categorial relvances inform utterances and their placement over the course of their production and reception. I have also hoped to indicate that, *ipso facto*, the production procedures themselves are reciprocally understood and employed by interlocutors, albeit in a tacit and practical way as culturally-standard matters.

It is my view that the development - one is tempted to say 'exhumation' - of a more inclusive methodology for ethnomethodology and conversation analysis might resolve several of the debilitating aspects of each pursuit - aspects that have often been noted and characterized (or, on occasion, mis-characterized) by the respective counterpart. In the course of a most thoughtful ethnomethodologically-based characterization of developments in conversation analysis since Harvey Sacks, Lynch and Bogen (1994 esp. 72-4) note Sacks's use of mechanistic imagery, e.g. a 'machinery' or 'apparatus' in order to describe the cultural, (interchangeable), methodicity of interlocutors' activities in their co-production of finely-ordered conversational interaction. Of course, we may note that cognate imagery has been used by 'mainstream' ethnomethodologists to describe their and conventional sociologists' methodologies dubbing them (as Garfinkel and Wieder have) 'alternative-technologies'. Nonetheless, it is undeniable that for Sacks the professional conversation analyst's task was to formally explicate such methodicities, and mechanistic (in the sense of 'grammatical') imagery could, for him, be employed as part of the conversation analyst's battery of technical devices that might be applied to such a task.

Since then, ethnomethodologists and other sociologists (particularly of the 'naturalistic' variety) have dubbed as 'mechanistic' conversation analysts' characterizations of conversational interaction. Indeed, these characterizations have even been seen, essentially, as a form of abstracted empiricism or as having a positivistic cast. Whilst this may - with some justification - be seen as the outcome of a further 'hardening' of Sacks's imagery by subsequent practitioners and the subsequent accumulation of a corpus of highly technicised work, one of whose underpinnings is a mechanistic imagery, we may still ask 'how is this apparently 'mechanistic' characterization of conversation given off by conversation analysts?'[8]

Part of the answer to this question surely lies in orthodox conversation analysts' disattending of the categorial order of conversation and of the procedural work deployed in and through this order. This disattending of the latter is important in the light of conversation analysts' attempted functional alternative for membership categorization, namely 'recipient design' and other 'particularisation / contextualisation principles' (Sacks, Schegloff and Jefferson 1974).[9] Here, with some partial exceptions,[10] any instantiated explication of the procedural operation of recipient design/particularisation is, to say the least, marginalised, treated as a fringe consideration: at best, it characteristically attains token acknowledgement. Again, it is as if analysts assume a *gestalt* alternation as between categorial and sequential orders, whereby one order can only be accorded foreground status if the other is relegated to the background. (This does not mean that background features are entirely inoperative: it instead refers to the *phenomenal status* of their operation.).

We might also claim that the relation between the categorial and sequential orders is more intimate than analysts have presently elaborated. One possible line of elaboration may perhaps be found in what sequential analysts, following Sacks, have termed 'tying techniques/devices', i.e. items that tie one utterance to an immediately preceding one, or items which 'skip-tie' (or 'skip-connect') to the last utterance but one in a sequence.[11] One tying device is where a pronoun in a succeeding utterance ties to a membership category in a preceding one: see, for example, this excerpt from a 'Goon Show' script from the 1950's:

> (Someone knocks at the door: one of the persons inside says 'Who is it?' and the caller replies 'It's me!')
>
> 1. A)   Who's that at the door?
> 2. B)   It's a man who calls himself 'me'.
> 3. C)   Ask him to prove it.

Here, the pro-term 'him' may be redressed by interlocutors (and overhearer) *via* a jointly-conducted tying operation which connects to the membership category 'a man', maintaining a consistent 'reference' across utterances 2 and 3. The tying operation and its 'product' (the achieved tie between 'him' and 'man') thus provides not just for utterances 2 and 3 as sequential objects but for their *specific* relatedness, their specific adequacy to each other.

To build on the sequential analyst's fruitful concern with tying, I wish to suggest, at this stage simply schematically, that operations of procedural knowledge such as the 'consistency rule' for the co-selection of membership categories may similarly work to achieve a specific relatedness between utterances in a given sequence. Thus, if a question contains one membership category and an answer contains another, and if the two categories may, *via* the consistency rule, be seen as deriving from the same membership categorization device (or the same standardized relational pair) then this may comprise one tying procedure for establishing the specific relatedness of *just this* answer to *just this* question, here and now. The consistency rule (see Sacks 1974a, esp. 218-220) may, through tying two categories, may operate also as an utterance design feature which achieves the specifically identifiable relatedness between *this* question and *this* answer. It is to be noted that the elegant characterization by Schegloff and Sacks of 'adjacency paired' structuring of utterances such as questions and answers[12] gives us the formal features of paired utterances (e.g. discriminative relations: the two utterances should identifiably come from the same pair type, e.g. 'question'-'answer') but does not refer to, nor does it provide for, the 'fine tuning' in the detail of utterance design that warrants just *this* answer as the answer to just *this* question, as distinctively adequate to this question here and now. Issues of the achieved relatedness of two or more particular utterances should also address the specificities of these design features as well as the more formal 'framework conditions' described by Schegloff and Sacks. One might conceive of the 'relation' between formal and specific adequacy in terms of necessary and sufficient elements in the achieved relatedness between (say) a question and an answer. One might also conceive of the 'two' sets of elements as related in that the distinctively identifying elements (also) 'deliver' the formal ones in instantiated ways.

One advantage, then, of dealing with the distinctively identifying details of particular questions and their answers, is, that it provides for a strong answer to the analytic concern evinced by Sacks towards the local sequential implicativeness of any utterance, i.e. 'why that now?' For all the undeniable elegance of Schelgloff and Sacks's analytic description of the formal features of adjacency pairs, that description only provides a weak answer to that concern, whereas attention to the fine-tuning of a given answer to its occasioning question as *only* relevant to that local pair, provides a strong answer. By filling in the identifying detail that operates through and also generates the formal features, the identifying detail (also) ties together two adjacency-paired utterances in ways that provide in a strictly local way what Speier has metaphorically termed 'interactional cement'. Such a respecification of 'adjacency pairs' would have the great advantage of preserving the original specifications by Schegloff and Sacks: indeed, such preservation is an important feature of respecification.

An additional gain from this approach is that, potentially, it feeds directly into recent concerns in ethnomethodology with 'haecceity' (previously 'quiddity') of social phenomena such as actions or settings. Garfinkel and Wieder (1992 esp. 180-4, and 203, endnote 2) have already written of the 'haecceities' of other kinds of 'pairs' (e.g. Lebenswelt pairs) that is their *in vivo* achieved relevances, the identifying details that compose them. Garfinkel and Wieder's analysis provides for the restoration of what they have termed the 'missing whatness' of formal studies of interaction.

My argument here is not that the building-in of the procedures for (say) the co-selection of proximal membership categorizations somehow 'deliver' (let alone 'completely' deliver) the respecification of the provisions of conversation analysis. Instead my argument is that the introduction of these co-selection procedures can be warranted and understood in terms of a far broader analytic project of respecification, as playing a small but, perhaps, not insignificant part in that project. To be sure, very many of the elements of conversation analysis might themselves also figure in such a respecification: I have already alluded to the phenomenon of pronominal transformation, which is surely a case in point.

Purely as an indication, consider the way in which the organization of membership categories into devices operates in the following transcriptions of reported speech from a homicide interrogation, where one of the co-participants, during his confession, artfully employs membership categories.

> A: hhhhh, I kept walk:ng (3) an:d I got
>   to the intersection (.2) off Broadstreet an'
>   (1 0) when this girl walked up to me an'
>   propositioned me (1 0)
> B: What did she say, exactly to yer, Lee?
> A: You look like a tough guy, (1 2)
>   Y' look like the member of a gang
>   I told 'er: I'm not a member of the gang:
>   I'm and independent (3) hhh an' she proposit-
>   ioned me again I asked her::? if she:d like to go to a
>   par:ty (.5) she said yess ( ) hh hh
> B: What did she as:k, actually say to y'ou?
>   hh hh
>   [Ye can word it ( ) use: rrr (3)
> A.   She asked me if I would like to get laid::

I have attempted a fuller explication of these utterances elsewhere (Watson 1983) and have space here only for a sketch. Let us for present purposes simply observe the way in which the categories 'member of a gang' and '(an) independent' map on to the M.C.D. 'types of tough guy' - a particular perspicuous instance of collections of categories as 'assembled objects'.[13] This mapping exercise, conducted through the consistency rule (see above), forms part of the 'cementing' procedures that particularise the suspect's alleged response to the species of his victim's prior assessment. Moreover, the selection of the category 'independent' over that of a 'member of a gang' may be viewed as an assembled object in another, related, sense. It preserves the relevance of the MCD 'types of tough guy' whilst assembling a link between one of these types, 'independent', rather than the other.

Given that the activity 'acting alone' might, conventionally, be predicated on the category 'independent' (as opposed to 'acting in concert with others', which might be predicated on the category 'member of a gang'), we may further note one of the procedural bases for the selection of that category. This basis is that the selection of a category- (and a device-) base may be topic-sensitive and, more generally, thematically-relevant. In this case, the selection of the category 'independent' is relevant to the topic (and overall theme) that the suspect acted alone rather than with his consociates at that time. This in turn operates - as the selection of categorial identities frequently does - to distribute blame, guilt or responsibility, deflecting it from some persons and attaching it to others. Derivatively, then, we may talk of an assembled object that is constituted through the assembling of the categories in the above case, namely a moral profile, a particular profile of blame-distribution - a distribution that is made on a 'categorial basis'. The confessing suspect claims incumbency of one category rather than another, whilst - and this is important - still preserving the 'tough guy' MCD: after all, he still has to make it plausible that he was a 'type' who was capable of fatally assaulting his victim. A great deal of highly specific and discriminative work is, therefore, done through the particularised 'fine tuning' in the mutual adjusting of these utterances, a fine tuning that is, in part, categorial.

One might also note that particularising work operates to realise yet another assembled object, that of the categorial pair 'police officer'-'suspect' (from the MCD 'parties to an interrogation'). For instance, the first-person avowal mode in relation to the victim and the offence operates as a realisation of the category 'suspect'. Thus we get a double reflexivity: the category 'suspect' (whether in the transcript or the participants or witnesses 'on the spot') informs our reading of the utterance and the utterance realises the category. One might, then, inspect utterances, and their serial organization, for their categorial haecceities, for their distinctive categorically-identifying specifics, and for the precise work that is done through these specifics.[14]

Ethnomethodology, Conversation Analysis and the Study of Membership Categorization Activities

In this section, we may ask the question: 'why has contemporary conversation analysis tended to fight shy of incorporating membership categorization analysis?' Also, although it is a more tangential issue, 'why has ethnomethodology never addressed Sacks's work on membership categorization?' After all, Sacks from the start treated membership categorization as a practice, an activity, one that was, through and through, culturally methodic, conducted through members' deployment of their procedural knowledge. A concern for such proceduralisation of action is something that is held in common both by ethnomethodology and conversation analysis.

Secondly, Sacks's concern with categorization comprises, again from the start, an explicative, rather than ironic, stance.[15] That is, Sacks sought to develop a form of sociology which did not set up in competition with lay members' conceptions or procedures but instead attempted to explicate those conceptions and procedures as they were built into conversational and other practices. This involved the refusal to employ downgrading terms such as 'false consciousness', 'latent functions', and other concepts from the battery of established sociologies, and the development of a conceptual armoury that did not treat members' conceptions and procedures as false, perspectival, misconceived or as otherwise degenerate versions of professional sociologists' conceptual apparatus. In turn, this non-ironic stance refused the characterization of society-members as 'cultural or judgemental dopes' unknowing or deluded about their own milieu, their own society, and as requiring correctives from the professional sociologist.

Sacks, then, avoided any attempt to use the categories of some natural or social science - or an idealisation of that science - as a template against which members' conceptions can be measured and, in all likelihood, found wanting. Sacks's project involved the explication of the formal properties (as given in practical sociological reasoning) of human action and interaction without resort to, say, ideal types of rationality whose conventional use was to throw into sharp relief the purportedly non-rational features of actual instances of action. To this end, Sacks increasingly concerned himself with using what Hugh Mehan Jr. has termed 'retrievable data', namely audio or video-recorded data and transcripts thereof, data that could be inspected repeatedly and minutely. From this corpus, Sacks's project was to develop proceduralised analytic description of naturally-occurring, naturally-situated social actions and interactions. Apart from a few quibbles, one might say 'so far, so good' so far as ethnomethodology and conversation analysis are concerned.

At this point, though, we can speculate that both ethnomethodologists and conversation analysts might feel that in Sacks's best-known analyses of membership categorization - and particularly in the earliest examples of his work on categorization phenomena - an element of cognitivism and a concomitant tendency towards the decontextualization of these phenomena may be discerned. Certainly, Sacks's early work on categorization does manifest some

significant derivations from the componential-analytic work that
formed part of its provenance.

Some of the representations in his doctoral dissertation did
give an impression of a static, decontextualized, somewhat rigid
'natural semantic grid' of categories rather than comprising a
thoroughgoing, radically praxiological approach to categorization
activities. This is, perhaps, only to be expected given the conditions of
production of these early writings, though it is arguable that some
residue from these writings persisted in Sacks's subsequent work on
categorization (see, again, the Editors' 'Introduction' to this collection).

Those whose analyses, by omission or otherwise, seem to be
premissed upon such assumptions about the character of Sacks's
categorial analysis may well find further substantiation of their position
from Sacks's frequent references to a 'machinery' or 'apparatus' that is
operative in conversational work (cf. Lynch and Bogen 1994), as
though there were something like an underlying 'grid' that structures
conversational work, giving rise to that work. One senses that one of
relatively few unifying features of the position of some
ethnomethodologists and conversation analysts is a wariness about
these apparent features of Sacks's approach, given that these
approaches may be taken as propounding a contextually-sensitive, non-
cognitivistic sociology.

If my sense of the existence of such a wariness is at all
warrantable, then I feel that it (the wariness) is ill-founded. Whilst
componential analysis did, to varying extents, make reference to
activities - asking for a drink in Subanun, and so on - it is clear that
even Sacks's earliest work focalises social action to a much greater
extent. Sacks's work comprises far more of a thoroughgoing
praxiological approach than does componential analysis/
ethnosemantics, and is much less concerned with the correct way (s) of
using a given term, and so on.

The best substantiation of this is to return to the published
version of Sacks's work (Sacks 1972) on the search for help initiated by
callers to a suicide prevention center. Here, Sacks points out the
potential problematicities concerning the 'literalness' or 'correctness' of
a given membership categorization for a given person on a given
occasion, but that members nonetheless have, as part of their
procedural knowledge, organized ways of jointly recognising the
appropriateness of given categories in given situations: indeed, these
situations are, in part, themselves constituted through these category
selections. In relation to suicidal, depressed or depairing callers' search
for help, those persons (and their counsellors at the center) typically

select membership categories from an assembled corpus, collection R, those to whom it is relevant for the person to turn for help - e.g. one's spouse, parent(s), and so on. For every caller there will be a person towards whom that caller has a right and an obligation to approach before all others with his/her problem. For a married person this will in all probability be his/her spouse. If that person is not consulted first s/he has rights to complain: 'Why didn't you tell me first? Why do I have to hear it from someone else?' The prioritised corpus of those to whom one can search for help gives order or methodicity to that search. This study was, then, one of the very first to formally and empirically describe the methodic bases of a given course of action (or interaction, that pertaining between caller and counsellor).

However, if for any reason the caller's first-place counterpart incumbent in a relational pair of categories, e.g. 'husband'-'wife', is unavailable for the purposes of a specific disclosure of personal troubles (e.g. regarding one of the spouses' adultery), then the caller may decide that second, third, etc. priority counterpart incumbents are, *ipso facto*, unavailable too. In that case, the person may call another corpus of categories, those whose incumbents have professional obligations to help, even though these incumbents may (and this is often a salient point for callers) also be categorized as 'strangers', where 'strangers' in general might be seen as unavailable for help.

What we have, here, then, are two examples of 'occasioned corpora' of categories - corpora that are occasioned in terms of (a set of grounds giving an account for) a search for help. The corpora are specifically assembled in relation to the categorial incumbencies; e.g. in the first corpus, the first place counterpart category depends upon whether or not the caller is married.

Whilst the componential-analytic 'spin-off' is undeniably still evident at this stage in Sacks's work, we can see that there is a definitive move towards the treatment of collections of categories in a more contextual way, i.e. in a way that places far more emphasis on contextual relevances. The corpora outlined above comprise *in situ, in vivo* assembled objects rather than comprising static semantic grids. Whilst the categories of Sacks's corpora seem, like componential-analytic ones, to be defined in terms of a criterial feature, Sacks's feature ('those categories relevant to a given search for help') is considerably more context-sensitive given its 'emplacement' in an occasioned corpus and its definition in terms of such a corpus.

There is immeasurably less fudging on who, the analyst or the subject, defines the criterial features of a term or a collection. Much of Sacks's emphasis on greater contextuality derives from analysis of (tape-recordings and transcripts of) naturally-occurring talk rather than his analysis being based upon the investigator's *post hoc* interview of or discussion with his/her subject(s). Moreover, Sacks's concern not to apply idealised logical or 'scientific' criteria to the ethnographic analysis of, say, colour categories again indicates a move away from any resort to an analytically-stipulated measuring-rod, or from an 'external' (out-of-context) standard.[16] In all, we might say that although there were some componential-analytic elements preserved in Sacks's earliest writings these elements were already beginning to be re-worked. This process of re-working took on a more and more radical cast as Sacks's thinking progressed, *pace* the references to an 'apparatus' or 'machinery', which might most usefully be seen as an explicative simile[17], a pragmatic device rather than as some kind of constructivist reification.

The culmination of Sacks's radical reworking of category analysis may be found in some of his later lectures, when the non-cognitivistic, contextual treatment of categories took on its most radical form. Oddly enough, this later treatment of categories has been accorded hardly any serious or extensive consideration, either by ethnomethodologists or by conversation analysts. This culmination in category analysis is to be found in Sacks's work on 'turn-generated categories' in conversation. This set of analytic concerns is important in that it allows us to make the argument that categorial relevances in the sequential organization of talk are in no way exclusively restricted to 'institutional talk': indeed, they are generic to *talk as such* (Watson and Sharrock 1991).

Categories, Context and Sequence

Perhaps the most obviously generic formulation of the categorial order in talk-as-such comes in Sacks's own work on turn-generated categories, particularly the 'caller'-'called' category pair in telephone conversations. He distinguishes between this generic category-pair internal to the turn organization of the conversation, and 'external' or contingent categorizations such *as* the age, sex, occupation of the interlocutors (Sacks 1992b [1971]: 360-366). The 'caller'-'called' category-pair comprises 'identities for conversation' in that it is generated through the (initial) turn-organization of the telephone call. Sacks refers to this category-pair as '...a series of terms that apply to people in a way that has them as *categories* and not merely the person they are, somebody with a name' (Sacks 1992b [1972]: 544, his emphasis; see also 542-53).[18] He points out that if the 'extrinsic' class of categories were in fact central to the organization of conversational interaction, then one would not be able to consider conversation as an independent system, as possessing a measure of autonomy and internal regulation (though, of course, Sacks never regarded such autonomy as an absolute or conversation as entirely freestanding: quite the contrary). Indeed, elsewhere, he gives an example not of turn-generated categories such as 'caller'-'called', but of category-generated turns. This is a case given by Ethel Albert, where she reports that in certain forms of ceremonial talk amongst the Burundi, older people speak before younger ones and this age-graded category-generated turn order may be defeased by another categorial order, e.g. that of status stratification: for instance, princes will speak before commoners whatever their respective ages (Albert 1964: 40-41).

This, then, is the contrast: turn-generated categories where (say) age-grade categories are distal as opposed to category-generated turns, where (say) age-graded categories operate as an integral structuring template for turn order. Other turn-generated categories pertain to particular sequence types, e.g. 'summoner' and 'summoned' in summons-answer sequences (though Schegloff (1968) writes, perhaps unfortunately, of these categories as 'roles'), 'story-inviter' and 'story-recipient' in invited story sequences (Cuff and Francis 1978). Sacks's notion of turn-generated categories must stand as the paradigm case of the contexuality of categories, given the embedding of 'caller'-'called' in initial turn order, with other categorizations, e.g. age, as furnishing a contingent context for the colloquy through recipient design (Sacks et al 1978: 43)) and the like. Certainly there is no sense in which his work on either set of categories ('internal' or 'external') can be seen as presenting them as repositories of decontextualized meanings.

Sacks (1992b [1970]: 163ff) attests to the pervasiveness and significance of turn-generated categories in telephone conversation, saying that: (163):

> A thing that called can hardly ever get out from under is
> that they are the called and that the other is the caller, and
> that there are all kinds of things affiliated with that

What is the nature of the 'affiliation' to which Sacks refers in this quotation? Clearly, the affiliation counts on the moral predicates of the categories. In his most highly elaborated paper on membership categories, Sacks describes standardized relational pairs of categories as loci for moral imputations. Writing of collection R (those counterpart category-incumbents to whom one can properly turn for help), Sacks (1972: 37) says:

> ...any pair of categories is a member of collection R if that
> pair is a 'standardized' relational pair that constitutes a locus
> for a set of rights and obligations concerning the activity of
> giving help.

And, obversely (Sacks 1974a: 226):

> .viewers use norms to provide the relevant membership
> categories in terms of which they formulate identifications
> of the doers of those activities for which the norms are
> appropriate.

Thus, moral/normative elements are, in more than one respect, accorded virtual defining status regarding categories and their combinations (i.e. their co-selections). To be sure, one major reason one might invoke for preserving analytic attention towards categorial phenomena in talk is that these phenomena highlight the moral organization of talk in a way that reference solely to sequential features structurally conceived neither necessarily nor consistently does.

If we focus particularly, perhaps, upon the above quotations and acknowledge that 'caller'-'called' may be conceived as a category-pair, we can then begin to 'foreground' the moral/normative elements attendant on the turn-organization of talk. As Sacks puts it, salience of these moral elements is, for interlocutors, maximised in the opening and closing phases of the unit 'a single conversation'. The caller may exhibit an orientation to the (members') fact that s/he has taken the called away from some other activity and has thus made an alternative claim on the called's time. Such claims are morally implicative. This orientation may be exhibited in the obligation of the caller to monitor the conversation for places where the called may display a readiness to close. Such an obligation of the caller may be exhibited in the making of close offerings, which take on the sequential form of offer-acceptance/declination. The called has an obligation to accept or decline a close offering, where, for example, a declination may make reference to the moral weightings of alternative calls on his/her time: 'No, don't be concerned, I wasn't doing anything anyway'.

What we have in this case is a *categorial distribution* of a particular adjacency pair type, i.e. an offer sequence, where the caller produces the first pair part and the called party produces the second pair part. This categorial distribution of sequence production amongst interlocutors stands in contradistiction to the 'main body' of the conversation where any ratified interlocutor may introduce an offer of any kind (though the making and receiving of an offer itself distributes identities). In the closing, or candidate pre-closing, sequences, however, the production of close offer sequences is ordered on the basis of who initially called whom and of the categorial identities thereby distributed through those two initial turns. That initial category-distribution furnished a production format for close-offering sequences. In this case, it is the overall sequential unit 'a single conversation' to which members conjointly orientate themselves in the timing and placement of that production format and, eventually, in the co-ordinated closing of a state of talk.[19] Moreover, it is clear that these procedural phenomena extend far beyond the case(s) of 'institutional talk': indeed, to tie them solely to institutional talk is to throw away the argument.

In addition to callers' offers of closings we might note that there are counterpart techniques specific to called parties. As Schlegloff and Sacks observe, a called party may refer to the caller's interests as a warrant for inviting the caller to close:

This is costing you a lot of money[20]

Schegloff and Sacks also observe that some techniques make reference not to any party's interests but to, say, some contingency, e.g. 'Someone's at the door'. These techniques are pair- or device-based, i.e. they apply 'across the board' (Watson 1978). Where a party's interests *are* invoked, the specification of those interests is a categorially-sensitive matter. The caller may characteristically, as we have observed above, initiate an offer to close (i.e. may introduce an offer-acceptance/declination adjacency pair type) whereas a called party may initiate an *invitation* to close (i.e. may introduce an invitation-acceptance/declination adjacency pair type), thus orientating the interlocutors to the caller's 'category-bound' obligation and prerogative to seek out, and find possible points at which to place, a candidate pre-closing sequence, i.e. a sequence that offers the option to move towards the closing down of the conversation. Clearly, the choice of *sequence type* - which, I maintain, is part of what Schegloff and Sacks term 'the specification of the interests of the other party' - is a category-sensitive, categorially-defined matter and is, consequently, integral to the 'recipient design' features of the telephone conversation. Those features may therefore be seen as diffusely 'category-bound' to 'caller' and 'called'. In this consideration of caller's and called's techniques, we can see the intricate and inextricable interweaving of categorial and sequential aspects of the talk. These aspects together comprise the warp and weft of the conversation: without the weft there is no warp and no fabric.

Sacks, then, treats 'caller'-'called' as 'identities-for-conversation', categorial identities that are furnished in regard of the opening sequences of the telephone conversation. On occasion we may even find that someone may parlay a turn-generated category into a full-time occupation: in his later years, the former world champion boxer Joe Louis became a 'greeter' in a Las Vegas casino, thus becoming the most noted person to turn a turn-generated category into a paying proposition.[21]

Sacks notes (1992b [1970]: 163) that 'caller'-'called' categories are a phenomenon that telephone interlocutors experience as a pervasive constraint, as something that, for instance '...called can hardly get out from under...', and is heir to a range of potential consequences that follow. For instance, there may be the accountable issue of the called having been called twice without having in the meantime called the other in return: hence 'Gee I've been calling you all day', and similar invocations of excusing conditions for not having (successfully) called. Furthermore, at the level of the topic organization of the conversation, the first topic, the 'reason for the call' is, typically, accountably cast in terms of the 'caller'-'called' category distribution. An interlocutor may often, *qua* caller, furnish a 'reason for the call' and this may have a foundational effect on the topic organization of that call, including the moral accountability of that organization.

If, for example, the person who has been called turns out to have got engaged, or has, perhaps, suffered some form of tragedy and has not already telephoned the caller to inform him/her of the fact, then that news, which ordinarily would be accorded first/primary topic status, might be treated by the caller as having been unwarrantably withheld from him/her. Thus the caller might well ask 'Why didn't you call and tell me?', and may even enunciate the suspicion that, for all the caller knows, the called might never have taken the trouble to inform him/her of that news. Clearly, too, the warrantability and illocutionary (e.g. accusatory or complaining) force of any such utterance may be redoubled when additional, extrinsic or distal membership categories are grafted onto the 'caller'-'called' pair, e.g. if it is one's mother who has called. The 'right to know' is, largely, cast in terms of such categorial identities (see above).

As a codicil to these general reflections on the notion of 'turn-generated categories', one might mention that the notion also applies far beyond 'caller' and 'called' in conversational sites. Other sites of interaction that are, primarily, non-conversational, also yield such categorial identities. In this sense, conversation is not distinctive as an interactional organization but is perhaps best conceived as *primus inter pares*.

Two examples of turn-generated categories in 'other' interactional organizations might here be briefly mentioned. These two organizations comprise visible orders. The first comes in the phenomenon of 'flow files' of persons walking through public space - serial formations of people walking, one party[22] following the other, in the same direction at a standard pace along an interactionally-maintained overall 'channel' for those heading in the same direction. The turn-generated categorial organization comes to be particularly highly marked when a 'flow-file' becomes a 'contraflow file', i.e. a serial organization of persons heading in the opposite direction to that of a given channel, i.e. heading down the 'up' staircase of an underground railway station.[23] There, a set of category-bound obligations of the first in the contraflow file, the pathfinder, is clearly visible: s/he has to exhibit particularly manifestly (i.e. in what Goffman terms a 'body gloss', a gesture or set of gestures in the round) the normatively dispreferred character of the file's contrary direction. S/he moves 'side-on', somewhat crab-wise, keeping to the side-rail more closely than those ascending the staircase, who walk full-frontally and often side by side rather than in single file. This and other kinesic and proxemic displays on the part of the first-position incumbent, the 'pathfinder', achieve the displayed *minimisation* of the contraflow *vis-a-vis* the main one, such minimisation being an utterly practical-moral matter.

Linked to flow-files (and often generated and transformed from them) is another visible interactional organization, namely queues or waiting lines. The queue comprises a set of visibility arrangements (to use Pollner's term) that display a turn order of service.[24] Again, here we have turn-generated categories, most vividly those of 'head' and 'tail' of the queue, but also, that of 'second in line' and further numerically-indexed categories. Again, the head of the queue who is 'next up' has special obligations to monitor (say) the point of service and also to monitor the ongoing service transaction for its upcoming completion point, etc. The turn-generated categories of the queue (first, second, etc. in line) might be said to be integral to the queue, whereas other membership categories that apply to potential or actual queue-members, e.g. 'firemen', 'mother-to-be', 'soldier' might again be said to be extrinsic or distal. It should also be noted that in both types of integral and distal category-orders, there may be more than one incumbent of the same turn-category, e.g. a mother and her children together may comprise a single turn-category in a queue. Indeed, multiple incumbencies may be precisely where integral and distal category-orders intersect.

However, none of this means that the distal status of categories is irrelevant. In queues in some areas of France, for instance, pregnant women, firemen and soldiers are, conventionally, permitted to move to first position irrespective of their order of arrival and consequent position in the turn order. This means that a 'priority' category may be mapped onto a turn-generated one, i.e. 'head of the queue'. To be sure, this phenomenon shows that 'context-sensitivity' and 'context-freedom' can be analytically formulated by reference to categorial orders as well as by reference to sequential ones.[25] The queue might be said to be context-free in respect of its integral turn order of categories but as simultaneously context-sensitive in respect of the procedural orientation of its members towards incumbents of distal categories. We might also observe that in the procedural rules that prioritise incumbents of some distal categories we might find one locus of cultural difference, i.e. in Britain the integral turn-ordering of queues operates in very much the same way as in France, but, for instance, in normal circumstances a fireman would not be allowed to go to the front.

Bearing in mind the above considerations of integral (turn-generated) and distal categorial identities, of multiple incumbency of single categories, of the grouping of categories into SRP's and MCD's and of the visible availability of all these, we are in a good position to appreciate (and analyse) the multi-faceted organizational detail of the following (from Bennett 1994: 101):

> 6 March, London   I come through Heathrow and in the queue parallel to mine an Indian family is held up at Immigration, the father, thin, dark, with burning eyes being questioned by a woman so stone-faced she could be at the East German border rather than at Heathrow. There are several sons, looking languid and beautiful and the mother with a small child in her arms
>
> "Who are these people?" says the official, jabbing at the passport. "I want to <u>see</u> all these people". Whereupon the father swiftly rounds up his family and marshals them in front of her   She does not even look up.

Concluding Comments

In this paper, I have, if somewhat speculatively, suggested that sequential and categorial phenomena in talk comprise 'two sides of the same coin', and that they are, in very many respects, aspects of each other. Conversational sequences are categorially instructed, both for lay speakers and analysts: the sense of the sequence - even its sense as a sequence - is, in significant ways, given by its categorial order. The categorially-instructed way in which speakers produce sequenced talk and in which Conversation Analysts frequently transcribe and examine talk comprises a lay method for building social or institutional structure into talk. As such, categorization phenomena in talk comprise instantiations of our commonsense knowledge of social structure, as, of course, do sequencing activities. By the same token, sequences of utterances may be treated as, *inter alia*, realisations of those categorial relevances. This being the case, I propose that both these aspects of our common knowledge be explicated and focalised on their own behalf. In this fundamental respect, I hope that this paper might be understood as an exercise in the sociology of knowledge.

It is in this sense that my observations on conversation analysts' transcription procedures[26] are, I hope, condign. If categorial and sequential aspects of talk are reflexively related or mutually determined, then to tacitly employ one aspect in service of an explicated treatment of the other is to let a regressive element into the analysis. It is to introduce a highly compromising constructive-analytic dimension into a methodological rubric which only finds coherence in its reasoned opposition to such constructivist policies. In other words, we are relegating an order of commonsense knowledge to the status of tacit resource when our task as analysts of the mastery of ordinary language is, surely, that of explicitation, namely to turn such resources into explicit topics that are 'visible' and available for analysis in their own right[27] - and, not least, are deemed worthy of such a rendering. This, too, distinguishes the approach I here attempt to recommend from those of constructive analysis. In Garfinkel's terms, the categorial order of conversational turn-taking is one of the 'radical phenomena' of conversation.

A further argument to be derived from my observations in this paper is that to refer to the ignored categorial order of talk as though it were only of relevance to so-called 'institutional talk' is to impose an artificial restriction upon what is in fact a generic matter. Indeed, it is to fudge the issue. Whilst some of the most perspicuous examples of this ignored order come from bureaucratic or occupational settings and transactions, others come from what has been termed 'natural conversation', which it has often been argued is the baseline from which 'institutional speech exchange systems' are derived and which they variously modify. As Sacks often indicated in his lectures, 'stranger', 'friend' and 'acquaintance' are categorizations too, and often inform both the organization and the content of the talk just as pervasively as does, for instance, a 'group therapist' - 'patient' category-pair - and ironically, much of Sacks's early data on 'natural' conversation was drawn from just such an 'institutional' setting.

Indeed, the generic status of many of the critical observations I have made above is evidenced by the fact that Schegloff's (1991:61) perceptive and important point about institutional talk - that because a doctor or police officer issues an utterance does not mean that 'doctor' - 'patient' or 'police officer' - 'suspect' are the identities that are salient for the interlocutors here and now (i.e. during this particular utterance or this sequence) - intendedly applies 'across the board'. It applies, for instance, to the transcription practices employed by West and Zimmerman in their analysis of female-male talk (West and Zimmerman 1983). [28] Our instructed reading of the transcript, i.e. that this is a male's utterance, this a female's, poses exactly the same orientational problem, and West's studies of cross-gender medical consultations merely compound that problem (West 1990).[29] I am not suggesting that we cannot find an empirical analytic basis through which we can address such an orientational issue: quite the contrary. However, I am expressing reservations about those conversation analyses whereby such orientational problems are, by dint of transcription and other textual procedures, treated as already- settled. Co-conversationalists may, in the practical activity of reciprocally arranging and monitoring their talk together, on occasion operate under such a categorial rubric but, for the analyst, this is to be shown, not tacitly endorsed or, even worse, reified into an overarching template for the inspection of the talk. Such a tacit endorsement again comprises something of a regression to the stipulativeness of constructive analysis. And there have been some stipulative studies of categorization in conversational and other sites, too, so a treatment of categorization and sequence as an interwoven order would be of mutual benefit to both 'camps' in the analysis of talk.

Such a policy respecifying the analysis of talk may well be perplexing, complicated and difficult to apply with no formulaic procedure being available. However, I should venture to suggest that this, surely, is precisely the strength of conversation analysts and ethnomethodologists - to deal coherently with complex arrays of 'found' detail. Another shared benefit of employing this impressive pool of skills is that in the process of our work we might together formulate a powerful reply to what might be seen as misconceived analytic formulations of context - formulations that are shared by a wide range of critics of varying degrees of sympathy, from M. Moerman (1988 [1989]) to P. Atkinson (1985, 1988) and beyond. What these critics seem to propose is that talk does not make sense without an ethnographically-furnished 'context' to be added on behalf of members, by the analyst. The transcription procedures in much conversation analysis gives far too much away to the position of these critics. A respecified analysis of talk may make even more clear that we can study members' speech as contextualising as well as contextualised and that members themselves furnish context within their talk. We do not need to skip from their own contextualising activities to the analysts' more or less independent furnishing of context and, at worst, the analysts' arrogation of definitional privilege concerning context.

A final comment: I am well aware that the corpora of ethnomethodological studies on the one hand and conversation-analytic ones on the other are not of a piece. Each corpus is characterized by a range of studies, some of which do not sit easily with the others. Many of the problems to which I have alluded here have already been flagged, to a greater or lesser degree, by some practitioners whilst at the same time having been elided by others. That this is so is encouraging: it augurs well for future debate.

Chapter Four

Ticketing Rules:
Categorization and Moral Ordering in a
School Staff Meeting

Carolyn D. Baker

Introduction

This chapter examines some features of the talk that occurred in a secondary school staff meeting concerning the rules governing the operation of a welfare system in the school. This welfare system involved the issuing of 'tickets' to students for good or poor behaviour and the translation of numbers of these tickets into 'levels' that carried specific privileges or punishments. The system governs the promotion and demotion of individual students and is designed to achieve a distribution of privileges and punishments in a rational and fair manner.

This welfare system was created by the school staff. They produced guidelines for the issuing of tickets to students, and they produced the rules for determining the promotion/demotion of students to one or another level depending on tickets accumulated.

The system was under continual review. The teachers could change the rules, or make new ones, in light of observed problems in the operation of the system. In the staff meeting discussed here, they were engaged in the work of proposing and discussing rule changes. What is of interest in this paper is how that talk was done.

In the meeting, members explicated the commonsense grounds of their own actual and possible actions, referring to both the realities and practicalities of the school and its members as they know these, and to principles of justice and fairness. They sought to achieve the rationality and the moral accountability of their actions in relation to the rules. Their talk is thick with descriptions that seek to align pragmatic and moral considerations. This meeting-talk is a case in point of other instances of moral- organizational work.

Previous ethnomethodological work on reference to rules and on using rules in organizational settings (e.g. Garfinkel 1967; Silverman and Jones 1976; Zimmerman 1974a) has drawn attention to interpretive procedures as sense-making and order-producing activities. Ethnomethodological studies of organizational work in educational settings have included studies of the practical, rule-referential work of assessment and of decision-making (e.g. Mehan 1983, 1991), of placement practices (Leiter 1974), and of categorization and classification practices (Cicourel and Kitsuse 1971). Studies of school administration and of staff meetings (Gronn 1983, 1984) have shown how 'talk is the work' of educational administration.

In such settings where organizational rules are being interpreted, worked with, or referred to, we can observe the production of the 'local adequacy' of rule-interpretation. In the setting under study here, it is possible to observe also the production of the 'local adequacy' of the work of *making up* the rules that will govern actions in future. In the meeting talk, members orient to the problem of finding/producing the local rationality and the local morality of their rules *for the school*, and of their rule-making practices *in the meeting*.

The talk that is generated around rules and rule changes involves much description of people and scenes. It relies on the production of types - categories - and category-bound descriptions of students. Membership categorization work underpins the reasoning that goes on by linking categories of students with category-bound activities in the production of actual or hypothetical scenarios. Thus the work of description (Schegloff 1988) through category selections is integral to the moral ordering being achieved in the talk (Jayyusi 1984, 1991b). This chapter will attend to the ways in which membership categorization devices are deployed by members of the school staff to persuade, to question, and to justify. In their accounting work, members show themselves to be professionally astute and morally adequate within the social world in which these student-types occur.

There is no questioning that the types pre-exist the talk. The types pre-exist the talk *for the members*. The categories/types are resources for describing. The problem of an infinite number of possible types - of categories as rhetorical devices - does not surface.

The Welfare System

The welfare system as described here was in operation in a new secondary school in New South Wales, Australia, in 1990 - 1991. Current rules for the tickets/levels system, and commentary on its operation, were formalised in various school documents.

One outcome of the operation of the ticketing system was the production of a computer printout, updated weekly, which showed student welfare 'levels' ranging from +4 at the positive end to -4 at the negative end, for all students in the school. These 'levels' were achieved on the basis of numbers of positive (yellow) and negative (white) tickets issued to students, discussed below. The printout looked like this in 1990:

Surname	First Name	10.8	17.8	24.8	31.8	7.9	14.9	21.9
Fraser	Helen	1	1	1	1	2	2	2
Fullan	Ben	1	1	1	2	2	1	1
Glass	Vicki	-1	-1	-1	0	0	0	1
Harding	Brian	0	0	0	-2	-2	-2	-1
Hume	Annie	0	0	0	0	0	1	1
Jason	Paul	-4	-4	-4	-4	-4	-4	-4

This shows the moral careers (cf. Cicourel and Kitsuse 1971) of students over the current school term. The printout was used as a 'glance-available' (cf. Jayyusi 1988: 68) index of the state of individuals and as a reading of the moral health of the school:

> [it's] like a state of the nation where each every student in the school's at. Um, what level they're at
>
> it's really important to do because of er as I said if someone goes zero, zero, zero and all of a sudden negative one and negative two in very quick time there's something going on in their life so. It's very helpful for that sort of thing, you know.
> [Interview with the Chair of the Welfare Committee, 1991]

The school also produced other documents regarding the welfare system. One of these was a sheet setting out 'guidelines' for issuing yellow and white tickets, including examples of the kinds of things students should be rewarded or punished for. The provision of examples such as 'consistent good effort or work', 'exceptional bookwork, assignments, test results etc.' for positive tickets and 'continued disobedience', 'rudeness and ill-mannered behaviour', 'defiant behaviour' and 'not to be issued for minor offences' for negative tickets relies on teachers' commonsense knowledge and situated competence to decide when such behaviours have occurred, what is 'minor' and not minor, etc., in order for the system to work. As will be shown in transcripts below, teachers recognized the problem of 'subjective interpretation' of these guidelines.

The text that is the referent of the staff meeting talk to be discussed here is a chart that indicates how many tickets of what colour during what time periods are needed for movement from one level to another, and what consequences correspond to these levels. This chart conveys a tidy logic and rationality to the system. It has rows and columns with no empty spaces and is laid out as if the bottom half (the way down) is the reverse story of the top half (the way up). That 'ALL STUDENTS START' at 0 suggests a game metaphor but also writes in a neutral, pre-operational position from which movement up or down can be seen as the logical outcome of students' own behaviours as reflected in tickets attracted.

HIGH SCHOOL - WELFARE LEVELS		
LEVELS - HOW PLACED ON THIS LEVEL	STAFF INVOLVED	CONSEQUENCES
+4 40 yellow tickets + no white tickets for 30 weeks	Year adviser Head Teacher Welfare Comm Principal	Certificate of excellence - Book prize. End of year BBQ or movie. Media coverage. +Level 2 and 3 privileges.
+3 30 yellow tickets + no white tickets for 30 weeks	As above	Certificate of Distinction Courtyard use Locker pass. +Level 2 privileges
+2 20 yellow tickets or no white tickets for 20 weeks	As above	Certificate of merit. Canteen pass Spectator at sporting events etc In draw for assembly prizes (movie pass).
+1 10 yellow tickets or no white tickets for 10 weeks	Year adviser Head teacher- Welfare Comm.	Letter home to parents Name published in Chronicle at the end of term (All positive levels).
0	ALL STUDENTS START	
3 white tickets	Year Adviser	Writing letter home to parents

		Interview with year adviser.
-1 5 white tickets	Year Adviser Welfare Comm.	Letter home to parents Playground or garden clean up. 5 half lunches Interview with year adviser.
8 white tickets	Year Adviser Welfare Comm	Warning letter home to parents. Interview with year adviser Playground or garden clean up as above.
-2 10 white tickets	Year Adviser Head Teacher - Welfare Comm School Counsellor Deputy/Principal	Letter home to parents Parents required for interview with Counsellor, Year Adv , and DP Student or daily conduct book. (2 weeks) Playground or garden clean up (10 half lunches) Exclusion from discos, excursions, representing school at sport One after school detention (1 hr).
-3 13 white tickets	Year Adviser Head Teacher - Welfare Comm School Counsellor Deputy/Principal	Letter home to parents Parents required for interview with Counsellor. Year Adviser and DP Daily conduct book continued Loss of school privileges continued 2 after school detentions Exclusion from the playground at lunchtime. (1 week). Restitution program.
-4 16 white tickets or the discretion of the Principal or Deputy Principal.	Year Adviser Head Teacher - Welfare Comm School Counsellor Deputy/Principal	Suspension - in school or out of school at discretion of the Principal. Exclusion from the playground until noticeable effort made to improve Restitution program.

This is a complicated chart and it is not necessary to master its details in order to see that as one reads up the chart, privileges accumulate, and get 'better'. At +2 students are awarded a canteen pass, which gives them rights to a fast lane to buy their food; at +4 they are given 'media coverage'. Similarly, reading down the chart, as things become more serious, more and more punishments accumulate and additional, and more important, of the senior staff become involved. As transcripts presented below show, teachers were aware that the proportion of students at different levels, and their speeds of ascent and descent through the levels, could be adjusted by changing the rules. In this respect, students' achievements of different levels were recognized not to be natural outcomes but the results of staff members' rule-making work. However, practical adjustments to the system (for example to achieve the 'right' proportions of students at different levels) could not be separated from moral questions (for example, notions of natural justice). To resolve such problems, teachers engaged in considerable accounting work.

The school's Welfare Committee was responsible for overseeing the operation of the system. Minutes of the Welfare Committee meetings show the extent to which the Committee attended to details of the ticketing/levels system - how seriously it was taken and how much work went into both operating it and fine-tuning it, showing faith in the ultimate, near-enough rule-governability of the system. At the same time these minutes document the members' appreciation of loopholes and such which it was their responsibility to spot and correct. In the minutes of a meeting held in early 1991, the following item appeared:

> 6   CANTEEN PASS RORT - SOME STUDENTS ARE TRANSFERRING THEIR CARD TO OTHERS.   THE LADIES IN THE CANTEEN DON'T KNOW THE STUDENTS NAMES AND THEREFORE THE SYSTEM IS BREAKING DOWN   THIS SHOULD BE ANNOUNCED AT   AN   ASSEMBLY   PRIVILEGES   CARRY RESPONSIBILITIES. A COMPLETE REVAMP OF THE CANTEEN CARD AWARD. CHANGE IT AS A REWARD GIVEN AT +LEVEL 3 (NOT +2 AS PREVIOUSLY) PUNISHMENT   TO   BE   GIVEN   TO   STUDENTS CONTINUING TO ABUSE THIS   ANNOUNCEMENT TO BE GIVEN AT MORNING ASSEMBLY THAT EXISTING CANTEEN CARDS ARE CANCELLED. [PRINCIPAL] TO EXPLAIN THIS AT NEXT FORMAL ASSEMBLY AND WILL GIVE DETAILS FOR NEW SYSTEM THEN

This was a highly elaborate and time-consuming system for monitoring the moral health of the school and for distributing rewards and punishments in ways that were seen to be rational and fair. Members of staff appeared to be committed to this welfare system, and this welfare system appeared to be central to the members' sense of and achievement of the social and moral order of their school. The welfare system was the topic of a considerable amount of informal comment and of formal consideration by staff, including a lengthy discussion at a staff meeting that I attended and audiotaped. My interest now is to look to their own accounts and their own accounting work to explicate how they produced and resolved problems in the system, and to find a locally relevant reason for the density of the work undertaken here.

Staff Meeting, 1990

I present some segments from a staff meeting recorded in late 1990 to illustrate the staff members' reasoning using membership categorization resources. The opening segment corresponds to the opening of this topic in the meeting. It presents the first half of a very long introductory speech by the Welfare Committee Chair. The Chair's talk is essentially a reading of the chart in a manner that adds temporal and causal connections to the spatial arrangement. In his accounting for why certain amendments had been proposed, and how the proposed amendments will work, he begins the work of finding and aligning pragmatic and moral issues by describing how (and why) students will now make their way across the levels.

Segment 1: Moral Categories

Bob	Principal
Gord	Deputy Principal
Len	Chair of Welfare Committee

[((voices talking, laughing))
1. Len: [Over over the last month or so we've been looking at the=
2. Bob: =Order, order
3 Len: the level system, and we've made a few changes, which have been suggested to the meeting now, what I'll do now is just show the people the changes we have made and open it up for discussion to see if people agree with the changes or see any problems with them. I'm handing around a copy of them now but it's pretty much the same as the sheet before, it shows that all the students start at level zero and go up positive one, two, three, four and they slip down negative one to negative four As far as the positive level goes or levels go, there's not many changes The major change is that it's gonna take more tickets to get up So to get to positive one you need 10 yellow tickets not 5. Then it goes up to 20, 30 and 40. The reason being there was, quite a few kids getting a lot of tickets and they were going to go through the system too quickly so we decided

to make it a little bit harder to get to especially
positive level 4. The changes with the negative
system, are almost th- opposite I guess where
there's you'd need <u>more</u> tickets to go down the
system. So if you look at the negative system now
negative 1, before you get to Negative 1, if you get 3
white tickets, the Year Adviser will send a letter
home to the parents warning them that the student's
about to trigger negative level 1   If they get another
2 white tickets they are placed on, negative level 1
and the consequences there, are a letter goes home
to parents again and they've got playground or
garden clean up five half lunches, and an interview
with the Year Adviser. If they further, if they get a
further 3 white tickets, they're not placed on
Negative 2 but triggers another warning letter home
to parents saying look they're still not trying, if they
get any more they'll go down to Negative 2.   So
after 8 white tickets they get the warning letter
home and another interview with the Year Adviser.
They need- now need, well they will now- then
need <u>10</u> white tickets to get to Negative 2. A letter
home to parents, parents requested for an interview
with the counsellor Year Adviser and Deputy.
They're put on a daily contract book, they've got <u>10</u>
playground clean ups and,
[continues for some time and concludes:]
So that's basically, what we thought is
improvement on the old system, so I'd just like to
leave it open now for any comments or questions or
mistakes we might have made in the new system
Yes, Al.

The chair has read the chessboard-chart as a snakes and
ladders board that has resulted in some observed problems of speeds
of ascent and descent ('there was, quite a few kids getting a lot of
tickets and they were going to go through the system too quickly so we
decided...'; 'before you get to negative 1, if you get three white tickets,
the Year Adviser will send a letter home to the parents warning them
that the student's about to trigger negative level 1'). 'Getting up' the
chart, 'slipping down' and 'triggering' level changes are portrayed as
moves the students make: as agents of their own ascent or fall. As well,
this opening speech calls on members' knowledge of several different
categories of students-in-relation-to the-levels, including those who 'go
[up] through the system too quickly' and those who 'need *more* tickets

to go down'. The Welfare Committee has redesigned the board for play, and seeks the comment of members of staff. Al was ready with a question:

> 4. Al: You went down three then plus- so mi- minus five,
>   minus ten tickets and then it goes down to minus
>   three. Is that <u>another</u> thirteen tickets?
> 5. Len: No An. another three.
> 6. Al: Another three So they're still dropping down very
>   quickly.
>   (2 0)

Al's first formulation plus question is treated as a check on how the calculations work for white tickets. His finding that it is three further tickets and not thirteen further tickets that will achieve negative three is joined to a further formulation, 'so they're still dropping down very quickly' (line 6), which is treated by Len as a request for a further account in relation to a problem.

> 7. Len: The last two they drop down the same
>   way as before, the other top ones have
>   slowed up quite a bit [( )
> 8. Al: [(Slowed up) right
> 9 Len: We just tend to (theorise) there won't be
>   too many students down here
> 10. Al: Yeah=
> 11 Len: =And once they get to that certain stage
>   they will, they tend to drop quickly
>   anyway.
> 12 Al: Uh huh
>   (6 0)

This account is produced in three parts: the first in terms of slowing the descent at higher levels while preserving the speed at lower levels; the second in terms of the volume of students at lower levels ('there won't be too many down there'); and the third in terms of a known natural attribute of students on the decline ('once they get to that certain stage they will, tend to drop quickly anyway'). This account, in which social facts are produced as moral facts (cf. Garfinkel: 1967 35) is a jointly-produced justification of how it is that the rules will have some students 'still dropping down very quickly'. The 'problem' in Al's formulation can be heard as the fact that students near the *bottom* of the chart are 'still dropping down very quickly'. In their solution they have appealed to known properties of students near the bottom: there aren't many of them, and they 'tend to drop quickly *anyway*': the social and moral 'fact' of students on the decline is produced as a robust fact that is independent of their rule-making practice.

The Chair's introductory speech, then, can be heard as inviting the production of problems to which the solution of appeals to social-moral facts can be applied.   Appeals to social-moral facts about students, their behaviours, motivations, the conditions of inevitable decline, and so on are part of the routine competence (both moral and pragmatic) of teachers as professionals. This talk is about more than the display of such competence. In the course of talking about changes to rules, they fill out for each other the grounds that could justify making the rules in one way or another. They display their routine knowledge of categories of students and of how the welfare system has worked/could work *given* these categories.   In so doing they produce accounts of the organizational and moral sense of their own actions *in the meeting* in devising and changing rules.

After the principal invites members of the research team to comment (which they do not do) and after another pause, Gary, another member of the Welfare Committee provides more justification for some of the changes. More categories of students essentially as moral actors are presented as part of the rationale.

(5.0)

14.Gary:Len hasn't mentioned just a couple of the reasons we, increased the number of tickets On Negative 4, one of the things we put in there is exclusion from the playground until a notable effort made to improve, that was to cut off people like uh, I won't say this is taped, but those people who got on to Negative 4, did their in-school suspension and then merrily went on their way collecting up to thirty odd tickets, and then nothing was happening to those so, once they get to the 16 tickets they're then, going to be drawn from the playground until they, there's a noticeable effort or to improve and get back to Negative 3 That was one of the things and the other one was to make it, once they got to Negative 2 we made it a little bit harder so we discourage kids from getting to Negative Two because they'd automatically trigger um a few more things that they may not be uh particularly like, like

> the one um one (hour) of school detention, after
> school detention or whatever.
>
> 15. Al: [Have those kids
> 16 ?: [How's (that going to be) organized?

This speech is presented explicitly as correcting an absence in the Chair's initial speech. It could be heard simultaneously as getting the researchers off the hook. However it could also be heard as documenting a silence/absence in the staff meeting: where are more problems, to which we can find solutions?

This speech does more moral-organizational work, for example in the explanation of why playground exclusion was introduced for those at negative level 4 who were 'merrily...collecting up to thirty odd tickets and nothing was happening' to them. That is, they were not being punished enough, given that they were 'merry' about collecting (white) tickets. On the other hand, the category of students approaching negative level 2 needed to be 'discouraged' from 'automatically trigger[ing] things they may not like', such as detention, that is, they had to be protected from the 'automatic' working of the system. As is done elsewhere in this talk Gary draws on membership categories and category-bound activities to describe the moral order (cf. Jayyusi 1984). Members' knowledge about categories of students and appeals to their *different* duties of care with respect to such categories are produced throughout the transcript. Thus the categories are used fundamentally in organising the distribution of sympathy in the meeting.

'Good kids' is a membership category which is independent of the category/levels constituted by the ticketing system. The problem seems to be one of matching the level-placements generated by ticketing with the categories 'already' in existence (what the kids 'really are'). In addition, this description of the Committee's reasoning suggests that the system can be adjusted to counteract its own flaws. It is said to have been too soft on one category and too hard on another. The adjustment is needed to match the array of moral characters that are still seen to pre- exist the system.

After this speech of Gary's the meeting continued to discuss the welfare system for a considerable period of time. On three occasions the principal attempted to conclude the talk on this agenda item by referring the issues to the Welfare Committee. As the talk proceeded, other members found problems in the system, and problems to which the welfare system could be found to offer adequate solutions. The welfare system appeared to be an inexhaustible resource for generating moral-organizational talk.

This talk can be characterized as finding/producing the local rationality (cf Heap 1990) and local morality of their rules and of their rule-making practices. In pursuing problems and solutions, staff members made use of overlapping families of practices, which included invocations of and appeals to social and moral 'facts' such as categories/kinds of kids and their associated activities (including, for some, behavioural 'slips'); describing, including 'scenic' practices with categories in actual and hypothetical scenarios; and accounting for the local production of this talk by tying their turns to each other's turns through devices such as 'I think' or 'because'.

Segment 2: Moral Calculus
The levels system was rife with regulations which were open to multiple characterizations of how they might work in regulating the overall distribution of students to levels and speeds of ascent and descent; and also of how students will feel and think about these same organizational features.

1 Jon: I can't see why you're trying to make it harder to go
        up Positively=
2 ?:   =No, I agree with that, I I think
3 ?:   Well, [I think
4 ?:   [I think it's a good thing that so many kids <u>were</u>
        (up)
5 Al: Because I think it- a lot of kids are up on Plus 3
        now, and at the end of the year they're gonna be
        knocked right back down to nought So if you can
        make it harder to get up there, you're only going to
        get the good kids and they're going to be
        demoralised come February when they're back to
        zero

In lines 1 - 4 above Jon and other speakers address the proposal to increase the number of tickets needed to go 'up' the levels system, as mentioned by the Chair in his first speech. This issue is pursued by Al, who supplies a complicated scenario about demoralised 'good kids' who will be knocked back to zero at the beginning of the next school year *if* they find it harder than it was this year to go up the levels.

He links this to the previous turns through the conjunction 'because'. This conjunction cannot be heard grammatically in the sense that he supplies the reasons for the prior comments. It is a method of tying his turn to preceding turns and in this way he, as an early speaker in the meeting, is showing another way (in addition to 'I think') in which turns can be introduced and what shape they can have. These early turns help to give the talk its trajectory. Related to Schegloff's (1991: 52-53) 'open question' about the problem of the 'procedural consequentiality' of setting/context, these coordinated entry methods seem to show both orientation of speakers to 'context' and speakers' formulations of the 'context' by means of these entries as consequential for what can/does occur.

The trajectory of the talk is directed also by the members' hearing of the kind of work that turns are able to contribute to: as proposed above, moral-organizational work that uses as its resources any member's commonsense knowledge of the school and its workings. Any competent member can say 'I think' and some are in positions to say 'I know'. Al is then challenged on some of the grounds of his plea and is called on to re-make the significance of his point, for as Tom points out in line 7 below, it is *understood* that students will return to zero -but that they will keep this year's privileges:

6 ?:   Well=
7. Tom: =They'll still have their privileges   (All those)
         people on the positive levels are going to carry on
         with their privileges [even though
8. Al: [So they'll still have the pass, but they'd be back to
         zero. Well I think that should be explained to them
         'cause a lot of them are worried about that

The moral that Al finds in his scenario, in the end, is that students should have these rules explained to them. The connection to the issue of *increasing* the numbers of tickets needed to go up has been lost, but the issue of demoralisation has been addressed, although in different terms. Much of this meeting talk is characterized by loose and fast-flowing topic-shifting that is nevertheless stitched together by and for the members through turn-initiations, particularly, here, 'I think':

9. Jon: I think more than drop or decrease the number of
         yellow <u>tickets</u> they need perhaps we should look
         why people <u>get</u> the yellow tickets. Perhaps people
         are giving out yellow tickets too <u>easily</u>
10 Len: R I don't think that's a problem, I think, statistically
         it looked like we did we had pretty much the right,
         numbers of tickets and kids were getting the right

number except we had one extra term this year to
play with. If we continued this same pattern next
year with the extra term plus the extra kids, there
would be too many students on Positive 4 that just
probably wouldn't mean as much as, trying to cut it
back a bit

11. ?:   Yes.

Throughout these segments, teachers appeal to statistics as a criterion of justice. Counting and accounting are also linked in the vocabularies used to describe the ticket-collecting through characterizations of the motivations and the moralities of students, as in 'merrily collecting', 'building up' 'amassing'. The categories are routinely placed into courses of action; activity-descriptions are morally laden. Related talk is about what the statistics should look like in order that justice can be found to be done. Their use of numbers, counts and statistics as robust facts on the one hand and as products of their own work on the other is not unique to this staff meeting.

In line 9 Jon stitches his new topic on to his initial point, by shifting it from a concern with *numbers* of tickets to *why* they are given. 'I think' looks to be a collectively-agreed practice used as a solution to the recognized impossibility of separating out or pinning down any one problem or observation within the welfare system. 'I think', as suggested above, appears also to work as an agreed form for describing the status of turns as candidate descriptions of the school world that 'count' and can/should accumulate to give this talk its open-ended character..

The moral calculus they produce is grounded in their competent descriptions of students and school life, but it also treats the working of the welfare system (including the statistics it produces) as *part of* these social and moral facts. In line 10 above, Len refers to a statistical criterion for determining whether teachers are giving out 'too many' yellow tickets. The statistics are made part of the moral order, for example in Len's allusion to the idea that if too many were on upper levels it 'wouldn't mean as much' so they have to 'cut it back'. The simulation-gaming features of this rule-adjustment talk draws precisely on their knowledge of this kind of calculus.

12. Jon: (   ) I think that the more, the quicker they get on to
the the lower positive levels probably the better off
Perhaps you should stretch the scale at the top, and
leave it the way it was at the bottom

13. Len: The lower levels of, you only have to get no white
    tickets for 10 weeks to get on Positive 1. Or 10
    white, 10 yellow tickets so

In achieving this apparently seamless talk speakers advance
themes also by offering formulations of preceding utterances. For
example Gord works from the immediately preceding talk about
numbers of numbers of yellow tickets to resurrect a point made earlier
by Jon (line 9) about what yellow tickets are given *for*. He introduces a
category-puzzle - an anomaly - in pointing out the case of a student
who has 'amassed' many white tickets and who also has 'amassed' a
number of yellow tickets. The strong inference is that students should
not normally be collecting both, or at least not in such large numbers
both ways. Again the logic of ticketing is seen to be a result of the
students' agency, but the anomaly leads to questioning the teachers'
work in giving out tickets.

14 Gord: The the only thing I can see uh one student who has
        amassed a a very large amount of ah white tickets
        um tells me today that he's also amassed 7 yellow
        tickets And I wonder if he's receiving them for
        what's considered to be just, you know, standard
        behavior. Now it's an improvement for him, but
        whether it's ah something that's uh outstanding or
        not, you know, I just worry about that a little bit
        because he feels that he is improving [(every
        now and again)
15.   [(((Several people talk at once))
16 Bill: Yeah I was just going to say that [(   )
17. ?:   [(   ) standardizing who gives. how we give yellow
        tickets really it's up to the discretion of the teacher=

The issue of whether teachers are following ticket-issuing
guidelines properly is raised at a number of points in the meeting, and
on other occasions. That some teachers might be cheating with tickets
(giving out too many white, too many yellow, 'at the drop of a hat', or
whatever) was a suspicion voiced and/or a claim made in these and
other recorded materials. This adds an element of intrigue to the
methods used by staff members in public talk about the ticketing
system, including at this staff meeting which must have been attended
by some of the members under suspicion. However in this analysis I
do not examine the possible 'overhearing audience' dimensions of this

talk organization (cf. Heritage 1985) although I recognize its importance to the moral-organizational work undertaken here.

Segment 3: The One White Ticket Problem

For the members, the 'problem' they face is hearably produced as a problem of achieving the ideals of rule- governability and of fairness/justice in a system that is observably (to them) open to subjective interpretation and open to unfairness/injustice.

The problem they face is also hearably the problem of aligning their practical decision-making (what rules, to achieve what outcome) with the moral accountability of these rules and of their defence or challenging of these rules in the staff meeting itself. The talk proceeds also to connect the getting of tickets with the giving of them.

These problems are available in the transcript segments presented above. They are given a focus in one phase of the meeting where they address what some of them see as the special problem of the 'one white ticket' given to students who are otherwise 'very good kids'. The Chair, Len, introduces the issue:

1. Len: Bob just reminded me too about uh the importance one white ticket can have to students when they're on Positive Level 3 or Positive Level 2   In in the system we've got now as well as the new system. These are kids that have built up say 20, 25 <u>yellow</u> tickets and then <u>one</u> teacher might for some reason give them one <u>white</u> ticket and that can affect them going past level 2, just the one white ticket so, if you sort of get in the habit of looking at the levels up there so you know where students are falling I suppose in the s. in the system that, you might think you might teach this kid a lesson or something by giving (them) one white ticket because they're showing off or something but, it could be very sort of

2. ?: Devastating

3. Len: Yeah, devastating for this one student because they're going <u>right</u> up there, they're just about getting to Positive 3 and there's about half a dozen kids I've got uh they won't get to Positive 3 this year now, (won't) even think about Positive 4 because they've just got one white ticket, over the year from one teacher   But if, if you're giving white tickets just be very careful and especially the very good

kids one white ticket can be quite important to their progressing up the system.

Len provides a strong characterization of the problem as something that happens accidentally and idiosyncratically to kids who have 'built up' many yellow tickets: 'one teacher might *for some reason* give them one white ticket'. Len provides a familiar case in point of such a good kid's behaviour ('showing off or something') and a possible logic for the teacher's reaction to it ('teach[ing] this kid a lesson or something'). 'Showing off' and 'teaching kids a lesson' are effective activity descriptors given that they are produced and understood as natural, normal actions and reactions of students and teachers respectively. They are both borderline activities, on or just over the very edge of responsibility, and amount to making a 'mistake' for students and teachers respectively. Here they are linked into a single hypothetical example that could cover many specific actual cases. This is 'scenic practice' with membership categorization, designed to make a moral point. With the etcetera clauses 'showing off *or something*', 'teach this kid a lesson *or something*' the application of this co-selection of descriptors [of a 'minor' student infraction and of an understandable, reasonable teacher reaction] is extended to other normal, understandable, student action and teacher reaction pairs.

It is another speaker who supplies the descriptor 'devastating' which Len uses to introduce a description of the motivations of students who are [or were] on the way up, who had 'built up say 20, 25 yellow tickets' and who 'won't even think' about positive 4 because of this accident. Implied here is that such students *should* be thinking of positive 4, and that teachers *should* be concerned that they are not.

Such a ticket could happen naturally, normally, but such 'devastation' of 'very good kids' can be avoided by consulting the levels sheet and keeping in mind where the students are. These mistakes in ticketing can be avoided by being 'very careful'. One could say that the giving of (white) tickets should, as a practice, take into account the membership category of its recipitent. 'Justice' seems to be a matter of aligning ticketing-level outcomes with pre-existing (pre-constituted) membership categories of students.

After more talk in implicit agreement that some rule is needed to cover this special case, the principal suggests referral to the Welfare Committee, and in the course of agreeing with the talk-so-far, presents his own scenario about how upsetting the one white ticket can be:

12. Bob: I think that is <u>one</u> area where the Welfare
Committee could meet to ah have some
discretionary powers on er there may be others, but
ah but that's the one that I certainly that strikes me,
the phone, you'd be a- amazed, well maybe you
aren't amazed but ah the impact that a white
<u>tic</u>(hh)<u>ket</u> from in this sort of situation, I've had
tearful <u>mo</u>thers on the phone ah and ah

13.   ((laughter and groans from others))

14.Gord:They can't hold their head up ( )
[((laughter))

15. Bob: [( ) Heads up,
((more laughter))
it's, it's it's the one, it's the one that perhaps hits
home to me the the the most, however, ah so maybe
that's certainly something that needs (   )

16   ((Somebody asks a question, B begins to reply and
is then interrupted))

17 Gary:I was under the impression that we'd already
de<u>ci</u>ded that [(   )

18 Bob: [That was fairly sexist I'm sorry. Tearful <u>par</u>ents.

The principal invites laughter in his description of 'tearful
mothers on the phone'. Are these mothers presented as taking the
issue too seriously? These teachers are taking it seriously enough.
'They can't hold their head up' extends the humour and the point that
some solution needs to be found.

19. Doug: (   ) then if any white tickets (say) that could be
referred to disciplinary committee over Positive 1,
so it gives them extra privileges as well

The meeting seems to be in agreement that this is a quirk in the system
that should be covered through the possibility for some sort of waiver.
But then Sam presents a counter-scenario in which the issuing of the
one white ticket is not accidental at all. His scenario equally depicts a
plausible, recognizable situation:

20 Sam:Well I've known this situation (   ) one
student in particular I said you're heading for a
white ticket I've been saying it for <u>weeks</u>, and then
eventually even though they <u>had</u> 20, 30 yellow
tickets=

21 Bob: =Ah yeah

> 22. Sam: And they probably thoroughly deserved it, 'N
> maybe I was feeling too reluctant, you know,
> ex<u>ac</u>tly this reason, oh they're a good kid, I'll give
> them another chance, um=

In the course of this talk, many different 'moral versions' of
students and teachers (and in one case parents) are introduced (cf.
Silverman 1987); the production of these moral versions through
category-work and/or scenic practice is part of the teachers'
professional competence. Now that the topic is the giving of tickets
rather than the getting of them, members begin to introduce scenarios
in which they quote themselves handling this problem in thought or in
talk: what was said or done, what could be said or done or written.

> 23 Bob: =Well, that that's part of the discretion isn't it? I
> mean thats the the Welfare Committee would come
> and see you and say you know what was the
> situation   That's the situation.   Fine, that stands
> But then you know
> 24. Gord: and your other uh where it says <u>other</u> whatever,
> you would say well you know after counselling or
> something you know, no notice was taken of
> 25. ?:   Yeah.
> 26 Gord: of warnings, you know, or something like that.
> And so that's on the ticket (   ).

Gord proposes how one could account on the ticket itself to
accommodate the idea that a good kid could deserve a white ticket.
The issuing of the one white ticket remains a highly accountable matter.
Sam, in his scenario in 20-22 above, says that he was 'feeling reluctant',
thus exactly the same kind of moral actor as the rest concerned with
the one white ticket problem. In his description of 'good kids' who
thoroughly deserve a white ticket he shows how long he held out - 'I've
been saying it for <u>weeks</u>' - which captures perfectly a version of how
any teacher, however much they appreciate 'good kids', could be
justified in issuing a white ticket.

At this point multiple 'moral versions' are put into play: Jim in
27 below talks about how hard it is to be good for a long time in a plea
for a one-white-ticket provision;   Len proposes that the Welfare
Committee investigate individual cases to see if they are really
'deserved' - and if not, the one white ticket can be quietly 'crossed out':

27 Jim: Couldn't you just build into it Len just, allowance
          for one white ticket in the in that time? Just as a I
          mean it's very hard to be good for so long and not
          just wanna break out (   )
28.   ((Laughter and comments 4 0))
29. Len: (   ) system I think it's probably best to do what Bob
          says and that's what I sort of do now, if I see
          someone just get the one white ticket I go and see
          the teacher and speak about the white ticket to them
          and if it's one like Sam, I say OK they deserve it and
          they get it, but if not if they sort of when the
          teachers realize there could be, some leeway there
          we might just [cross that one out and let them have
          another chance
30 Jim: [Well yeah, that's the fairest if you're prepared to do
          that that's (really fair)
31 Len: Yeah, I don't mind=

There appears to be agreement that the crossing-out of the
ticket and giving 'another chance' will occur at the discretion of the
Chair in consultation with the teacher. Another speaker provides a
formulation of why they *cannot* build it in directly into the written
rules, by providing yet another category, this time of students who will
exploit the provision if it is there. Again we see the use of quoted
speech as the 'activity' indicating the implied moral category
('exploiters').

31 ?:   =But I still think=
32. ?:   =But once you sort of put it (in the framework of)
         system here, the kids think oh beaut, I've got this
         one thing and I can get one white ticket and
         ((somebody interrupts - unclear what he says))
33 ?:   yeah.

More and more of these versions and associated scenarios
involving character and motivation ('oh beaut...I can get one white
ticket'; ' said you're heading for a white ticket I've been saying it for
weeks') could be produced, as part of the routine professional
competence of teachers. They are not produced randomly; they are
produced as part of the work of accounting and are placed at points in
the talk where, for example, rule-decisions are hearably being made.
    Topics are inserted, dropped, and resurrected using the locally
organized conventions for entry into the talk, such as 'I think' and
'because', which advance the elaboration of problems and solutions in

the system. In this meeting, few issues are settled formally. But understood as moral-organizational work, this talk appears to be custom-built. Even if the rules of the system cannot cover each and every social/moral fact or problem that members raise, talk about the rules and about their rule-making is 'talk as the work' (cf. Gronn, 1983) of achieving moral accountability and moral community.

Organizational Work: Finding Social Order

I have emphasised the selection of categories and activities in the descriptions put forward. The pervasive work with membership categorization devices in and around accounting for decision-making in this instance, shows us 'culture in action'. Culture is made retrospectively and prospectively in the moment of the meeting. What happened before is hearably, recognizably sketched through category-based vignettes or even brief phrases such as 'merrily collecting'. What could happen in future is also warned of in these ways ('oh beaut'). The production and recognition of such items for their status as documents of the underlying school culture attest to members' cultural competence. Central to this work is the production of categories of moral actors and of courses of moral action.

Members of this school staff might be seen to be in the impossible position of trying to perfect a system that is observably, to them, not perfectible. However, my analysis has suggested that they take themselves to be in the not only possible, but normal, position of attempting to achieve a *near-enough* rule-governability for their system. In this respect they are in the same position as any other committee or community attempting to make or use rules in ways that are seen to be rational and fair. Similar practices of looking for and finding the local rationality and the local morality of one's actions could be expected to be found in the course of any work in reference to rules.

What may distinguish this instance, and provide the locally relevant reason for the density and other properties of this talk, is that here the members recognize that the system is both of their own making, and self-operating. They are working with dual notions of 'structure' and 'agency' throughout this talk: the system is both (either, alternately) independent of human action and design in its 'automatic' and universal workings - some of these because of human nature, natural facts - and yet recognizably dependent on their rule-making work and their discretion. With the exception of the principal's reference to (tearful) parents, there is no appeal in this talk to any external constraint or external accountability.

In their talk they look for and 'find' the local rationality and the local morality of their rules and of their rule- making work. In their talk they also look for and 'find social order', not as a *'theoretical exercise'* but as a *'practically and socially organized'* one (Sharrock and Button 1991: 162). They find social order in the sequential and consequential production (and hearing) of descriptions of actors, motives, actions and statistical patterns. Membership categories and the courses of moral action they are implicated in, are central to these descriptions. For each other, for the observers attending the meeting, and for readers of the transcript, their talk counts, and works, as *'courses of instruction'* in 'how to *adequately, competently* describe the social actions which take place before [their/our] eyes' (Sharrock and Button 1991, 163).

Chapter 5

Lies, Recollections and Categorical Judgements in Testimony

Michael Lynch and David Bogen

As commonly defined, lying involves two elements: a statement that is contrary to fact, and an intention to deceive (see Bok 1979).[1]   Accordingly, the exposure of a lie through cross-examination is said to require the demonstration, first, that a witness gave untrue or misleading testimony, and second that the witness was well aware of the untruth and intended to deceive the court.   Although lawyers assume that witnesses lie on the stand with great regularity, they also acknowledge that convictions for perjury are exceedingly difficult to obtain.   The relevant facts may be unknown, ambiguous or disputed by the parties to the case, and it may be difficult to demonstrate beyond a reasonable doubt that a witness intended to deceive the court.   It is often held that the difficulty arises from the fact that intentions are private matters, inaccessible to scientific as well as commonsense scrutiny.   Nevertheless, for the courts, the exposure of a witness's intentions and motives is a practical requirement, even though 'intentions' and 'motives' may be regarded as epistemologically problematic.

There is no question that the possibility of a witness's lying presents the courts with a chronic problem, and many of the procedures and strategies used by participants in a trial to corroborate testimony or expose inaccuracy and contradiction are addressed to that problem. We should not, however, suppose that the courts are engaged in an 'epistemological' undertaking. The task for the courts is not to articulate a general theory of knowledge or to address the doubts of a philosophical sceptic. Nor is it necessarily the case that court inquiries are analogous to professional psychological research. A court's judgements about truthful or untruthful testimony is unlike a systematic study of the relationship between witness behaviours and audience attributions.[2] Academic methods and standards of judgement for the most part are beside the point. Marcus Stone (1995 [1988]:51), for example, goes so far as to argue that professional psychological research offers no help for an interrogator who hopes to expose a witness's lies.

> No current body of psychological knowledge has any practical value for application to the problem of credibility in courts If it were otherwise, the legal profession would have seized on it long ago
> There is no known psychological technique or test which can penetrate the mind of the individual in isolation, to ascertain if he is lying. This insight can certainly not be derived from so-called body language   .   An understanding of lying must be practical, based on common sense, experience of life and the courts, and free from psychological jargon or theorizing

To support his claim about the irrelevance of psychology, Stone (1995: 69-70) cites the negative findings from Paul Ekman's (1985) research on lying. Ekman acknowledges that a lying witness's overt comportment may not yield discrete, unequivocal signs of lying. Aspects of a witness's demeanor, such as hesitation, a wavering tone of voice, an averted gaze, sweating, and so forth, are commonly associated with lying, but these 'signs' may in some cases be attributed to sources of anxiety, distraction, or anger which have nothing to do with lying.

In a criminal trial, judgements about truthfulness and lying involve 'holistic comparison[s]' of various reports about a common reality, after they have been tested or challenged adversarially' (1995:51). The temporal and interactional conditions under which the courts make their judgements differ considerably from the simplified and controlled conditions of the psychology laboratory. Stone (1995) concludes that it is 'the psychologist who can learn about lying from the cross-examiner, and not the converse.' This recommendation is compatible with an ethnomethodological view of the relationship between situated practical actions and academic analyses.[3] However, it should be added that psychologists, and also sociologists, may learn less by appropriating cross-examiners' general remarks about lying and credibility than by examining what lawyers and witnesses *do* during cross-examination. Lawyers are no less prone then anyone else to account for their practices by invoking natural-theoretical conceptions of knowledge and judgement. Often, these conceptions are individualistic, emphasising heroic qualities of a skilled cross-examiner's technique for 'penetrating' the inscrutable mind of a reluctant witness.

A radically different view of lying, and of its accountability, is put forward by Harvey Sacks. For him, the idea that lying is undetectable because private is a figment of what might be called educated common sense. Sacks (1992a: 558) says:

> People have the conception that psychological terms are properly used by virtue of special knowledge of the persons you're dealing with (And by 'psychological terms' I mean conventional, lay sets of terms like 'thinking,' 'having a reason for doing something,' etc.) Now that's a kind of thing that people who have had some university training are specially wont to insist on, i e , 'You don't really know about somebody until you . etc.' But our language is not built in such a way. Persons use psychological terms with the same freedom and 'lack of knowledge of other persons' as they do any other terms.

Like Stone, Sacks denies that professional psychology can equip us with an ability to detect lies, but he goes a step further when he says that a formal education can obscure what a student already knows when acting in everyday circumstances, namely that 'lying is perfectly observable, in the same sense that anything else is' (Sacks 1992a: 559). Presumably, Sacks was not saying that lies are always perfectly obvious (having studied with Goffman he would be well aware of the interactional strategies for concealment). Instead, he is saying that lies are essentially public actions. The fact that lay and professional psychology gives an inadequate account of how lawyers, counsellors, teachers, parents and peers are able to tell when someone is lying, should not lead us to conclude that judgements about lying are necessarily arbitrary or unfounded. Instead, as Sacks observes, persons often quite freely speak of what others *can* know, remember, or say. The point is that the ability to tell when someone is lying arises from sources other than a knowledge of an inner, occult process. This holds for psychological practice, no less than it does for legal practice and everyday language use. The question for Sacks, and for us in this paper, is how *do* persons come to assess the truth of what others say about their own, first-person, experience? This is a large question, and we shall address it by examining a few instances of interrogations conducted under different circumstances. As we understand the phenomena of lying and exposing lies, they do not boil down to a matter of one individual's judgements of the truth-value of statements made by another. Instead, they arise in and through the temporal and interactional production of interrogatory dialogue. In keeping with the theme of this book, we focus on some of the categorical resources through which intersubjective accounts of what a witness *can say* are generated in the course of specific interrogations.

Evident Lies and Moral Entitlements to a Possible Past

Contrary to the idea that lies involve private intentions to deceive, and that accusations of lying are essentially problematic, on some occasions persons treat lying as an evident, and even obvious, matter. Take, for example, the following transcript from English, Hampe, Bacon and Settlage (1964: 94, quoted in Pollner 1975: 420) of dialogue between a doctor and mental patient.

Dr: Remember last week you promised you wouldn't lie to me any more when you told me that you weren't nervous about masturbating and that stuff

Pt: Yes.

Dr: But you did lie to me again. The very next lie—you told one of my assistants that when you were brought home from the hospital after you were born you heard a broadcast

Pt: I thought I did.

Dr: You knew that was a lie

Pt: I made myself believe it I wanted to . . .

Dr: Inside yourself, Gerald?

Pt: Yes.

Dr: You knew that was a lie.

Pt: I couldn't have remembered a broadcast when I was five weeks . . I can't remember anything that happened when I was five weeks old

Dr: Of course not. And yet you lied to my assistant here. You knew your dead Aunt didn't speak to you, that it was a hallucination . . .

Pt: Yes, it's what I said. I said the first day I came here
        I was still believing that I heard her voice.
Dr: Well, how about now? Are you hearing voices
        now?
Pt: No.

Note the way the psychiatrist tells the patient that he 'couldn't
have remembered' a broadcast shortly after his birth, and that he 'knew'
his dead aunt did not speak to him. We might ask, 'How can he know
this?' Although different schools of psychiatry may recommend
different strategies for handling patients who lie or hallucinate, they do
not exhaustively instruct the practitioner on how to tell the difference
between valid and invalid perceptual accounts (Pollner, ibid, and
Coulter 1975: 385-396). It seems unlikely that psychiatric doctrine, or
even a singular insight into the particular patient's mind, enables the
doctor in this instance to challenge the patient's story. The patient
yields when challenged, saying 'I couldn't have remembered a
broadcast when I was five weeks ... I can't remember anything that
happened when I was five weeks old.' He concedes that he is not
entitled to such memories.

It might be argued that the authoritative terms of the doctor's
accusation — 'You knew that was a lie' — together with the patient's
concession, are little more than effects of psychiatric power. In support
of this, it can be said that the doctor shows none of the restraint against
accusing the patient of lying that he might have shown with persons
who are not under his administration, and it also can be said that the
patient, for his part, may be attuned to the hazards of disagreeing with
the doctor's assessment of his own experience. The doctor seems
unwilling to countenance the possibility that the patient might be a
person with highly unusual capacities to perceive and remember, or
that he might have a cultural background that sanctions communication
with the dead. Although the doctor's authoritative stance and the
patient's grovelling compliance are prominent in the scene, for our
purposes it is important to recognize that both parties give lip service to
an evidently normal version of what can or cannot be remembered:

Patient: I can't remember anything that happened when I
         was five weeks old.
Doctor: Of course not.

The doctor uses an expression ('Of course not.') which affirms
what the patient has just said and reprimands him for having to
acknowledge something that should be so obvious. He reprimands the

patient not only for lying, but for saying something patently absurd. As Wittgenstein (1969: 67,71) points out, there are some things about which we cannot be mistaken:

> Could we imagine a man who keeps on making mistakes where we regard a mistake as ruled out, and in fact never encounter one?
> E g. he says he lives in such and such a place, is so and so old, comes from such and such a city, and he speaks with the same certainty (giving all the tokens of it) as I do, but he is wrong.
> But what is his relation to this error? What am I to suppose?
> . . . I should not call this a mistake, but rather a mental disturbance, perhaps a transient one.

Something similar can be said about lying. In the present case, for a man to report having heard a broadcast five weeks after his birth may seem less of a lie than a symptom of insanity. Who but a madman would imagine that anyone would believe such a story? In a way, by accusing the patient of 'lying' the doctor credits him with enough sanity to know the difference between a sensible and nonsensical account of his own past. From a psychiatric perspective the patient's confession might be said to indicate an 'insight' into his disorder.[4] Whether sincerely or not, the patient expresses agreement with the doctor's account of what he *can* or *cannot* have remembered. It is crucial to recognize that these conditional terms (can/cannot) articulate the patient's *possible* experience in terms of a public, normative standard.

We can begin to appreciate Sacks's assertion that 'lying is perfectly observable' by focusing not only on lies and lying, but more generally on how what a witness says about the past (including the witness's own remembered past) is couched in terms of what *one can say*. In this sense, a witness does not own the details of her or his own past. In the above instance, the 'perfectly observable' character of the patient's lies derives from an assessment of the obvious falsehood of what he is alleged to have said. This assessment is not, or not only, a judgement about cognitive abilities or capacities (one cannot say what one is incapable of knowing or remembering); more immediately it is a question of moral entitlement.

In the sense we are considering it, moral entitlement has to do with grammatical, conventional, and sometimes legal, associations between categories of persons, actions, scenes, and identities. A strong logical sense of 'can' and 'cannot' may be gained by considering the expression 'a man cannot be a bride' (Sharrock, Hughes and Anderson

1986). In this instance, the category 'man' is excluded from the identity 'bride'. By definition, brides are women. A less strict, but for present purposes a more apt, sense of categorical exclusion has to do with moral rights. For example, the statement 'a man cannot pretend to be a bride' proscribes a logical possibility (according to the statement, it is possible, but not morally right, for a man to pretend to be a bride). Modifying a proscription can have grammatical consequences. For example, when same sex marriage is permitted, associated terms (bride/groom; aunt/uncle) may be retained. As a matter of grammar, and/or of legislated right, what a person category can or cannot be, or do, is not a matter of personal aptitude. A partner in a same-sex couple can *try* to act the part of a bride in a wedding ceremony, and the 'bride' and 'groom' may even perform a secret marriage ceremony, but they *cannot*, as a rule, openly claim the associated entitlements if the relevant laws exclude them from the category 'married couple'. The formulation of a rule, as opposed to the description of an ability, raises different possibilities for contesting the matter in question. So for example, 'women cannot vote' (stated prior to their enfranchisement) may be challenged by an effort to change the law (perhaps through acts of civil disobedience in which women present themselves at a polling place), whereas a statement like 'women cannot do higher mathematics' may be challenged by a demonstration of aptitudes and abilities contrary to the assertion. A statement of ability may support a legislative change, so that efforts to demonstrate that 'women *can* do higher mathematics' would be consistent with a movement to remove legal and informal barriers against admitting women into mathematics programs. The point of our raising the distinction between abilities and entitlements is not to establish an absolute demarcation between two domains of usage, but to note that the relevant sense of 'cannot' in an expression like 'an adult cannot have sexual intercourse with a minor' has to do with public rights and not inherent capabilities. This distinction becomes critical when we examine so-called 'mental' or 'cognitive' capacities associated with what can or cannot be said, known, remembered, forgotten and the like.

Like many other matters, moral entitlements and exclusions often are associated with specific occupational categories, and not just with what anybody would be expected, or required, to do or to know.[5] Ekman provides some apt examples of this, although he does not fully work out their significance in his psychological analysis of lying and memory. He observes that a 'memory failure is credible only in limited circumstances.' He gives the example of a doctor, who when 'asked if the tests were negative can't claim not to remember' (Ekman 1985: 30).

Although the doctor may very well have forgotten the test results, he 'can't claim not to remember' them because it is a doctor's legal and professional responsibility to produce records of such tests under the appropriate circumstances. To say that he forgot the results would not effectively excuse him from the responsibility to produce the relevant reports. Ekman also gives the example of a policeman who is asked by a suspect whether the particular room is 'bugged'. Like the doctor, the policeman cannot claim a loss of memory in response to this question. Although one can imagine that the policeman might fail to remember that the particular room was bugged, to acknowledge such failure opens up the question of responsibility for the relevant item of knowledge. (The policeman might disavow responsibility by saying that the room in question was under another policeman's jurisdiction, but this differs from claiming a memory loss). Even if true, such 'memory failure' would come across as an evasion or, if not an evasion, an admission of incompetence. The policeman *cannot* claim not to remember because members of his occupation are expected, as a matter of duty, to collect and retain such information in files if not 'in their heads'.[6] This has less to do with psychology than with legal regulations and moral responsibilities that apply to particular occupational categories and their record keeping practices. As Jeff Coulter (1983b:135) puts it:

> . . . to have forgotten certain matters can lead to being held responsible not (merely) for a 'cognitive malfunction' but for a moral lapse. This intertwining of the 'psychological' and the normative is much neglected in extant memory models, but appears at once when materials taken from everyday life are examined.

Because of the parallel vocabularies, it is easy to conflate conventional and legal responsibilities for collecting and reporting information with individual capacities to remember. The two, of course, do sometimes go together, but compared to cognitive organization of memory, the social logic of memory is, as Coulter says, a 'much neglected' topic. More than that, an appreciation of this topic can motivate a critical reconception of mental phenomena. Such a reconception can accord primacy to public settings of conduct rather than the 'inner' states of the individual. This reconception also has methodological implications. A lack of access to the witness's mind no longer must be viewed as an essential source of uncertainty that is only partially overcome by interpreting overt behaviour. Without opting for behaviorism, we can analyse public, interactional conduct as an ordinary (and ordinarily accountable) basis for the production and recognition of stories about the past, including those included under the category of lies.

Ekman's example of a doctor who 'can't claim not to remember' the test results is beguilingly simple, but what Coulter calls the 'intertwining of the 'psychological' and the normative' can be far more complicated than a stable association between a personal category and an activity type. To a large extent, a recipient's determination of what a speaker is entitled to say is derived from the details of *what* they say. In other words, an assessment of the person's competence and credibility is strongly connected to the plausibiity of the stories they tell. This is not to say that competence and credibility can be reduced to the plausibility of a single, isolated story, because reputational considerations come into play which may lead a recipient to doubt an otherwise unremarkable story, or to believe a story that, told by someone else, would seem incredible. However, as the following example (Sacks 1992a: 113) suggests, grounds for suspecting a lie are sometimes found in a finite array of details in a story. One notable feature of this excerpt, which Sacks extracted from a call to a social service agency by a man (B) who reports a marital problem, is that the recipient (A) challenges B strictly on the basis of what he says in the immediate call.

(1)	A.	Yeah, then what happened?
(2)	B:	Okay, in the meantime she [wife of B] says, "Don't ask the child nothing" Well, she stepped between me and the child, and I got up to walk out the door. When she stepped between me and the child, I went to move her out of the way And then about that time her sister had called the police. I don't know how she what she . . .
(3)	A.	Didn't you smack her one?
(4)	B:	No
(5)	A.	You're not telling me the story, Mr. B.
(6)	B:	Well, you see when you say smack you mean hit.
(7)	A.	Yeah, you shoved her. Is that it?
(8)	B:	Yeah, I shoved her.

In his analysis of this instance, Sacks speaks of an 'inference-making machine'. This is a way of emphasising the strong intersubjective grounds deployed by the recipient (A) for projecting untold elements of the story told to him. According to Sacks, 'A' had no independent access to the event, and yet he is able to demand the correct version from the story teller (B), who presumably had been present at the scene. Lies of omission are often said to be more difficult to detect than lies of commission, but in this case an omission becomes explicitly and strongly accountable. Moreover, the recipient (A) not only remarks that something was omitted, he proposes exactly what was omitted ('Didn't you smack her one?'). Moreover, after B's denial, A insists 'You're not telling me the story, Mr. B.' Mr. B then begins to yield the missing details, first by objecting to the word 'smack' and its implication of a bodily assault. When the interrogator (A) substitutes 'shove' for 'smack' (suggesting more of an effort to get past the wife), B accepts this modified version.

Sacks (1992a: 115) points out that there is nothing extraordinary about the interrogator's achievement in this case. Parents, for example, routinely challenge their children's accounts by demanding that they 'tell the whole story'. Sacks also suggests that there is good reason to suppose that the 'inference' in question is based on rather simple resources, analogous to recognising the missing letter in the alphabetical series (a), (b), (d). A machine attuned to the canonical series can supply a missing item, just as the spell-check function in a word-processing program can correctly identify a common word from which a letter is missing. Such machine 'inferences' only succeed with highly standardized and clearly demarcated sequential objects. For Sacks, the possibility of making such inferences (inferences that come immediately to mind, and which require no special insight or ability) is set up by the fact that story scenes and sequences of events are duplicated with great specificity and regularity. The fact that conventional stories may vary between different historical and regional societies, as well as under different local circumstances, is beside the point. As conventional objects, they are locally stable (or, at least, stable enough) so that members can make use of them as contextual resources for achieving, or insisting upon, a determinate order to a story told on a particular occasion.

With respect to the above sequence, Sacks proposes that, as 'members of the same society that these two people are in,' we can reconstruct the logic through which the recipient of the call challenges the caller's account by saying 'Didn't you smack her one?' and concluding that 'You're not telling me the story, Mr B.' Sacks (1992a: 116) describes the sequence as a series with a missing element.

> What we have is roughly something like this: A knows that
> the scene is 'a family problem ' So (a) is the family quarrel,
> (b) is the guy moving to the door . (d) is the police coming

And (c) is the grounds for the police to have come That is, apparently on some piece of information the police have come, and that piece of information is the thing that A has guessed at. A apparently knows, then, what good grounds are for the police to be called to a scene. And he's able to use those good grounds, first to make a guess, and then to assess the correctness of the answer to that guess.

It is important to keep in mind here that A's judgements in this case are *categorical*. Although B relates a story about what, for him, is a singular episode involving himself, his child, his wife, her sister, and the police, as Sacks observes, 'A knows essentially only the set of terms that B uses to name them' as *a* child, *a* wife, *that* wife's sister, and the police. In this case the story includes both too much and not enough detail. By mentioning that 'her sister had called the police,' B includes a phase of the story that begs the question 'What grounds did she have for calling them?' Although it is imaginable that the sister called the police for no good reason — for example, that she overreacted or was trying to frame B— the story does not include any hint of such special motive or circumstance. Instead, the account is vulnerable to a default inference to the effect that the sister called the police for a good reason, to protect B's wife from his assault. 'Didn't you smack her one?' offers just such a reason. This 'good reason' derives from the entire sketch: the generic identities and implied alignments of the family members, the described sequence of actions, and the climactic entry of the police. The relevant actions and alignments come into play as part of a recognizable story. The specific membership categories have a critical role for the sense of the story (and of what is missing from it). This can be appreciated by performing systematic substitutions. As Sacks (1992a: 119) puts it :

To get a sense of the way in which the inferences that can be made from a story are geared to these categories, we could try, for example, using different categories. What if it were, not "her sister," but 'a neighbor' who had called the police? A possible inference in that case would be that the grounds for calling the police had something to do with 'creating a disturbance'; crying child, husband and wife yelling at each other. Or, for example, just shuffle the one category around a little bit. Would the same inference be made if it was 'my' sister, not "her" sister who had called the police? The rules with respect to who owes what to whom, and who takes care of whom may be so formulated that those things matter a great deal. The inference in this case might then be, not that the husband had produced some activity which served as good grounds for calling the police, but that the wife had done so.

Even when considered in simplest terms, the story sequence is more complicated than a series of natural numbers or letters in the alphabet. Nevertheless, as Sacks suggests, an analogy can be drawn between seeing that an item is missing from a series of consecutive letters or numerals, and seeing that something has been left out of a story. In as much as a standard order of actions and events has unchallenged priority in an account of the past, this default order can be cited in the absence of any evidence of its actual occurrence. Such generic resources not only can be used to elicit admissions of what was 'missing' from an other's account of his own past, they also enable persons to claim the disposition to perform creditable actions, even when the actions in question were not in fact taken. This provides the basis for a particularly interesting type of knowledge claim, which Wittgenstein (1958: 187) elucidates with an analogy between claiming to know a mathematical progression and claiming a disposition to do a particular action.

> When you said "I already knew at the time . . . ." that meant something like: "If I had then been asked what number should be written after 1000, I should have replied '1002' " And that I don't doubt. This assumption is rather of the same kind as: "If he had fallen into the water then, I should have jumped in after him".

Testifying that 'I already knew at the time . . .' does not *represent* an actual past experience or mental state; rather, it avows that the speaker *would have done* a particular action if the appropriate occasion had arisen. The speaker claims a disposition to do a particular action-in-context, an action associated with specific entitlements and credits. An utterance like 'If he had fallen into the water then, I should have jumped in after him' takes the form of a counterfactual conditional: an assertion of what *would, should, or could have* occurred (or in this case, what a speaker would have done) under conditions that did not in fact obtain at the time.[7] There is nothing particularly mysterious about this, as it is one of many ways that persons take on board the entitlements and responsibilities of the generic categories into which they include themselves. Accordingly, describing the past implicates an entire range of claimable, assertable, and disclaimable rights and responsibilties associated with being a certain *kind* of person with a typical biography. This is not only a matter of recalling details by reference to 'context', it often is a method for developing a particular sense of context, and, by virtue of doing so, claiming a moral status.

The conditional and contextual reconstruction of a past

Thus far, we have emphasised how a recipient without independent access to a witness's past experiences can nevertheless deploy strong intersubjective resources for assessing the plausibility and completeness of the witness's stories.   Although this emphasis enables us to appreciate Sacks's assertion that 'lying is perfectly observable, in the same sense that anything else is,' as noted above we should not conclude that lying is *perfectly obvious*. If this were the case, lying would not be such a useful practice, and it would not present such severe problems for participants in the courts and in many other areas of daily life.   Analogies with mathematical progressions, and formulations like 'the inference-making machine', can suggest too determinate a sense of how an interrogator may be led to accuse a witness of lying or omitting relevant facts.   Materials from courtroom interrogations and government tribunals provide vivid documentation of the discursive slippages and loopholes a witness can exploit to avoid and defend against accusations of lying.

Consider, for example, the following excerpt from the testimony at the 1987 Iran-contra hearings, in which a witness (Oliver North) implies a context for his actions, and of what he may have known and what sort of person he was 'at the time' in question (his interrogator John Nields is counsel for the US House of Representatives majority on the investigating committee):

Joint Senate-House Hearings on the Iran-contra affair, Afternoon Session, July 7, 1987, ML/DB Transcript

Nields: Were you ever told that the president (0.4) had authorized the TOW:: shipment to proceed?
          (0.2)
North: I was et some point, yes.
          (0.8)
Nields: To the best of yer recollection, whe:n?
          (2.0)
North: Well I kno::w I was told that in eighty-<u>six</u> as I was preparing the chronologies, I was pr<u>o</u>:bably told that in eighty-fi:ve or I would've asked (.) more questions than I <u>did</u> about it.
          (1 4)

Nields: (W[ho)
         [
North: [I don't reca:ll it specifically.

The question concerns North's knowledge of a shipment of US missiles (TOW missiles) to Iran in 1985. When elaborating upon his answer, North works backward from an acknowledged incident ('I was told that in eighty-six') to an earlier time ('eighty-five') at which point, he now says, his actions implied that he knew about the president's authorisation of the missile shipment. His recollection is organized by reference to what he would have done if he had not known ('I was probably told that in eighty-five or I would've asked more questions than I did about it'). By his account, if he had not known in 1985 that the TOW missile sale to Iran had been authorised by the President, he would have inquired about the warrant for executing the deal. The matter of fact—or in this case of *probable* fact—is implicated by what he recalls *not doing*. This is a claim to the effect that if he had not known at the time that the deal was authorised, he would have asked more questions about it. Although the utterance takes the form of a recollection, it is equally salient as a moral claim. North asserts that he was disposed to act appropriately in the situation. He claims not to be the sort of person who would act without first securing proper authorisation. His recollection is packaged as a defense of the moral status of the biography in which that recollection is situated.

Modal formulations ('might have,' 'could have,' 'probably would have,' 'should have,' 'must have,' etc.) do not necessarily weaken or mitigate the status of the facts or incidents a witness is asked to recall. Instead, they can enable interrogators and witnesses to claim reasonable grounds for recovering a singular past. The use of such expressions opens up logical relations enabling and expressing an entire range of possible, probable, contestable, and incontestable inferences and conclusions. By using such formulations, a witness can present recollections that seem plausibly tied to public criteria, arguments, and moral judgments (Brannigan and Lynch 1987: 115-146). These criteria, arguments and judgements do not necessarily make up a stable and inflexible body of normative standards shared by members of a community, because they are brought into play singularly, rhetorically, and contestably.

While there is no getting around the importance of what the witness says about the past, and about his knowledge of the past, it seems clear from these instances that a witness does not unilaterally control what *can* be said on behalf of his past or his knowledge.

Although North and the other Iran-contra witnesses were quite resourceful, as the following excerpt shows they were not in full control of the entitlements to the details of their own pasts (see Coulter 1983b: 135)   Notice how the interrogator (Nields) manages to frame the witness's (North's) (non)testimony by describing a scene that North surely would want to deny if he could:

> Nields: Did you suggest to the Attorney General that maybe the diversion memorandum and the fact that there was a diversion need not ever come out?
> North: Again, I don't recall that specific conversation at all, but I'm not saying it didn't happen
> Nields: You don't deny it?
> North: No
> Nields: You don't deny suggesting to the Attorney General of the United States that he just figure out a way of keeping this diversion document secret?
> North: I don't deny that I said it. I'm not saying I remember it either.

(From *Taking the Stand: The Testimony of Oliver North* New York: Times Books, 1987· 33)

As this exchange makes clear, North's avowal of non-recall neither confirms nor denies that he invited Meese to suppress the 'fact of the diversion.' Nields does not simply let this stand unchallenged. He follows North's initial disavowal with questions which emphasise that North does not deny suggesting to the Attorney General that he suppress evidence of potentially scandalous administrative conduct. Nields dramatises the latter point by citing Meese's formal title as 'the Attorney General of the United States,' and then juxtaposes this with a colloquial restatement of North's position, 'that he [Meese] just figure out a way ...'. This formulation highlights the illegality of the described scene, and takes an incredulous stance toward North's failure to *deny* that it happened. The reference to the Attorney General places the described transaction under the jurisdiction of appointed government officials acting in their official capacities.   This contrasts to the administration's claim that in November 1986, when Meese purportedly began his investigation of the Iran-Contra diversion, he was acting in the capacity as 'friend of the President,' and not 'Attorney General' (see Halkowski 1990).   By repeatedly soliciting North's confirmation that he does not deny what someone in his position certainly would want to deny, Nields shapes North's 'non-response' into an informal *nolo contendere* plea (see Graham 1978).[8]   North conspicuously passes on the opportunity to contest Nields's version of the event, either by recollecting a different version, or (as he sometimes did) objecting that the question insinuated that he had done something that he would never be inclined to do. North persists in saying that he does not remember the incident, and by so doing he contributes nothing further to the story of the event beyond Nields' description of it. However, he comes close to making a damaging admission by not contesting the possibility that he may have suggested to Meese that he suppress the evidence.

As the above instances illustrate, interrogators are able to press witnesses by raising normative claims about what they should or should not recall about their own pasts. By neither confirming a plausible description that damages his case, nor burdening himself with the task of contesting its plausibility, a witness who fails to recall may avoid the horns of a dilemma. Interrogators are not left empty handed, however, as the witness's professed lack of recall itself can be subject to judgements of plausibility and further interrogative pursuit (cf. Atkinson and Drew 1979).   In the following cross-examination by Defense lawyer Barry Scheck of a prosecutorial witness Dennis Fung, a criminalist (evidence-collection functionary) from the Los Angeles Police Department, in the televised trial of former American football player O.J. Simpson, Scheck employs conditional formulations to suggest in detail what Fung must have done and known.

1.   Scheck: Okay, Mr Fung. Let me ask you directly, on June 13th in the morning, did Detective Fuhrman point out four red lines, red stains to you on the bottom of the Bronco door?
2.   Fung: I don't recall him doing so.
3.   Scheck: When you say you don't recall, are you saying it didn't happen?
4.   Fung: I'm not saying that. I'm saying I don't recall if he did or if he didn't
5.   Scheck: All right If you had seen four red stains on the exterior of the Bronco door on the morning of June 13th, you would have taken a photograph of them; would you have not?
6.   Fung: That would depend, but I don't know. But that would depend on the circumstances
7.   Scheck: Let's try these circumstances. You were pointed out a red stain by the door handle?
8.   Fung: Yes.
9.   Scheck: You were photographed pointing to that red stain, correct?
10.   Fung: Yes

11	Scheck:	And you're the person that's supposed to direct the photographer during the collection process?
12.	Fung:	Yes.
13.	Scheck:	You're supposed to photograph items of evidence of some importance that are pointed out to you by the detectives?
14.	Fung:	Yes
15.	Scheck:	In the circumstances of this case, if you had seen four red stains on the exterior of the Bronco door, would you not have directed the photographer to take a picture of it?
16.	Fung:	It would be likely. Yes
17.	Scheck:	If you had seen four red stains on the exterior of the Bronco door, would you have not done a presumptive test on June 13th?
18.	Fung:	Possibly, I -- If it was necessary, I would have.
19.	Scheck:	If you had seen four red stains on the exterior of the Bronco door, would you have not swatched them?
20.	Fung:	I would -- I would possibly have swatched them
21.	Scheck:	If you had seen four red stains on the exterior of the Bronco door, would you not have included that observation in your reports for that day?
22	Fung:	If I thought it was important to the investigation, I would have included it in my notes, yes.
23.	Scheck:	Looking back at the circumstances of this case, would not those four red stains have been an important detail that you would have certainly included in your notes?
24.	Mr Goldberg (prosecutor): Calls for speculation.	
25.	The Court: Overruled	
26.	Fung:	From my perspective now?
27.	Scheck:	Let's try your perspective then
28.	Fung:	I don't recall my exact state of mind then, but it -- I don't know exactly if I would have put it down or not.

(Reporter's transcript of proceedings, *The People of the State of California v. Orenthal James Simpson*, Superior Court of the State of California for the County of Los Angeles, Case No BA097211, Volume 124, April 12, 1995.)

In line 3, Scheck asks Fung if his failure to recollect Detective Fuhrman's having pointed out four red stains (presumptive blood stains) on the defendant's vehicle on the date after the murders, implies that this 'didn't happen'. (Fuhrman had previously testified that he had pointed out the stains to Fung on the date in question.) Fung's answer (line 4) makes explicit that he does not mean to imply whether the incident did or did not happen. This is reminiscent of the logical explication provided by Oliver North's line, 'I don't recall that specific conversation at all, but I'm not saying it didn't happen.' Scheck then pursues a more resolute answer by framing a series of questions in a variant of the classic 'if-then' propositional format (lines 5, 15, 17, 19, 21). In this instance he uses a form of counterfactual conditional: 'If A had been the case, then B would be the case' (see Hempel 1966: 56 and Goodman 1983).[9] This is a standard way logicians use to formulate natural laws, but here the 'law' in question is formulated as a temporal relation between perceiving something and taking an action: 'if you had seen A, you would have done B,' or, interrogatively, 'if you had seen A, would you not have done B?' This is not an empirical generalisation, it is a methodological rule. Given that Fung (line 2) initially professes not to recall seeing the 'four red stains' in question on June 13, Scheck's repeated questions appear to suggest that if Fung *had* seen them, he would have made sure to record the evidence with photographs, test results, and notes. When Scheck states (and Fung confirms) that Fung was photographed pointing to 'that red stain' by the door handle (lines 7-10), he is referring to a different stain that had been entered into evidence. Scheck uses the fact that Fung produced a record of *that* stain, as further evidence of what he would have done if he had seen the four stains in question.

According to Fung's earlier testimony, the prosecution directed him to collect evidence of the four red stains, after Detective Fuhrman mentioned them during a preliminary hearing a few weeks after the murder. Fung acknowledges the later investigation, but fails to recall Furhman's mentioning the stains to him on June 13. Scheck's line of questioning seems designed to expose Fung's inability (or unwillingness) to corroborate Fuhrman's testimony about finding the four blood stains the day after the murders.   The absence of corroboration might be relevant as a basis for impugning Fuhrman's testimony about finding the stains, and suggesting that Fuhrman or someone else planted the blood stains on the Bronco door after Fung's initial crime scene investigation. In addition, it might suggest that Fung neglected to collect relevant evidence in a timely manner. As millions of television viewers witnessed, such arguments were employed by Simpson's defense team.

It seems appropriate to say that Scheck is making use of an 'inference making machine' to compel Fung to acknowledge a conclusion derived from a set of antecedents. In this case, the logic of the argument can be schematised as follows:

(1) If Fung had seen the four red stains on June 13, he would have directed a photographer to document this fact, and would have done a

presumptive blood test, collected a sample ('swatched' the blood stains), and made an entry into his notes.

(2) Fung followed such procedures on July 5 (took photographs, etc.), but not on June 13.

(3) Either Fung did not see the four red stains on June 13, or failed to collect or document the relevant evidence from the crime scene. Assuming that these two alternatives are his only alternatives, the argument places Fung in a dilemma: either he acknowledges an inconsistency between his own and Fuhrman's testimony, or he admits to incompetence.[10]

The logic of Scheck's argument cannot meaningfully be specified in terms of necessary and sufficient conditions.[11] This is because Scheck deploys irreducible suppositions about a singular incident in relation to an idealised protocol. He repeatedly holds Fung's recollected (or, in this case, non-recalled) actions to the terms of a standard protocol. Scheck does not (or not only) invoke commonsense knowledge of relevant events and actions, he deploys highly specific substantive, normative, and methodological accounts of Fung's professional activities. In a way, Scheck proposes to be an expert about what someone in Fung's position ought to have known and done at the singular crime scene. In other words, the lawyer professes to know more about a criminalist's situated practices than an incumbent of that occupational category seems able to say on his own behalf.[12] Not surprisingly, Fung does not entirely go along with Scheck's account of his practice. Fung prefaces each of his 'confirming' responses with qualifying expressions ('it would be likely', line 16; 'if it was necessary', line 18; 'I would possibly have', line 20; 'if I thought it was important', line 22). Without entirely contradicting Scheck's propositions — 'If you had seen A, would you not have done B?' — Fung combats the implication of a determinate or lawful relationship between circumstance and action. It is not enough to say that these qualifications suggest an uncertain, contingent, or probable relation between the circumstances at the crime scene and what someone in Fung's position should have (or typically would have) done; they also bring into play the matter of situated judgement. Fung suggests that as a competent investigator, he does not simply see particular items of evidence and then document them according to standard protocols, he makes a number of judgements about what is relevant and important (enough) to photograph, document, and collect. And, presumably, aside from what he did in fact record and collect, Fung implies that what he remembers about the crime scene also depends on the judgements he originally made about the relevance and salience of particular collectables. In other words, while he acknowledges the salience of the methodological rules Scheck formulates, he also implies that he did not follow those rules mechanically.

The salience of speaking in this instance about an 'inference-making machine' is suggested by the repetitious logical framing of the successive questions in Scheck's line of interrogation. It should also be clear, however, that Scheck does not simply set a determinate machine in motion, he struggles to instantiate it, and his repeated questions attempt to insist upon and reinforce a particular line of logical derivation. The witness, for his part, successively (but not necessarily successfully) resists the logical force of the questions by suggesting a less mechanistic role for inference-making in his practice. A further complication to the logic of this dialogue is the fact that it is oriented to an overhearing audience that includes a lay jury (in this case, one with well-established demographic characteristics), a judge, and a massive public. Even if, as so many ethnographies of work in the Goffmanian mode suggest, it is commonplace for members of an occupation to share an insider's understanding that their actual practices do not, and cannot, follow the specifications of an idealised manual of procedure, such ideals apparently have special rhetorical and evaluative significance when a practitioner's actions are subject to a formal-legal scrutiny by a body of outsiders. When setting up his line of interrogaction, Scheck repeatedly invoked official manuals and protocols, and Fung and other prosecution witnesses seemed extremely reluctant to dismiss the salience of such idealised accounts.

By juxtaposing the witness's non-testimony with a description of events that 'one such as he' should certainly recall (or, in the case of an incriminating description, should certainly want to deny), an interrogator can suggest to the overhearing audience that the witness's professed inability to recall should be counted against his credibility. Even though a witness's audience may have no independent access to the events the witness recalls or fails to recall, and they may have no determinate criteria for deciding the plausibility of the testimony, they can, and typically do, make judgments about the truthfulness of that testimony, and they do so without any need to peer into the witness's mind.

Conclusion

A lack of recourse to the witness's mind should not be viewed as an essential source of uncertainty that is compensated for by indirect inferences about memory. Instead, in certain respects what a particular witness can recall (credibly, plausibly, sensibly) is an irreducibly public matter. This also applies to what the witness can fail to recall. Confusion about this matter is common not only in psychology and philosophy of mind. Such confusion was encouraged, for example, when Iran-contra witnesses were asked to recall specific White House meetings in which the arms sales to Iran and the 'diversion' of proceeds to the contras were planned and approved. President Reagan and others gave variants of what might be called the breakfast defense: 'How would you be expected to know what you had for breakfast on a particular date six months ago?' Such a defense relied upon a credulous audience to 'forget' that the relevant mode of recollection for a bureaucratic official is to consult the files and retrieve the appropriate records. In this case, the plausibility of such a defense was aided and abetted by the destruction of such files and records, such destruction amounting to a particular kind of forgetting.

In less blatant ways than in Reagan's 'breakfast defense', individualistic conceptions of memory are relevant to the rhetorical production and interpretation of testimony. Interrogators and their audiences selectively call into play judgments about what particular witnesses could or should have remembered, and about the memorability of particular events for someone who lived through them. Such judgments do not take the form of lay psychological 'theories' in the sense of being general conceptual models of how the mind works. Instead, as was especially evident in Scheck's interrogation of Fung, these judgements are sensitive to contextual and rhetorical portrayals of events, scenes, agents and actions (see Burke 1945). In brief, they are embedded in locally organized, and selectively contested, protocols and narratives.

Harvey Sacks's lectures and writings demonstrate how conversationalists and story-tellers routinely deploy membership categorization devices in which conventional categories of, e.g., family members, are bound together with typified attributes and activities (Sacks 1972). In a far more technically specific way than Alfred Schutz's phenomenological account of commonplace social typifications (Schutz 1964), Sacks's analysis shows how such conventionalised categorical associations organize the production and intelligibility of vernacular accounts. Both Schutz's typifications and Sacks's membership categorization devices can be construed as instances of ordinary, situated ideal types that members use to organize and coordinate their communicative actions. So, for example, in the above instances, when a psychiatrist admonishes a patient for lying, or a social service employee demands that a caller tell the 'whole story', or an interrogator presses a witness to acknowledge a plausible account of what he had done in the past, the interlocutors organize their accounts and admissions by reference to what *can have happened* in specific scenes of action performed by recognizable types of social agent.   However, an emphasis on formal devices or machineries can be misleading. Although generic categories and associations are used, they are given singular reference to singular characters and actions in stories presented as recollected events.   The 'Attorney General' mentioned by Nields and acknowledged by North, refers to a singular person (Edwin Meese) who is described as having met with North on a specific occasion in November 1986, and Barry Scheck's account of what a police criminalist is supposed to have done at a crime scene is referenced to Fung's singular actions on June 13, 1994.   The occupational titles and actions, and the legal circumstances and practical competencies associated with those titles, are relevanced by an immediate scene of interrogation.   These categorical specifications help project and organize what a witness can remember or reasonably claim to forget, and what an interrogator can press the witness to recall, but they do not *compel* specific inferences and deductions.

Many of the conceptual, narrational and logical resources through which recollections are cast and lying becomes accountable are not cognitive, at least not in a psychological sense.   What a speaker is entitled to say, or fail to say, about his or her own past is not determined by the state of the speaker's mind, or even by the lay-psychological theories held by his or her interlocutors.   Instead, a speaker's reconstruction of past scenes can be projected, assessed, and even produced on demand through what Ian Hacking (1995: 218) calls 'memoropolitics,' the work of 'hooking a narrative onto the person in the dock.'   As noted, this involves normative demands upon what incumbents of categories can say, not say, or be said to have done, but the organizational frame provided by a narrative is far more specific, singular, and complex than a simple association of category types with general types of conduct.

It may be tempting to conclude that professional sociology, or the professional analysis of social interaction, can yield insights into lying and discursive recollection that psychology cannot.   Although we do believe that lies and their detection are best viewed as contextually-embedded interactional accomplishments which employ typified categories of social action and identity, we do not think that sociology can serve any better than psychology as a source of general techniques for detecting lies or otherwise organising and understanding accounts of the past.   Although the sequences we examined exhibit intricate ways in which abstract categorical resources are used to project, solicit, recount, gloss, and evade the description of singular biographical episodes, they are not readily detached from the circumstances of use (both the past circumstances described, and the present circumstances of interrogation). In our view, the most powerful organizational resources used by interrogators and witnesses for generating testimony are records, files, protocols, and 'master narratives' of singular historical events (for more elaborate discussion of this (and other issues) see Lynch and Bogen 1996). The details of testimony are solicited by reference to agent, agency, and action categories, but in a highly specific and intensively documented way. What a witness can say is bound up in complex series of actions, and transactions at specific times and places involving large casts of characters. Abstract category devices and inference making machines may be featured at every point in the solicitation, reiteration and elaboration of testimony, but rarely as complete devices that can be detached and meaningfully described separate from the singular elements of an historical event.[13]

Chapter 6

Narrative Intelligibility and Membership Categorization in a Television Commercial

David Francis and Christopher Hart

In this chapter we offer an ethnomethodological analysis of a television commercial. We have selected this particular phenomenon for analysis, not out of any commitment to the notion that TV commercials are especially significant as social phenomena, nor because we believe that through the analysis of one commercial we will be able to accept or reject, or otherwise comment authoritatively upon current sociological theorising about advertising, the role of the media in modern society, or any other topic of conventional sociological concern. Insofar as we have a specific motivation for this study, it is largely a methodological one, to show that ethnomethodological analysis can usefully be brought to bear on such a phenomenon as a TV commercial, lacking, as it does, many of the obviously 'interactional' characteristics with which phenomena more usually investigated by ethnomethodologists are imbued. Thus a TV commercial falls, analytically, within that class of phenomena which have come to be called 'texts'. [1]

Ethnomethodological studies of texts have analysed them as situated accomplishments of commonsense knowledge; rather than conceiving of a text as possessing features which pre-exist the operations of commonsense understanding, ethnomethodological studies treat such understandings as *constitutive* of the text. The task for analysis, therefore, is to explicate the organized character of such constitutive commonsense accomplishments. Such studies, which draw upon the sub-tradition of ethnomethodology known as 'membership categorization analysis', predominantly have focused upon *strictly verbal texts* of various kinds (e.g. newspaper headlines - Eglin & Hester 1992, Lee 1984). In this chapter, we seek to show that this form of analysis can be brought to bear upon a text in which verbal elements are very much secondary to visual ones. Where *visual* materials have been studied, these usually have taken the form of *pictures*, capable of being reproduced on the printed page (e.g. Lynch 1985).

The TV commercial we seek to analyse consists in a stretch of *film*, rather than a single picture or string of pictures. Furthermore, it contains no speech; although it has a verbal dimension, this consists in a 'theme song', which is played/sung over the action - and which is, in part, 'lip synched' by one of the characters. As a stretch of *musical film*, the TV commercial poses some distinctive 'data' problems in relation to accepted methodological canons in ethnomethodological inquiry. Consideration of such problems provides a way into examination of the availability of the text to commonsense, intersubjective understanding.

Analysing a TV Commercial: Methodological Considerations

There is a long-standing maxim in ethnomethodological inquiry to the effect that, when confronted with a methodological problem, look to see whether it can be transformed into a researchable phenomenon. As a stretch of musical film, the TV commercial which comprises our object of analysis raises a problem of 'data reproducibility'. A distinctive feature of ethnomethodological and conversation analytic inquiry is a commitment to the reproduction of materials, in order that fine grained analysis may be conducted in a way which provides the reader with access to the detail of the phenomena. In relation to the analysis of a TV commercial, such detailed reproduction is problematic. While we have the commercial on video-tape, there is no way by which its *filmic* character can be reproduced on the printed page. There are no 'transcription practices' available for the detailed representation of such materials. Neither is there any realistic way in which the relationship between the visual and the musical dimensions of the commercial can be reproduced. It might therefore be argued that only the videotape constitutes a complete and literal record of the TV commercial, and that by contrast any description or representation we might provide stands as an incomplete and selective 'version' whose veracity, by dint of the unavailability of the video-recording, the reader is unable to judge.

However, such an 'empiricist' argument misunderstands the status of data in ethnomethodological inquiries. The detailed reproduction of materials is undertaken in order to *facilitate* analysis, not as a means for gaining pristine access to some 'analyst independent reality'. All theoretical inquiries into the phenomena of daily life presuppose the availability of those phenomena to mundane, pre-theoretical description and understanding. Thus, for example, for a phenomenon such as a TV commercial to be captured on video-tape - as we have taped the TV commercial which comprises the object of inquiry in this chapter - presupposes that this phenomenon has been mundanely 'found'; in other words, that it is commonsensically recognizable-describable-reportable as such. While the mundane availability of phenomena *qua phenomena* comprises a 'seen but unnoticed' background to other theoretical inquiries, ethnomethodological studies seek to place this at the center of their investigations. Uniquely, in our view, ethnomethodology addresses the recognizable-describable-reportable character of phenomena and seeks to explicate a phenomenon's intelligibility as an *operational accomplishment* of socially organized processes of intersubjectivity and commonsense understanding. Ethnomethodology insists that any and all understandings of social life and social phenomena can only be constructed 'from within' socially organized processes and practices of intersubjective understanding.

In line with this conception, and taking the maxim 'turn your methodological troubles into phenomena for analysis' as our guide, we wish to consider the phenomenon of narrative intelligibility as a prerequisite of the 're-tellability' of stories[2]. We take it that, while we cannot 'reproduce' the television commercial as a stretch of video or as a slice of musical film, we can 're-tell' the story which comprises it. As will presently become clear, the commercial has what can be characterized as a *narrative structure* - crudely, it tells a kind of story. This observation is not a *finding* of our inquiry; rather we take it that 'anyone' can see that this commercial tells some kind of story. Thus, we have no difficulty in informing readers what the commercial is 'about', by *recounting the story*. Our commonsense ability to say what it's about is a mark of the text's 'self-narrating' character; we take it that - in relation to a narratively constructed text - the question 'what is it about?' will normally (and adequately) be heard as requesting just such a recounting or summarising of the story. Thus narrative would seem to be a constitutive common-sense feature of this particular commercial; describing the commercial *as* a narrative, and re-telling its story, is to give an account of it which is 'reflexive' in just the way that Garfinkel (1967:8) noted as the *reflexive* character of members' accounts:

> Members' accounts, of every sort, in all their logical modes, with all of their uses, and for every method for their assembly, are constituent features of the settings they make observable.

We take it that members might find some commercials not to be describable in such a narrative way. Faced with the same question, 'What's it about?' (as opposed to the very different question, 'What's it *for*?'), with reference to a different commercial, they might, for example, assert that 'It's not *about* anything - it's just a set of images' and find this to be a relevant and correct response.

In our view, these considerations do not solve the methodological problem of the reproduction of the commercial, so much as *dissolve* it. Since our phenomenon is the TV commercial *in-and-as-its-commonsense-intelligibility*, giving representation to that intelligibility is a pragmatic and tactical issue rather than an epistemological one. The problem of how to represent our materials is one and the same as how to make our understanding of the commercial's narrative character intersubjectively available (to ourselves *and* to the reader) for the purposes of our inquiry.[3]

Two Descriptions of the Commercial

The TV commercial is for Greenalls, a brand of English beer. It was shown as part of a campaign for Greenall's beer, broadcast on British television in the mid-1980's. We will refer to the commercial as 'Miss the Boat', since this is the name by which it was known within the advertising agency which created it.[4] This is not a name which was available to the television viewer of the commercial.

We will now present two 're-tellings' of the commercial, which we refer to, respectively, as a 'commonsense narrative description' and a 'technical description'. Having given these descriptions, we will then consider the differences and similarities between them.

'Miss the Boat': (1) A Commonsense Narrative Description

> It is apparent that the commercial consists in three scenes In the first scene, we see a crowded quayside and a tramp steamer preparing to leave the harbor. Most of the

crowd, who are noticeably foreign-looking (Asian/Arabic), are carrying belongings and walking away from the vessel; we may conclude that they are passengers leaving the ship. We see a youngish guy carrying a holdall, rushing in the other direction against the flow of the crowd and towards the ship. He jumps over a barrier and various piles of cargo as he runs along the quayside in the direction of the vessel. An official in a cap runs toward him, but the young guy runs past him, holding up what appears to be a passport. He is stopped at a barrier by a customs official who demands to examine the passport Allowed to pass, the guy continues to sprint down the quayside until stopped again, this time by a bald man with an eye patch, who physically restrains him, waving his arms in a gesture of 'no further'. The result is that the young guy misses the boat; we see the mooring rope of the ship being cast off and get a view of the quayside from the ship as it moves away. The young guy registers his disappointment, both facially and by throwing his passport down in frustration The camera pans to his feet and we see a cabbage lying on the ground. The young guy kicks the cabbage as though it were a football. The cabbage hits a dockworker and a game of football spontaneously develops This ends when the young guy kicks the cabbage at a dockworker who is crouching in front of some cargo netting, in the manner of a goalkeeper. The force of the cabbage/football knocks the goalkeeper backwards into the netting, and the young guy and the dockworkers throw up their arms in celebration of the goal . The scene closes as the young guy turns towards the camera, and begins to sing along with the theme song, which has begun earlier in the action

The commercial then fades to a second scene. Initially, we see a close-up of a glass of beer being drawn from a beer pump The camera pulls back to reveal a pub scene, initially we see two barmaids behind the bar and then other persons in the pub. As these persons come progressively into view, they notice the camera, and smile and wave in a welcome greeting As the camera pulls further back to show the whole of the pub interior, the pub crowd as a whole turn towards the camera and signify greeting, several by raising their glasses. The theme song has continued over the top of this scene.

There is then another fade to the third and final scene. The pub scene fades to a shot of the tramp steamer sailing out to sea. There is then a close-up of the guy and the burly stevedore standing side by side on the quayside, apparently watching the boat sail away The stevedore lifts his eye-patch to reveal a perfectly good eye, from which he wipes a tear The young guy turns and looks quizzically at the stevedore. This shot freezes for several seconds before the commercial ends. During this last shot, the name Greenalls appears in the bottom right of the frame, and the theme song fades away

In referring to this description as a commonsense narrative description, we make reference to the fact that this is the kind of description that 'any competent viewer' might provide in response to a request to 'tell in some detail what the commercial is about'. We further take it that, armed with such a description, any viewer who had not seen the commercial might, upon seeing it, have no difficulty in recognising it as the one described. Rather than simply assert that this is the case, still less to regard it as a hypothesis in need of validation, we wish to approach this 'sameness' as a phenomenon for inquiry in its own right. As a further resource towards this end, we now present a second description, designed to give some detail of the filmic construction of the commercial. Since we take it that this filmic construction is, from the point of view of an 'ordinary viewer' a *seen but unnoticed* dimension of the commercial, we refer to this as a 'technical description'. Technically, then, the commercial consists in 32 separate camera shots. Since the whole commercial lasts only 48 seconds, most of these are extremely brief; as a filmic production the commercial is marked by the fast editing technique which is nowadays characteristic of many television commercials. Here, then, is a second description of the commercial, as a sequence of separate camera shots.

'Miss the Boat': (2) A Technical Description

1. Panoramic view of a busy dockside, with a ship moored top left. Stream of people moving along quayside away from ship. Bottom center ('foreground') a guy is seen jumping over a barrier rail, moving in opposite direction to the 'stream'.
2. Action shot of young guy, holding a passport in one hand and a bag in the other, jumping over a barrier
3. Two men in uniform (official cap, dark trousers, white shirt and tie) standing by a barrier, one begins moving rapidly along quayside, gesturing with his arms (right to left across screen)
4. Close-up of young guy running along quayside (left to right on screen), waving passport in front of him

	Stream of (foreign-looking) people moving in opposite direction
5	Young guy runs passed uniformed man, who has his arms raised in gesture of 'halt' Guy runs up to barrier where second uniformed man is standing, pursued by first uniformed man
6.	Close-up of young guy between the two officials, thrusting his passport at them as they grab him One official takes passport from guy, whose expression then registers disappointment/impatience
7	Mid-distant view of rear of ship moving away from quayside, mooring rope being cast off and dropping into water
8	Full frame close-up of official looking at passport (facing left to right).
9.	Close-up of young guy (facing right to left), looking agitated, 'pleading' with official.
10.	Head and shoulder close-up of official, holding out passport
11	Action shot - young guy running along quayside, jumping over pile of baggage
12	Action shot - young guy running along a railed walkway which is parked on the dockside, jumping off the other end and running towards a large, bald man who can be seen in the middle distance
13	Close-up of burly, bald man, wearing eye-patch over left eye He is facing screen right, with arms up and shaking his head Young guy enters screen right and is grabbed by bald man Bald man pushes guy back and waves his arms in a gesture of 'no'.
14.	Mid-distant view of ship, side on and now clearly visible as a 'tramp steamer', moving away from dock
15	Close-up of young guy, throwing down his passport in anger/frustration Camera pans to his feet - several cabbages lying on the quayside Guy kicks the nearest cabbage as though it were a football
17	Close-up of (first) dockworker, surrounded by several others, eating a bun He is struck in the face by the cabbage.
18.	Shot of cabbage at the feet of the group of dockworkers One kicks it.
19	Close-up of (second) dockworker, kicking the cabbage

20. Action shot of young guy standing on quayside - he 'traps' the cabbage as it rolls towards him. Dockworkers enter shot (foreground), moving towards him.

21. Action shot of young guy, surrounded by several dockworkers who are 'tackling' him.

22. Close-up of first dockworker, now standing in front of pile of crates and netting, crouching in a 'goalkeeper' posture.

23. Close-up of young guy, 'dribbling' the cabbage

24. Action shot of young guy kicking the cabbage.

25. The 'goalkeeper' is hit in the stomach by the cabbage, knocking him backwards into the pile of crates, which collapses over him.

26. Close-up of young guy and other dockworkers, throwing up their arms and shouting in celebration of the 'goal'.

27. Close-up of 'goalkeeper', lying slumped in the pile of crates.

28. Rear shot of young guy and others, looking towards the 'goal'. Young guy turns to face camera and begins to 'sing' *(lip synch with theme song)* - "BUT EVEN MORE"

29. Scene fades to a close-up of beer splashing into a beer glass.

30. Shot of two 'barmaids', standing behind a pub bar on which two Greenalls beer pumps are visible. The barmaids are looking at the camera and have their mouths open in expressions of surprise and joy Blonde barmaid raises her hands in wave of greeting. Camera pulls back to show men at bar with glasses of beer in their hands - they turn to camera also with expressions of joy and greeting Camera continues to pull back, revealing more of the pub interior, filled with numerous people engaged in 'pub activities' (e.g. young woman playing pool) - people in the pub notice the camera and react with joy - several raise their glasses in a greeting salute/toast.

31. Pub scene fades to shot of cargo boat sailing away, out to sea.

32 Close-up of young guy, facing camera, with bald man at his shoulder. Bald man raises eye-patch to reveal a perfectly good left eye. He sniffs tearfully and wipes his eye with a handkerchief. As he does so the word GREENALLS appears on the screen,

bottom right. The young guy turns to look
quizzically over his shoulder at the bald man.
*(This shot freezes for approximately 4.5 seconds before
the screen blanks.)*

Comparing the Two Descriptions

These two descriptions differ in a number of ways. The second
is longer and more detailed than the first, and takes the form of a
numbered list denoting the order of the camera shots which comprise
the commercial together with a description of the 'contents' of each
shot. In these respects, it makes sense to speak of the second
description as more 'technical' than the first, a difference which is
marked in the titles we have given to them. Notwithstanding these
differences, however, we take it that any reader can recognize from
reading these two descriptions that they are both descriptions of the
same television commercial. One way to begin to develop our analytic
interests is to ask how such a finding is possible. What is it about the
construction of these descriptions which makes them recognizable as
two contrasting descriptions of the same thing? After all, it is not as
though it would be impossible to construct a very different kind of
description, one which might give the reader considerably more
problems of intelligibility and recognition than either of the above. We
have in mind what we might call a behaviouralised or 'thin' description,
such as might be constructed by leaving out much of the contextual
detail of the setting and action given in both (1) and (2), and by
referring to the characters in more decontextualized and uninformative
ways (e.g. 'a man running, stopped by another man, then by a third
man......' and so forth).

We take it that readers might find such a description
problematic by contrast with both (1) and (2) in that it 'doesn't tell the
story'. Conversely, while (1) and (2) are different in the ways just
mentioned, we take it that they are recognizable as alternative
descriptions of the same story. Readers might find that the difference
between them is that, whereas the narrative description is constructed
so as to make the story unproblematically available, the construction of
the technical description is such that recovering the story from it
requires a little more effort on the reader's part, the description visibly
having been constructed with reference to other relevancies than
'simply' the telling of the story. Of course, both descriptions are
'selective', in the sense that more could be said, things could be
described in greater detail, or with a slightly different emphasis, and so
forth. The technical description illustrates such a difference of

emphasis; here 'telling the story' takes second place to highlighting the *filmic construction* of the commercial. As member/analysts, we have employed our understanding of the depicted events to describe the commercial in terms of the visually depicted scenes which comprise it. Thus, we feel remarkably confident that *both* the 'narrative description' and the technical description are accounts which, upon viewing the video-tape of the commercial, *any competent member would recognize* as a description of those depicted events.

In this sense, both descriptions are the product of a *member's commonsense analysis* of the visual content of the commercial. Both descriptions are *members' descriptions*. Both instantiate culturally available commonsense knowledge, which has been employed to express in words what it is that is depicted visually. To speak of 'analysis' here is not to suggest that the content of the commercial is experienced as problematic. As member/viewers, we have quite literally seen the events visually depicted as such a narrative; we have had no difficulty in transforming the visual experience of the commercial into a verbal re-telling which 'captures the essentials' of the narrative. To speak of such a re-telling as the product of an analysis is to note that it can be examined for its methodic process of commonsense construction.

Can Commercials Afford Stories?: Scenic Framing and the Co-Selection of Descriptors.

We now begin to investigate the way in which the narrative intelligibility of the commercial is a product of members' commonsense analysis. We will explore the ways in which the commercial is *designed* as a story. Our interest lies not so much in the 'accuracy' of any particular version of this story, but in its 'availability', that is, in how the intelligibility of the story is *built into* the filmic and musical construction of the commercial. For example, with reference to Scene One, we take it that what we have called the self-narrating character of the commercial refers to the fact that the shots making up this scene can be understood as depicting a single temporal course of action 'unfolding' before the viewer's eyes. Specifically, then, our analytic interest centers around how it is that a textual story in the form of a musical film provides for its own *re-tellability*. How is it that we have been able to re-tell the story of 'Miss the Boat' and do so *mundanely*, that is in a way that we feel confident would enable any competent member to recognize the commercial *as the one described?* We assert that, as a stretch of film, 'Miss the Boat' is constructed so as to *afford* (Anderson &

Sharrock 1993) such a description[5]. Such affordance is a methodical accomplishment.

In a lecture concerned with stories and storytelling (Sacks 1992b: 18-19), Sacks poses the question of what provides for the recognizability of something as a story:

> A first thing I want to come back to is the issue of that those things which I'm calling 'stories' are stories Now, it's obviously a story. What we're asking here is, is there some set of features that stories have so that one can have some principled basis for using what is after all a lay characterization. What we want to find are some features that have been put into it which provide for its recognizability as 'a story'. We want, then, some features that are not just there incidentally, carried along artifacts of its being a story, but features that are put in, in the making of a story

Sacks goes on to propose that one set of such features involve the phenomenon of 'co-selection':

> One gross, recurrent thing that is present for stories is that across its sentences one finds that a lot of the words, particularly those that are 'carriers of the story' so to speak, i e. the nouns, verbs, adjectives, can be said to be *co-selected* ....We have a partial picture of persons, in producing their talk, engaged in selecting words out of various formulations of word classes They do it by reference to syntactic constraints on word classes and things like that, and in various ways fix in on a word class from which the word is selected - where many of them can be replaced with another. And one thing to look to is that range of talk within which it looks like a set of words of some sort are selected by reference to each other, or selected by reference to some stateable thing, e.g. a 'topic' . . What I'm saying is if you take what I'll call the 'descriptors' in talk, then you'll find that when people are telling stories, the descriptors are co-selected.

These remarks draw attention to the ways in which stories involve the use of words which can be understood as 'hanging together' in terms of their reference. In his work on description as a social activity, Sacks emphasised both the potentially infinite variety of descriptions which might in principle be given of any object or event,

and the fact that many descriptors have multiple senses. In the light of
this, he sought to problematise how it is that members are able to
understand the reference of particular words on a given occasion of
their use, and to do so 'automatically'. Conceived in these terms, the
issue is one of the socially organized basis of the selection of
descriptors; what resources are available to speakers and hearers such
that how and why some object is described *this way*, rather than in
some other way which might be seen to be (at least in some sense)
equally 'correct', is *mundanely apparent*. Sacks's analyses of this issue
emphasised the idea of *category collections*; descriptors are co-selected
with reference to such collections. As a process of co-selection,
descriptor/category use is organized by virtue of the ways in which
selected categories and category predicates 'go together' with reference
to commonsensically available collections from which they are drawn.
Such collections (or membership categorization devices) are of various
kinds in terms of their socially organized properties. Sacks notes that
some membership categorization devices (collections of categories)
have the property of being 'duplicatively organized'. In other words,
the categories making up the device 'belong together' in such a way
that, when mapped onto a given population of persons, one can find
that these persons constitute an instance of a commonsensically
recognizable social unit or setting.

   Equipped with these resources, we can return to the two
descriptions and unpack them as products of members' category
analysis by examining the *co-selection of descriptors* in and through which
the narrative is constituted. As a first observation, we note that there
are *three* 'kinds' of descriptors to be found in this description: (a) of
persons, (b) of *activities* and (c) of *objects*. In what sense, according to
what 'selection principle', might these descriptors be said to be 'co-
selected'? We suggest that a basic from of co-selection involved here is
what we will call '*scenic framing*'. That is, the descriptors employed are
such as to provide a consistent sense of scenic orderliness to the
persons, activities and objects which constitute the narrative. This
scenic orderliness, then, amounts to a structure of commonsense
relations between persons, activities and objects which has the
character of a 'relational configuration' (Lynch and Peyrot 1992). Thus
we note that the narrative description begins with a reference to a
'crowded quayside'. This description sets up a relevant context, in
relation to which subsequent descriptors can be understood as
consistent. To illustrate this point, we consider the link between the
categories of 'customs official' and 'passengers' and their associated
activities. We note that the categories employed to describe various

participants to Scene One, 'passengers', 'customs official', 'dockhands' and so forth, are hearably consistent with one another in terms of the *scenic characterization* of the setting as a 'quayside'. As the name of a recognizable and commonsensically known setting, 'quayside' also constitutes a possible 'duplicatively organized category device'; in the context of the viewer's description one might speak of an 'occasioned' membership categorization device *'Parties to a Quayside Scene'*. We refer to this as an occasioned device, to mark the fact that the categories employed are ones which in other circumstances might be found to have little in common and not to 'go together' in the way they do here. Thus, 'customs official' and 'dockhand' might, on some other occasion of use, be found to belong to the collection *occupations*, and as such have little to connect them with the category 'passengers'. It is only in the context of the setting as a 'quayside' that these descriptors are hearably consistent.

The same 'relational configuration' is central to the technical description. As indicated above, Scene One is comprises 28 separate camera shots of varying lengths. The entire scene lasts some 35 seconds out of the total length of the whole commercial of some 48 seconds. The shots making it up vary in length, the shortest being approximately 0.2 seconds, the longest (the last shot of the scene) being approx. 3.5 seconds. In describing these 28 shots as Scene One, we are noting that their construction is such as visually to convey a sense of a single time-space location. Thus, as the camera switches from shot to shot, these separate shots can be viewed (are mundanely seen) as representing 'the same place' (a quayside). This sense of setting is, of course, technically accomplished in the filmic construction of the shots. Thus, the commercial opens with a brief (approx. 0.5 secs.) panoramic shot of the quayside, taken from a high angle such that the whole setting is panoramically visible. The numerous items visible in this shot - described in the narrative description as a stream of passengers, a ship, a building recognizable as some kind of warehouse, piles of cargo, and so forth - constitute a visual 'gestalt', such that in describing them - as we just have done - it is commonsensically 'natural' to identify them in *scenic terms*. They combine to convey an immediate sense of a recognizable socio-spatial scene, such that subsequent shots can be seen as further representations of 'the same place', and even 'the same things' - as close-ups of what was seen panoramically in the opening shot.

In describing 'quayside' as a setting, we draw attention to the fact that there is more involved here than simply reference to a physical place. A quayside also can constitute a *social scene*, that is, a setting constituted by certain categories of persons standing in certain typical relations to one another, which relations involve certain typical courses of action. In this sense, we can speak of the *relations between* such persons as reflexive and mutually implicative. Thus, 'customs officials' and 'passengers' are more than simply two types of persons one might find on a quayside; they comprise a *'course of action' category pair*. Since a quayside is a possible point of entry or departure from a country, it constitutes one location for activities associated with national immigration/emigration. Such activities center around and make relevant the categories of 'passenger' and 'customs officers'. The pairing of these categories provides the viewer with a resource for seeing particular persons as occupants of one category or the other. Thus, the fact that the officials in the commercial are commonsensically recognizable as customs officers is the product of a mutually reinforcing concatenation of visual features; partly the fact that they are wearing uniforms (peaked caps, shirts and ties, etc), partly a product of their quayside location and partly visible in their actions towards others in the scene (e.g. the young guy), who are see-able as passengers. Conversely, the young guy is see-able as a 'passenger', in part by his actions of running towards the ship, but also by virtue of the fact that he is holding a passport in his hand, which he presents to the official when he is stopped at the barrier. In these ways, then, the visual construction of the commercial makes available a configuration of mutually elaborative category-predicate relations, involving persons, activities and objects.

Returning to the narrative description, as each new descriptor is introduced, a sense of *scenic orderliness* is sustained and reinforced, involving further mutually implicative relations between persons, activities and objects. For example, consider the latter part of Scene One, when the young guy has 'missed the boat'. As a reminder, the narrative description describes what happens in these terms:

> The young guy registers his disappointment, both facially and by throwing his passport down in frustration. The camera pans to his feet and we see a cabbage lying on the ground. The young guy kicks the cabbage as though it were a football The cabbage hits a dockworker and a game of football spontaneously develops. This ends when the young guy kicks the cabbage at a dockworker who is crouching in front of some cargo netting, in the manner of a goalkeeper The force of the cabbage/football knocks the goalkeeper backwards into the netting, and the young guy and the dockworkers throw up their arms in celebration of the goal

In this description certain persons are identified as 'dockworkers' and a particular object is referred to as 'cargo netting'. These descriptions are the product of a contextual analysis on the part of the viewer. That the persons so identified are dockworkers and the object is cargo netting are *scenic inferences*. In response to a challenge "How do you know that's what they are?" the viewer might find "What else could they reasonably be?" to be a proper and adequate response. For example, the persons identified as dockworkers would not appear to be passengers, since they are not going to or coming from the ship, neither, from their dress would they seem to be describable as officials. Observably, they are dressed in 'working clothes' and are 'standing about' on the quayside, just as a ship is leaving the dock. The fact that the ship has just left might also be found to explain how they are available to become involved in an impromptu football match, their work for the present being over. The intelligibility of the scene and the identities of those in it is an accomplished orderliness of an analysis of 'categories in context' (Hester 1994).

The Central Character: Course of Action Analysis and 'Motivational Texture'.

If one principle of co-selection of descriptors comprises the 'scenic framing' of the location of the story as a quayside, a second dimension of co-selection comprises the action descriptors which provide the 'motivational texture' of the narrative. The narrative description is *egologically ordered* (Schutz 1962), that is, organized around an individual and his 'project'. It describes a 'young guy' and his actions in such a way that it is clear that he is the central character of the action. This centrality is constituted both by the ways his actions are described and in the ways that references to others are contingent upon how they stand with reference to him.

The availability of the young guy as the central character of the action is something which emerges in and through the succession of shots and by virtue of the unfolding action these reveal. The use of close-ups, and the way in which these are interwoven with mid-range and long-range shots is crucial here. For example, in the initial, panoramic shot, the young guy can be seen in the bottom of the frame, jumping over a barrier to avoid the stream of people coming down the quayside. The next is a mid-range shot of the young guy vaulting over a barrier, holding a document in one hand and a bag in the other. Shot 3 is a close-up of two officials, standing by a barrier, and the fourth is a close-up of the young guy, running and holding the document (which the viewer can now see to be a passport) in front of him. Shot 5 tracks the progress of the young guy as he runs past the first official and up to the barrier where the second official is standing. Subsequent shots (8-10) show the official perusing and then returning the passport, enabling the young guy to continue on his way. His progress is then tracked in a further sequence (shots 11-13), culminating in the encounter with the 'bald man' who prevents him from going any further. In these ways the sequential ordering of the camera shots makes available a distinction between 'primary' or 'central character' and 'secondary characters'. Secondary characters are those who appear in the action by virtue of their involvement with the central character, their relevance is provided by the course of action in which he is engaged. The viewer sees them only insofar as and for so long as they are implicated in the young guy's progress. These characters appear as they become relevant and once this relevance lapses so they properly disappear from the action.[6]

What the filmic construction also makes available is the link between the identity of the central character and his 'project'. Thus, his actions are described in such a way as to make it available to the reader to understand that he is engaged in a *consistent course of action* - he is described as 'rushing', 'jumping', running' and so forth - and the actions of other persons are referred to in terms of this course of action - for example, he is 'obstructed' and 'restrained' by them. Furthermore these descriptors are consistent with a *purpose* which, in a reflexive fashion, they make available to the reader as the project which motivates the young guy's behaviour and thereby *explains* this consistency. He is 'rushing', etc. in order to catch the boat. This project is confirmed by his reactions to the behaviour of other parties: when the young guy has eventually 'missed the boat', he 'throws down his passport' and, 'in frustration' kicks a cabbage. In these ways, the narrative description conveys that the young guy's actions can be seen as constituting a single course of motivated conduct, a sequence of actions informed by a consistent purpose. Everything the guy does displays his wish to catch the boat. Also, the constituent elements of the quayside setting have been described in relation to the egological center of the action; the significance of objects, persons and so forth has been constituted by the relationship in which they stand to the guy and his purpose. Specific elements of the scene impinge upon the central character's motivated course of action in a direct way - they comprise circumstantial conditions which he must negotiate in order to pursue his purpose and reach his goal.[7]

What we have referred to as 'scenic framing' and 'motivational texture' are mutually defined and mutually intelligible; the guy's course of action is *embedded* in the quayside context, which in turn is seen in terms of how it impinges upon the course of action and thus upon his *categorial identity.* He is not simply a 'young guy', but a *'young guy far from home'.* The viewer can comprehend the central character's course of action *as such* by virtue of the way his actions are 'foregrounded' against an intelligible scenic 'background' *within which* he acts. This foreground-background involves seeing that the young guy is engaged in a course of action which is predicated by its setting; he is trying to catch the boat *because* he is in a foreign place, a place which he wishes to leave. It is not that the young guy's actions simply *happen* to be taking place in a quayside setting, rather that they are doing so is crucially constitutive of what those actions *are.*

The Action and the Song

So far we have been concerned solely with the visual dimension of the commercial, and with the ways in which the visual depictions which comprise Scene One are intelligible as a narrative. We now turn to consideration of the aural dimension. Approximately four seconds into the commercial the theme song begins. The song continues throughout the remainder of the commercial, both as a musical background to the action and, at a particular point, as a 'lip synch' by the central character. Once again, the question we pose concerns the work of category analysis in and through which the viewer is able to find that the song and the visual action are related. We take it that the visually depicted action and the song are hearable - and are heard - in mutual conjunction as two elements in a unity; in other words, they are heard by means of the *documentary method of interpretation* (Garfinkel 1967) as documents of a single, complex whole. In order to provide the reader with some sense of the interplay between song and visual action, we now offer a *third description* of the commercial, intended to show the juxtaposing of the song lyrics with the visual narrative:

SONG	VISUALS
	Open on young guy with holdall, pushing his way through crowded quayside towards rusty old-cargo-cum-passenger ship
	He's momentarily held up by customs officers who insist on checking his passport Our guy watches
I MISS MY HOME SO FAR AWAY	despairingly as he sees the mooring ropes being cast off and the gangplank being withdrawn

TAKING IT EASY ON A SUMMER'S DAY. .	He races forward again, hurdling barriers and piles of luggage.
I MISS THE FRIENDS I LEFT BEHIND. .	He finally reaches end of quay where he comes up against a giant of a man with an eye-patch who stops him and shakes his head
THOSE TIMES WILL NEVER LEAVE MY MIND	View from the ship of our guy waving helplessly
	He turns away in frustration and kicks a cabbage that's been knocked onto the floor
I MISS THE TEAM...	It whistles through the air, hits a dockhand, ricochets around his workmates and comes back to our guy who wallops it
THE ROAR. .THE SCORE...	into cargo net, taking the 'goalie' with it
THE WARMTH...THE FUN	Dockhands congratulate our guy, who
(LIP SYNCH) BUT EVEN MORE .	turns to camera and sings

(At this point the quayside scene fades into scene two, which comprises a single tracking shot, beginning with a close-up of a beer pump and pulling back to reveal the interior of a crowded pub)

Focusing upon the song itself for a moment, we note that the lyrics take the form of a 'lament' by an unidentified person, "I". In order not to presuppose the analysis we seek to explicate, we will refer to 'The Singer of the Song' as that person who refers to himself through the use of "I".[8] The Singer of the Song expresses his feelings about 'home'. In referring to it as a lament, we are noting that the lyrics express a consistent set of feelings about 'home'. The lyric takes the form of a list of (some of) the things that the Singer of the Song misses about 'home'. Since the song is sung over the visually depicted action of the commercial, the viewer's analytic task is to make sense of this lament in terms of the narrative action. We take it that the viewer can find, with little or no difficulty, that the Singer of the Song is expressing feelings which can be associated with the young guy who is the central character of the visual narrative. As such, they are also recognizably consistent with the young guy's course of action in attempting to catch the boat. We further take it that when, in the closing camera shot of

Scene One, the young guy turns towards the camera and begins to 'sing' (lip synch) the song, this simply 'confirms' what the viewer already knows, i.e. that the feelings expressed in the song are the young guy's feelings and that, in this sense, the song is 'his song'.

In arriving at such an understanding, the viewer has made sense of the relationship between the song and the visual action in accordance with what we will refer to as 'the viewer's maxim'. This maxim concerns the phenomenon of category boundedness, that is the commonsense relationship between category incumbents and predicates such as activities or feelings. It is a variant of the 'hearer's rule' which has been noted in previous studies (Sacks 1972, 1974a). It can be stated as follows: 'If, for some predicated activity or emotion, you can see this activity or emotion as associated with (done by, felt by) a given incumbent of a category to which this activity or emotion is commonsensically tied, then see it this way'.

How does this maxim provide for the viewer's understanding of the link between the song and the visual action, the finding that the song is 'the young guy's song'? We begin by noting that the viewer's maxim presupposes that there are 'grammatical' links between emotional states, category identities and social circumstances.[9] These grammatical links between the identity and circumstances in which the individual relevantly (and observably) stands and the emotional state avowals which he can intelligibly make are such that, for example, should relevant circumstances be found not to obtain, then the avowal of or claim to a certain emotional state *is rendered unintelligible*.[10] Thus, rather than find that an individual is dissembling, exaggerating or disguising his true feelings, persons may find that, as an incumbent of a given category, he is laying claim to feelings which it *makes no sense* for him to claim to possess. Conversely, knowing that an individual possesses a given identity and stands in certain category relevant circumstances, persons may find that, his avowals (to the contrary) notwithstanding, he *must* be experiencing certain feelings.

An avowal of the feeling 'missing home' presupposes that the individual who avows it is 'away from home' in some relevant sense. Schegloff (1972) has noted that 'home' is an indexical expression the specific reference of which is occasioned by the circumstances of its use. We suggest that the viewer has no difficulty in finding a relevant sense of HOME by hearing the song in relation to the visual action. Given that the young guy is seen attempting to catch the boat, and thereby to leave the 'foreign looking place', it is available to the viewer to find that HOME refers to the place which the boat would have taken the young guy, were he to have caught it. The first line of the song, I MISS MY

HOME SO FAR AWAY, can be heard as setting up a locational contrast between HOME and FAR AWAY. This contrast is an indexical one; in other words, the viewer is obliged to look to the relevant context of its use to find its meaning.   Insofar as the quayside setting is visibly 'foreign' and given the fact that ships are vehicles for worldly travel, the locational reference of 'HOME' can be understood in what we propose to call 'worldly distance' terms. While 'home' might have a multitude of possible references, it is apparent that it is here referring to the guy's desire to leave this 'foreign' place for his own 'part of the world'.

What that part of the world relevantly consists in for him, subjectively or *emotionally*, can then be found in the lyrics of the song and confirmed in the visual action. What is 'missed', the relevant sense of 'home', and the feelings expressed in the lament, are accomplished methodically by virtue of two structural features of the lyrics; their sequential order and their categorial organization in terms of paired contrast categories. Sequentially, the lyrics can be heard as a list of items which are missed. While it might be possible to hear these as a list of (unconnected) things which are missed by someone, it is clear that, by virtue of the categorial identity of the Singer-of-the-Song as 'young man far from home', the items are hearable as consistent with one another and as expressing a single, general emotion.[11] The young-man-far-from-home laments the absence of these items, and in so doing provides for the *situational embeddedness* of the emotion 'missing home'.

'HOME and FAR AWAY' is merely the first of a number of 'contrast pairs' which are set up by the category descriptors used in the song. Insofar as each line of the song can be heard *sequentially* as adding a 'new' item to the list of "things missed" *and* as elaborating the emotion which the song *as a whole* is thereby found to express, the song lyric sets up a series of *occasioned contrast pairs*. These pairs can be represented as follows:

HOME	/	(FAR) AWAY
COMFORTS	/	RIGORS
FRIENDS	/	STRANGERS
TIMES (PRESENT)	/	TIMES (PAST)
TEAM (MEMBER)	/	TEAM (NON-MEMBER)

This contrast pair structure provides for the understanding of the lyric as an unfolding *motivational account* of the visual action. Inasmuch as the first set of categories list the things which the guy is 'missing', the viewer can find that the second half of the pair characterises what he 'has', i.e. the place/time/relations, etc within which he is visibly located. If we think of this structure as a kind of 'gestalt', it is clear that the 'first' contrast (HOME/FAR AWAY) provides a thematic for understanding the following contrasts. In other words, the young guy's actions can be understood as motivated by a desire to substitute the left hand side of this structure for the right hand side. The situational embeddedness of 'missing home' thus is constituted as involving a number of elements, including missing the 'comforts of home', 'friends' one had there, the 'times' one had with them, the 'fun' of what one did with them, and so forth.

For example, in the second line the Singer sings TAKING IT EASY ON A SUMMER'S DAY. We take it that the viewer, in hearing this as the *second* line of the song, in relation to and as coherent with the *first*, can hear this lyric as making reference to the 'comforts of home' which are being missed as a result of being 'away'. Thus, this line suggests a contrast pair COMFORTS / (RIGOURS), which can be mapped onto the initial contrast between HOME and AWAY. A third such contrast pair is made relevant by the use of the descriptor 'friends'. In the third line of the song the Singer sings I MISS THE FRIENDS I LEFT BEHIND. Hearing this lyric in relation to the visual action, the viewer can find relevant a contrast between 'friends' and 'strangers'. We note the structural similarity between contrast pairs and 'standardized relational pairs' or SRP's (Sacks, 1972). As Sacks has pointed out, the SRP 'friend-friend' links structurally with its opposite 'stranger-stranger', such that members, in finding that they stand in a category relationship or relationships describable in terms of the second pair, can simultaneously find that a relationship of the first pair type is 'noticeably absent'. We can express this structural relationship diagrammatically, as follows:

SRP (a)	STRANGER	-	STRANGER
$\updownarrow$			
SRP (b)	FRIEND	-	FRIEND

(where $\updownarrow$ stands for 'contrasts with and makes noticeably absent')

This structure further explicates the situational embeddedness of the avowed emotion 'missing home'. One way in which persons can find that they are 'away from home' is to find that they are 'among strangers'. We take it that this contrast pair structure can be mapped onto the visual action, and specifically onto the actions of the 'young guy'. The visual action, consisting as it does of his attempt to catch the boat and leave behind what he 'has', thus amounts to his efforts to get away from 'strangers', and the 'foreign place' he is in, and get back to the place and time where he was among 'friends'.

In these ways, then, we take it that the song lyric is hearable as a motivational commentary upon the visual action of the commercial. Furthermore, as the song lyric and visual action together *unfold*, the viewer can find that the visual action 'reflects back' on the lyric, such that the category relations described in the lyric are *symbolised and exemplified* by the visual action. We take it that just as the unfolding lyrics of the song can be heard as fitting the unfolding visual action, so conversely the visual action can be seen as providing a set of *visual instructions* for understanding the lyric. In other words, the aural-visual relationship is a reflexive one, and connections can be found, so to speak, in *both directions*.

The reflexive relationship between song lyrics and visual action provides the viewer with resources for understanding the subsequent events in Scene One. In particular, the unfolding of the story involves a change in the relationship between the central characters and others and a corresponding change to the emotional texture of the action. To explicate this we remind the reader of the lyrics, up to the point at which the action of Scene One fades into Scene Two:

> I MISS MY HOME SO FAR AWAY
> TAKING IT EASY ON A SUMMER'S DAY,
> I MISS THE FRIENDS I LEFT BEHIND
> THOSE TIMES WILL NEVER LEAVE MY MIND
> I MISS THE TEAM, THE ROAR, THE SCORE,
> THE WARMTH, THE FUN, BUT EVEN MORE

It is notable that the reference to the TEAM and its associated features accompany the visual action of the impromptu quayside football match which is initiated when the guy kicks the cabbage in frustration at having missed the boat. In this impromptu football match, the relationship between the central character and the other parties to the action is transformed. Whereas in the opening section of Scene One the young guy and other characters in the scene stood in some kind of *opposition* to one another - others were in various ways 'obstructing' the guy in his attempts to catch the boat, in the ways we have outlined - the guy and other characters now come together in a single course of joint action, engaged upon a *common project*, the football match. As we have noted, the game develops 'accidentally' from the guy's action of 'kicking the cabbage', an act of anger and frustration at missing the boat. The cabbage strikes a 'dockhand' in the face, falls to the ground, and is then treated as a 'football'. By virtue of this development, the relationship of the guy to the 'dockhands' becomes one of co-players - in this new course of action the guy no longer is surrounded by others who stand towards him as 'obstacles' in his path, but now as *colleagues* in a common venture.

This transformation in the action is interpretable as standing in a definite relation to the ongoing lyrics of the theme song. Thus, there is a matching between the *collective and co-operative* character of the 'game' and the lyric's reference to TEAM; also, the specific nature of the game - a *football game* - since 'the team' (or 'my/your team') is a conventional formulation widely used within British popular sports culture by football fans to refer to the football team which they support. This association between visual action and song lyric is further developed by the lyric's reference to ROAR, SCORE and FUN. These words are sung as the guy scores a *'goal'*, by kicking the cabbage football into the goal represented by the netting in front of which the dockhand 'goalie' stands. The action of Scene One ends as the guy and his fellow players throw up their arms in joint celebration of his 'goal'. The guy turns to face the camera , which moves into close-up as he lip synchs' the line BUT EVEN MORE. At this point Scene One fades into the opening shot of Scene Two, the close-up of beer splashing into a beer glass.

'GREENALLS' as a Master Category

We have noted the readily available narrative intelligibility of Scene One as depicting a settled sequence of events involving a central character engaged in a 'motivationally transparent' course of action. The fact that the commercial observably has a narrative format which provides 'viewing instructions' for understanding the scenes sets up for the viewer the task of finding a narrative connection between Scene One and Scene Two. The narrative format of the commercial would seem to instruct the viewer to find Scene Two as linked with Scene One. Scene Two follows Scene One sequentially, but in what sense does it follow *narratively?* What 'storied' connection might the viewer find between them?

In order to explicate this, we note firstly the way in which the lyric of the song develops in relation to the visual dimension:

SONG	VISUALS
OH GREENALLS	close-up of beer
	splashing into pint pot

MY GREENALLS	close-up of the pumps, and pull back to see people at the bar laughing and joking.
GREENALLS	camera pulls further back to show the whole, busy pub. Everyone turns and raises glasses to camera.
MY GREENALLS .	Dissolve back to quayside where we see
MOST OF ALL I MISS MY	our guy next to the big bloke with
GREENALLS. .	eye-patch. He lifts eye-patch and wipes
(fade)	away a tear from his perfectly good eye.

Super: MOST OF ALL I MISS MY GREENALLS

We note that the name 'Greenalls' does not occur in the song lyric until Scene One has faded into Scene Two. The song line OH GREENALLS, MY GREENALLS is sung over the opening moments of Scene Two. This line thus explicates, and thereby *connects*, two things. As the name of a brand of beer, it informs the viewer what sort of beer it is that is pouring into the glass (or rather, it confirms this, since the name 'Greenalls' can be seen on the beer pump which becomes visible as the camera close-up begins to pan out). Also, it can be heard in relation to the previous lines of the lyric as a *summation* of all that the guy is missing about 'home'. We have made the point above that the song lyric is more than simply a list of things 'missed'. By virtue of the structure of category contrasts and their interrelationship, the lyric is hearable for the unity of feeling it expresses. In relation to this unity, GREENALLS is not simply another in the list of things the guy is missing; the singer - now explicitly identified as the 'young guy' - sings that GREENALLS is the thing he is missing 'most of all'.

In this respect, it is available to the viewer to hear GREENALLS as a 'master category' in relation to the structure of category contrast pairs outlined above. This hearing provides (retrospectively) further explanation of the situational embeddedness of his feeling of 'missing home' and a further way of understanding the urgency of the young guy's actions on the quayside. As an explanation of the guy's motives, the song can be heard as revealing why he is desperate to get 'home'. With reference to the things he is missing, the thing he misses most is GREENALLS. Thus the fact that the young guy is 'missing home' and in particular is 'missing GREENALLS' provides the viewer with resources to make sense of the fact Scene Two depicts a pub and a crowd of people. Since, at the opening of Scene Two, in the very first shot, the word 'Greenalls' can be seen on the beer pump, it is available to the viewer to see that this is a Greenalls pub, and that the 'Greenalls' to which the song has been referring is just this beer and this kind of pub. What kind of pub? As the camera pulls back, the pub interior is revealed as crowded with people, and not just 'any' people, but co-incumbents of the category 'young guys and girls' and thus candidates for the descriptor 'friends' in respect of the young guy in Scene One. Furthermore, the lyric BUT EVEN MORE...OH GREENALLS accomplishes more than a formulation of the guy's feelings; it serves also to specify the kinds of persons who are his friends. The visual content of Scene Two, showing as it does a 'friendly crowded pub', and not just *any* pub but specifically a 'Greenalls' pub, provides the viewer with resources for identifying the parties to the pub scene as 'Greenalls drinkers'. Thus, these persons are tied to the young guy in two, mutually reinforcing ways. They are both candidate members of the device FRIENDS and manifest members of the category 'Greenall's drinkers'. In this way the action of Scene Two gives *concrete reference* to the guy's lament in Scene One, and thereby provides for the narrative contiuity of the text. *This* is what he is missing; it is for want of *this* that he was desperate to catch the boat. [12]

As with Scene One, the visual and the aural dimensions of the commercial can be understood in the manner of a 'gestalt'. Thus, the viewer can find his understanding of the significance of the pub setting and the song lyric confirmed by the visual action in Scene Two. We have noted that, as the camera pulls back to reveal, first the barmaids behind the bar and subsequently the crowded interior of the pub, the persons so revealed wave and smile in greeting towards the camera. We note that the viewer might find a specific ambiguity in this action: who is it that is being greeted? We take it that, insofar as there is an ambiguity here, it is constituted by the possibility of a *dual understanding* of this greeting. It is not that the viewer has no available addressee for the greeting, but rather that there are two available candidates: the young guy and the *viewer* themself. Thus the viewer can find that, while the greeting might be understood as directed towards 'themself', it might also be understood as addressed to the guy. This ambiguity is not loose but, we suggest, systematically generated. As a

final step in our analysis, we seek to unpack this dual understanding of
Scene Two.

Finding Relevance for the Viewer

First we will consider the way in which the action of the
'greeting' provides for its own understanding as possibly addressed to
the 'young guy far from home' who the viewer has seen as the central
character of Scene One. We noted earlier that the combination of the
action of Scene One together with the song lyric makes relevant the
standardized relational pair, 'friend - friend'. This paired structure has a
reflexive character; if person A stands towards person B as a 'friend',
then person B stands correspondingly towards person A. One thing
which follows from this is that members can find that the descriptor
'friend' is only properly and correctly employable in respect of a given
other where it can be anticipated that other will employ that same
category in respect of themselves. This reflexive organization applies
also to the distribution of category predicated emotions. Thus, we also
noted earlier that in circumstances in which one is absent from one's
friends a proper emotional response is to be 'missing' them. The
reflexive organization of the SRP means that one can anticipate that
they will (should) be experiencing the same emotion - since self is
correspondingly absent from them, they will (should) also be "missing"
self.

We take it that the reflexive properties of this SRP structure
provide a resource for finding the guy to be a candidate object for the
collective greeting expressed by the pub crowd towards the camera. In
relation to the narrative of Scene One, the action of the crowd in Scene
Two can be found to involve validation of the young guy's membership
of the 'friend-friend' relationship in respect of them. This membership
both justifies and occasions such an action as a greeting. Since greetings
are category bound and category implicative it is available to members,
on the occurrence of a 'first greeting', to inspect the relationship
between the speaker of the first greeting and its addressee, the party
who should produce the 'return greeting', to find that these persons
stand in a category relationship which is either appropriate or
inappropriate for the performance of an exchange of greetings. The
relationship between categories and activities is such that the very
occurrence of a 'person directed' first greeting can itself be taken as
adequate grounds for inferring the relationship between the two parties
to be a proper one, such as a relationship of acquaintanceship or
friendship. Where such a relationship is not obvious (immediately
recognizable), a first greeting therefore can be taken to constitute a

claim to such a relationship between the parties, one which is inspectable for its validity. In this respect, then, the sequential logic of an action pair such as a greeting exchange is implicated with the combinatorial logic of identity categories.

A further feature of greetings as action structures is that there may be relevant contextual circumstances which preclude the close ordering of the first and second parts, such as normally obtains in the case of greetings in ordinary conversation. In such circumstances members may recognize a necessary and inevitable temporal separation between a 'greeting' and a 'return greeting'. Paramount among such circumstances is the non-co-presence, in interactional terms, of the parties. Thus, greetings may be sent by one party to another who is non-co-present, in a form which is non-interactional - for example by mail.

The greetings performed (in various ways - raising glasses, waving, smiling) by the participants to the pub setting in Scene Two can be presumed to have an 'object', that is a party towards whom those greetings are directed. Since the situation is not a conversational, interactional one - the greeting is directed straight to camera - the viewer, as we have already suggested, is presented with a dual sense of the addressee of the greetings. They can be understood both as actions *within* the narrative, and as *textual* actions addressed to the viewer as *recipient of the text*. This second dimension is provided by the viewer analysing the greeting in the context of its occurrence within and as part of a media text. To speak of the commercial as a 'media text' is, at the very least, to note that it is intended for consumption by what Jayyusi has called a 'public at large' (Jayyusi 1991a). This constitutes one significant way in which media texts differ from phenomena of a more interactional and 'local' character, such as conversational activities. It is not that a media text is not 'recipient designed', but that it's designed character can be presumed to be *impersonal*, its intended recipient is anyone who occupies the category 'viewer'. To be viewer of a media text is to engage with it under a set of auspices. Central to these auspices is the adoption of a stance which we will call the stance of the 'properly oriented audience member'. Among other things, this stance involves the giving of proper regard to the audience-produced character of the text, recognising that the text is not something which has been produced 'just for you' individually or 'personally' but, instead, orienting to the text as something 'produced for anyone'. In this respect, one orients to the text as a viewer by treating it as a *commonsensically knowable object*, as something for the understanding of which what 'anyone knows' is both adequate and relevant for its proper comprehension.

A second aspect of the stance of the properly oriented audience member concerns respecting the normative requirement to specifically disattend the 'actual production features' of the text, in favour of engagement with it as a 'virtual production'. We take it that to be a viewer is to have available as a *seen but unnoticed* feature of media texts the distinction between virtual and actual production, the noting of which Cuff (1978: 8) attributes to Harold Garfinkel:

> In this respect, an observation by Harold Garfinkel seems pertinent. He calls attention to a whole class of events staged for public consumption, e.g stage plays, puppet shows, radio and television programs Two sorts of accounts of these events can be given: a 'virtual production account' and an 'actual production account' A virtual production account describes 'what literally happens', i.e the 'virtual happening' as it is designed for public consumption. The actual production account describes what is involved in staging or producing this virtual happening. Garfinkel illustrates this distinction from Disneyland: the virtual happening of 'Mickey Mouse's tea-party' can also be accounted for by describing how this event gets staged in such terms as 'someone dressed up in a mouse suit'.

One may take it that, knowing that an event is a virtual production, the viewer has it mundanely available that the 'virtual effects' can be understood in terms of what was *intended* to be conveyed. In this sense, the viewer can analyse the text to find that normal 'real world' constraints upon the occurrence of events are not properly expectable in relation to the 'intended effect'; in other words, that in viewing the text, the reader should operate a 'principle of dramatic license' (or what is sometimes referred to as a 'willing suspension of disbelief'), in order that the intended effects may be realised. The relationship between these two dimensions of understanding may be experienced in varied ways. Thus, on some occasions members may find that the 'production aspects' of a staged performance are such as to obstruct a 'proper' attention to and engagement with the virtual events, while on other occasions they may find that such aspects can be relegated to their proper scenic place.

The viewer's orientation to the text as a virtual/actual phenomenon and as designed for 'any viewer' is relevant to both understandings of the greetings actions. On the one hand, the viewer can take account of the produced nature of the commercial as a text for public consumption, to find that the normal constraints upon concerted interaction need not apply as they would in interaction between co-present participants. Thus, that the 'pub crowd' in Scene Two and the 'young guy far from home' in Scene One are not interactionally co-present - indeed, the fact that their relationship is a purely *virtual* one, is no obstacle to the viewer understanding the greeting possibly to be directed to the young guy. In orienting to the commercial as a virtual artefact, viewers can find that the virtual distance in time and space between the pub crowd and the young guy both occasions the greeting and stands as no obstacle to its expression. In other words, the viewer can take it that the real world improbabilities and difficulties of 'taking literally' that the pub crowd in Scene Two are addressing their greeting to the young guy in Scene One are *specifically irrelevant* for the purpose of viewing the commercial *as* a commercial. It is enough that, in the virtual world of this commercial, such a connection can be made.

The second understanding of the pub crowd's greetings - that they are addressed to the viewer himself. - also requires the viewer to orient to the text as a virtual text *designed to be viewed as such*. In this respect, then, the two understandings are mutually implicative and mutually reinforcing. That the commercial is a text designed to be viewed and thus also known to be a virtual production can be seen as *built into* the very structure and content of the text. Put differently, we are proposing that, in this respect, the commercial comprises what we propose to call a 'knowing text'. The defining feature of a knowing text, it would seem, is that it demands of the viewer that they employ their knowledge of its dual virtual/actual production character to attend to it in the manner for which it was 'accountably intended' and see in it the effects that it has been 'designed' to provide. This also means that such a text requires of the viewer that the self identification of themself as *'viewer'* be recognized as implicated in a proper understanding of specific actions and events within the text. In this respect, then, the competent viewer of 'Miss the Boat' arguably is one who understands the narrative as consisting, at least in part, in things that are specifically addressed to them *as* viewer, as well as things put there for them, the viewer, to find.

Chapter Seven

Conclusion:
Membership Categorization Analysis
and Sociology

Stephen Hester and Peter Eglin

It is the fundamental premise of this collection that the theoretical payoff of ethnomethodological membership categorization analysis is a view of culture as *internal* to action. In Chapter One we sought to explicate this by drawing a contrast between a decontextualized model of culture (as membership categorization devices, membership categories and predicates) and its ethnomethodological alternative as culture-in-action. In Chapter Two we developed our argument by demonstrating with respect to data that the proper understanding of the use of categories in interaction is as 'categories-in-context.' In Chapter Three, Watson extends the argument by pointing to the unexplicated interplay between sequential and categorial order in conversation. In chapters Four, Five and Six respectively, Baker, Lynch and Bogen, and Francis and Hart variously exhibit this attentitiveness to the locally ordered and locally ordering character of culture-in-action as membership categorization *analysis*.

Our first objective in the Conclusion is to address a second feature of the internality of culture in action. In contrast to the macro-micro distinction so dear to sociology's mainstream, the studies collected here may be used to exhibit the incarnation of social structure *in* agency. We will review them in support of this contention. Our second objective is to argue, in keeping with the thrust of other recent studies in ethnomethodology (Button 1991; Garfinkel 1991), that MCA contributes to the *respecification* of sociology's foundations and practices as topics for ethnomethodological inquiry rather than as taken for granted resources of sociological work. We wish to show how membership categorization analysis, as ethnomethodology, can offer a novel point of view on traditional sociological problems by respecifying the study of such issues as the relation of individual and society, the link between social structure and social action, and the connection between motivation and action. It is our contention that all sociological areas, as traditionally investigated, whether demarcated as 'theoretical' or 'substantive', not only rest for their intelligibility on, but constitute forms of, membership categorization analysis on the part of the sociologist.

The Incarnation of Social Structure in Agency

It is conventional to locate ethnomethodology in the territory of micro-sociology, even of micro-interactionism. This location is understood to restrict the findings of ethnomethodolocial inquiries to the realm of 'face-to-face interaction,' leaving it with nothing to say about the relationships among institutions or about the presumed influence of the culture and structure of the 'surrounding society' on the character of the interaction among 'individuals.' As Sharrock and Watson (1988), among others (e.g. Schegloff 1987), have rather conclusively demonstrated, however, this set of distinctions between macro and micro, culture and action, structure and agency and, above all, society and the individual quite fail to capture the nature of ethnomethodology's phenomenon and that of its claims. In order to appreciate this failure it is not necessary to formulate that phenomenon but simply to inspect, for example, the subjects and topics of the studies collected here.

In Chapter Two Hester and Eglin consider the work of identifaction, motive-attribution and moral assessment done via the selection and use of categories and predicates in descriptions of 'problem children' in teacher-psychologist talk, and of suicides in news headlines. In Chapter Four Baker elucidates the methods teachers use in a particular school setting to accomplish justice for students for all practical purposes. For Lynch and Bogen in Chapter Five '(not) remembering' is not a matter of cognition and the salience of information, but of the relationships between recollections of the past, credibility and the ties between actor-categories and actions. They reveal the use of these relationships and resources in interrogatory dialogue obtained from the Iran Contra Hearings and the O. J. Simpson trial. In Chapter Six, Francis and Hart examine some methods of membership categorization analysis used in accomplishing narrative intelligibility in a TV commercial. Finally, in this chapter we investigate the accomplishment of sociology itself as a professional mode of inquiry through its practitioners' use of methods for formulatiing social structures.

Notice that in each case above analysis does not begin with, nor anywhere rely on, a pre-supposed distinction between (features of) 'society' and (features of) 'the individual,' but speaks to the accomplishment and realisation of (many of) sociology's 'structural' phenomena *in, as* and *through* members' particular, concerted, interactional practices. Thus, the studies variously address the production and recognition of such 'structural,' institutionalised phenomena as: deviance, social problems, social control, education, the school, justice, suicide, news media (Chapter Two and, in part, Chapter Four); justice, law, government, the State (Chapter Five); advertising, the economy, production, consumption, mass media, communication, culture (Chapter Six); the discipline of sociology, the professions, 'society' (this chapter).

Also properly to be included in this list, but separated here for heuristic purposes only, are all the social identities in terms of which persons participated in, or were constituted by, interaction in the settings concerned: teacher, pupil, psychologist, newspaper, news reader, fiancé-fiancée, boyfriend-girlfriend, (police) officer, young man (Chapter Two); teacher, student (Chapter Four); doctor, patient, lawyer, defendant, criminalist, detective, (Chapter Five); friend, viewer, consumer (Chapter Six); sociologist, society, individual (this chapter).

It is both inadequate and irrelevant to replace these categories or identity descriptors with the putatively a-social term 'individual' and then seek to build society back in from outside (structural determination) and from inside (internalisation). For, as is sociologically commonplace, in academic discourse 'individual' is itself a concept freighted with heavy political and historical baggage. Whatever these particular origins are, one prominent vehicle for the concept's re-production is the social-scientific disciplines, notably sociology itself. In this way, we may place sociology's categorizational practices alongside those of other members as another set of methods for making society (see our last section below).

In seeking to show the 'stuctural' relevance of ethnomethodological membership categorization analysis we are not to be heard as motivated by a desire for rapprochement with structural sociology traditionally, conventionally or constructively conceived. For, as we are at pains to show, we abjure the distinction generating the question in the first place. There is simply no need to bring back together that which we choose, as a theoretical option, not to see as separate in the beginning. It is not as pristine 'individuals' that persons are formulated as problems at school, described in the newspaper as tragic events, encountered in public on the sidewalk, appealed to in television commercials, or cross-examined in court - *except* when formulated as objects for mainstream sociological theorising in professional sociology's texts. Whole ranges of persons' particular characteristics are just what are *not* relevant, without special account, to particular courses of interaction in which they are involved. Instead it is identities *for* the organization / setting / occasion / activity / turn in question that are relevant. In the exercise of the multiple methods which members use for producing and recognizing categorial identities they thereby produce society. We have called this collection 'Culture in Action' just because we believe that membership categorization analysis addresses these key conceptual notions of sociology. Whereas conventional sociology separates these theorised 'entities,' only to be then afflicted with the problem of their re-combination (Schegloff 1987; Sharrock and Watson 1988) membership categorization analysis, as ethnomethodology, shows their embodied confluence, their mutual incarnation, in the detail of 'society.' As Garfinkel might put it, these studies display 'contrary to the entirety of the social science movement, incommensurably asymmetrically alternate sociology, the local production and natural, reflexive accountability of immortal, ordinary society really, evidently and these ordinarily' (Garfinkel 1991: 17).

The Contribution of MCA to Respecifying Sociology's Foundations

We want to trace three implications of MCA for the practice of (professional) sociology. Firstly, MCA affords a way of studying members' methods of formulating social structures. Secondly, it provides a means of specifying the dependence of professional sociological inquiry on ordinary lay members' methods of practical reasoning. Thirdly, it allows us a perspicuous method of respecifying formal sociological knowledge and inquiry as comprising a professional variety of membership categorization.

Membership Categorization and Social Structure

Whilst most of the work in MCA has been concerned with personal membership categories and categorization devices, and notwithstanding the 'argument for incarnation' already made, the collectivity categorizations introduced in Chapter One provide an additional way of studying 'social structures' ethnomethodologically, as Coulter (1982) indicates. That is, 'social structures' or 'institutions' are describable and analysable in MCA terms. It allows us to see how members use categories of social configuration or collectivity-categorizations, such as the 'stock exchange', the 'army', the 'military-industrial complex', the 'school', the aristocracy', the 'middle class', the 'state', 'capitalist society', 'them' and 'us', as well as membership categorization devices like 'family', 'stage of life' etc. The use to which such collectivity-categorizations may be put are as investigable as any other type of membership category or categorization device. Thus, social configurations may be used to provide the sense for a membership category, to impute a motive, contest an explanation, provide for the intelligibility of an action, and a whole host of other practical activities. The key point is that in MCA, as opposed to structuralist sociology, the uses of these collectivity-categorizations are respecified as members' phenomena and there by as topics of inquiry rather then as resources for sociological theorising. Moreover, such a respecification sidesteps orthodox sociology's dichotomy which as we have seen, both provides such sociology with its characteristic topics and problems (including 'bridging the micro-macro divide') and establishes a basis for criticising 'interpetive sociologists' for 'leaving out the social structure' (power, class, patriarchy, etc.). As we have argued above, following Sharrock and Watson (1988), social structure may be viewed as 'incarnate' to social 'interaction'. What we wish to add here is that MCA affords a way of examining how social structures are articulated in the talk-in-interaction of everyday life.

The Dependence of Professional Sociology on the Language of Everyday Life

It is well known that ethnomethodology's pedigree owes much to Alfred Schutz. It is perhaps less well known that Schutz's 'phenomenological sociology' reveals fundamental inconsistencies between its program and that of ethnomethodology. In particular, whilst Schutz recognizes the importance of common sense knowledge and its role, for ordinary members of society, in ordering the social world, he fails to consider how social scientific practice itself is irremediably grounded in that selfsame common sense knowledge of everyday life. For Schutz, the important thing is to ensure the consistency (adequacy) of the social scientist's second order constructs with the first order constructs of the ordinary members of society. He does not consider how social scientific second order constructs are already 'infected' by first order constructs.

The irrevocable and inevitable connections between ordinary language and that of the technical language of sociology and the other social sciences *has* been recognized in a variety of contexts. Caton (1963: viii, cited in Turner 1974: 8), for example, observes:

> Technical language is ... a part of some language like English or French and a part defined only by reference to some particular discipline or occupation or activity among the practitioners of which it is current ... Further, it seems clear that numerous ubiquitous words and phrases occur in technical contexts in the same senses or used in the same ways in which they are used in everyday contexts: eg, articles, the verb 'to be', 'all', 'some', 'too', 'at lease', 'there is', 'and', 'or', 'if.. then', 'hardly', 'very', etc   For example, surely the quote the 'are' of 'Cannines are vertebrates' is the 'are' of 'Dogs are animals'.   Also, most of the kinds of utterances involving technical language appear to already found in ordinary language - I mean requests, assertions questions, explanations of what one was referring to, etc

Furthermore,

> There are two further relations between ordinary and technical language which I do not think have been sufficiently emphasised. First, that the clarification of what someone is saying usually is achieved by using devices which are already a part of ordinary language and which are taken over into and used in dealing with technical language.   And second, that whatever technical language a person may acquire is, and, as things are, has to be acquired against the background of ordinary language

In a similar vein Coulter (1974: 108) remarks:

> Sociologists generally share the natural-language of their subjects, and this has involved them in a tacit pre-understanding of their identification of the environment (social and physical) in linguistic categories.   Ethnomethodology seeks to explore the dynamics of members' understandings as observable features of social settings, whilst holding that such dynamics also characterise the sociologists' procedures for recognising data

More recently, Sharrock and Watson (1989: 433) declare:

> [S]ociology itself is a natural language pursuit, one carried on and reported in some one of the variety of natural languages and one which requires, depends on and employs the (largely) unexamined descriptive resources of such language.

MCA shows how the use of devices, categories and their predicates provides for the intelligibility of the substantive domains and topics of sociological inquiry. Thus such resources are deployed in making available for study such phenomena as 'schools', 'classrooms', 'criminals', 'courtrooms', 'bosses' and 'workers', 'men' and 'women'. The intelligibility of these social identities, institutions and activities, and therefore of the substantive sub-disciplines of sociology, depend upon the use by members, of MCA. Jayyusi (1984: 3) makes this point, for example, with respect to the domain of the sociology of deviance. As she indicates, this comprises 'the morally displayed and premised descriptions of persons by other persons (either lay or 'officials').' She continues,

> Indeed, the very sociological term 'deviant' is a normative description of members produced by, and incorporated or presupposed within, the corpus of sociological work 'Labelling theory' attempts to address the process of labelling someone 'deviant'. However, the categorization 'deviant' obscures the very diverse procedures, implications and consequences behind the production, use, display and practical intelligibility of various categorizations subsumed by that sociological rubric: murderer, marijuana user, prostitute, alcoholic, child molester, etc.

Sociologists do not then, as a rule, make problematic the nature of the contexts and the actors they investigate. Speaking, for example, of the domain of education, Sharrock and Button (1991: 159) state:

> sociologists of education make studies to find out what goes on in classrooms, but they do not require explicit, specially developed methods to find relevant data. They certainly do not set out to study some activities and then *discover* that these events take place in classrooms (or that their taking place in classrooms is the 'best explanation' for them). They might discover, say, that teachers are more prejudiced against certain kinds of students than we had imagined, but they do not discover that these events are events-in-a-classroom, nor that the categories 'teacher' and 'pupil' are the best pair of categories for collecting together their observations. They start to collect observations as events-within-

a-classroom and they order them, furthermore, in terms of the relationship between 'teacher' and 'pupils' from the very beginning They do not, that is, derive the categories 'classroom', 'teacher' and 'pupil' on the basis of a set of observations, but organize their observations and descriptions on the basis of those categories which are *in place from the very beginning*. They are, of course, in place from the very beginning because they are *institutionalised* (so to speak) in the social setting that is being described, because they are *socially sanctioned ways of describing* events which take place in that setting

The point applies not only to the identification of types of person and setting for investigation but also to the identification of persons' talk and other actions as instances of acts, processes, beliefs, motives and conditions comprising the sociological topics of inquiry. In achieving sociological translations of members' actions the sociologist is employing in unexplicated fashion his/her own competence in categorizational sense-making to render members, their features, actions and settings as instantiations of sociological concepts.[1]

Professional Sociology Respecified as Membership Categorization
The EM and, in particular, MCA conception of social structure discussed earlier allows us a particular vision of sociological practice and especially sociological practice of the 'structural variety'. This we would suggest is a 'professionalized' form of membership categorization. Thus, our interests are not limited to lay membership categorization, nor to the tacit membership categorization of professional substantive sociological work. Rather they extend to the work of professional members whose stock-in-trade is a distinctive collection of social configurations and membership categories, and where a major part of what is done with them is to examine the interconnections between categories of actions, categories of persons and categories of social configurations. If, indeed, members' MC 'analysis' is folk sociology, then professional sociology is folk sociology writ large. MCA provides us with a method of seeing this in the detail of sociological inquiries. Though not expressed in the full-blown language of MCA we are using here, this direction of inquiry has to some extent been anticipated by Sharrock (1974: 45) in the following passage:

Sociologists routinely treat the activities of society's members as being somehow related to on or another corpus of knowledge: it is supposed that there must be some connection between what members know and what they do. The use of such notions as 'culture', 'perspective', 'ideology' and 'world view' has not only been intended to convey the idea that members' activities are to be construed by reference to some corpus of knowledge but also that the corpus of knowledge itself must be viewed as being in some way associated with the collectivity in which the actors have membership. The problem for sociologists has not, then, been that of finding a relationship between any member's knowledge and his activities but, instead, that of interpreting the relationship between a collectivity's corpus of knowledge and the activities of its members

This, we suggest, hints at the respecification of sociology's foundational methods as a topic of EM enquiry. More directly related to our present programmatic remarks Jayyusi (1984: 52) says:

> Much of members' social theorising is organized through the production and provision for collectivities in talk as morally organized groups and the characterization and description of individuals and their actions as relative to, and accountable in terms of, their membership in such groups.

We can clearly do no more here than indicate in a preliminary way what we take to be the promise of this avenue of inquiry. We will develop brief illustrations for three standard sociological perspectives. The conceptual machinery comprising the various sociological perspectives and the uses to which they are put in sociological inquiry is a form of 'professional' MCA. Thus the perspectives differ in terms of three major conceptual elements of MCA: (a) the models both of the singular actor (membership category) and collective actor (collectivity-category) they employ, presuppose or afford, (b) the membership categorization devices in which these actors are collected, and (c) the features or predicates they attach to such theoretical categories of actor.

For a first example, in the *structural consensus perspective*, society is posited as a 'system' with constituent 'roles' into which persons are 'socialised'. These ideas can be seen to be deployed according to the logic informing the use of categories, devices and predicates. Categories are the 'roles', devices are the institutional collections of roles (such as comprise religion, family, education, work, etc), and predicates are 'role expectations'. Much sociological practice under the aegis of this perspective consists of the 'discovery' and 'fabrication' of sociological categories of persons whose assigned social characteristics (predicates), derived from the social configurations within which they are sociologically located, account for their behaviour.

Similarly, for a second example, we may note, after Jayyusi, a characteristic turn in *Marxist sociology* by which collections of persons are turned into morally-organized collectivities:

> The concept of 'hegemonic' class, for instance, in the Marxist tradition is routinely made to work by constituting, through its situated use, a collectivity morally organized with respect to the ideas, values, commitments, etc. that are said to be hegemonic. It can also thus constitute another collectivity (the 'hegemonized' one) as one that is morally organized in a subordinate way, but which could be organized differently.

That is, each form of society (or historical stage) is marked by the ascendancy of a particular class-category which is one half of a standardized relational pair - 'freeman and slave, patrician and plebeian, lord and serf, guildmaster and journeyman, ... Bourgeoisie and Proletariat'. Moreover, category-bound activities are predicated of these pairs: 'in a word, oppressor and oppressed, stood in constant opposition to one another, carried on an uninterrupted, now hidden, now open fight ...'. Revolutionary reconstitution of society is a matter of category transformation. Theories of capital accumulation and of revolution involve extended predicates of the contending class-categories. Category and predicate provide methods for assigning actors and actions their proper identities, methods, in short, for reading history and society. A similar re-specification might be offered, one would think, for feminist theorising that depends on the relational pairing of the categories 'men' and 'women' (with associated 'qualifications') as 'parties to patriarchy'.

Finally, for a third example, in the *symbolic interactionist* tradition social action is accounted for in terms of the cultural predicates (knowledge, belief, values, norms, definitions of the situation, etc.) which are tied to particular collectivities (for example, industrial workers, drug users, taxi drivers, cocktail waitresses). It may be further understood as the outcome of category-bound strategic practices construed as deriving from, say, demand characteristics of the social configuration in which they are located. Thus the demands of the courtroom (say, for disposing of cases) become the category-tied motives of such courtroom personnel as 'public defender' and thereby are made to account for, say, their routine involvement in plea bargaining.

The subject matter of membership categorization analysis - membership categories, membership categorization devices and category predicates - infuses lay and professional sociological practical reasoning. The studies in this collection attest to the pervasiveness of this phenomenon and demonstrate, we hope, the vitality of this particular form of ethnomethodological inquiry. Through this concluding excursus on MCA's relationship to, and re-specification, of sociology we hope to have shown, in addition, its promise of radically recasting the discipline from which it sprang.

Notes

Chapter one
1. Early summary accounts are provided by Speier (1970, 1973). The following sketch of the central concepts of MCA is largely taken from Hester (forthcoming).
2. They begin with Sacks (1974a) and Schegloff (1972). Jefferson (1974: 198) touches briefly on MCA, and Schegloff (1988) returns to Sacks's treatment in the context of posing the problem of description. However, after Sacks himself apparently turned away from MCA inquiries to concentrate more on sequential CA, Schegloff, Jefferson, Pomerantz, Charles Goodwin, Marjorie Goodwin, J.M. Atkinson, Heritage and other analysts who developed this prolific field paid relatively little attention to categorisational topics in their work. Curiously, in two published papers directly dealing with members' management of identity reference (Sacks 1979; Sacks and Schegloff 1979) the language of MCA is virtually absent. In another set of studies, illuminating fragments of MCA have been subordinated to sequential conversation analysis (Brannigan and Lynch 1987: 127-128; Halkowski 1990; Marlaire and Maynard 1990; Maynard and Zimmerman 1984). For MCA studies in the context of the Manchester School's 'ethnographic conversation[al] analysis' see the next section below. For critical reflection on the 'separation' of CA and MCA see Watson (1994) and Chapter Three in this collection.
3. There is a 'branching texture' to the organisation of membership categories and membership categorisation devices, in that, depending on context, a category may be used within a device or it may operate as a device in its own right. Similarly, erstwhile devices may be 'transformed' into categories (cf. Eglin and Hester 1992: 254, 250; Jayyusi 1984: chp 4; Schegloff 1972: 95ff).
4. This section is adapted from Eglin and Hester (1992).
5. Further and subsequent conceptual innovation can be found in Hester (1990, forthcoming) where the notions of 'category disclaimers,' 'category substitution,' 'category warrantability,' 'category mistakes' (pace Ryle), and 'anticipatory categorisation' are developed.
6. The argument in this section is a revised version of Hester and Eglin (1992a). See also Hester (1994).
7. For a critique of this 'once-and-for-all' conception of decontextualised meanings, see Coulter (1971) and Hester (1985).
8. One of the dangers with the distinction is that of appearing to endorse an old shibboleth to be found in critiques of EM, namely that sense-making varies with the 'degree of indexicality' of category use: some categories are more indexical than others, goes the argument (e.g. Abercrombie 1974; Goldthorpe 1973). See Benson (1974) for the EM corrective.
9. We have found that it is easy to be drawn into a debate over pre-existent versus constructed collections, with family and sex at one end and supposedly 'topic occasioned' collections at the other Following Sacks's recommended test of whether a collection is natural or topic-occasioned, namely can one answer the question 'What are the members of the class?', we descended into the murky waters of arguing over the significance of the relative ease with which one can provide

categories for the sex collection compared to the apparently indefinitely extendable list of imaginable members of various topic-occasioned classes. While, as we have shown, it is easy enough to make problematic the answer 'males and females' to the sex test in the direction of showing that there could be different answers on different occasions for different purposes so that the possible members of the collection sex comes to resemble those of topic-occasioned collections, we reminded ourselves of the essential EM point of indifference to all such questions, namely that all issues and questions of order and sense are unrelievedly local and indexical. This means that the question 'Does the collection exist prior to particular occasions?' is misleading from an EM point of view since its answer would involve another situated, local course of practical reasoning, another instance of order production, and it is that locally achieved state of affairs which is EM's phenomenon not the production of conceptual stipulations. This means then, to repeat, that Sacks's distinction is potentially misleading. EM's interest is in the occasionality of *all* collections, as they are used by members. This does not negate the possibility that for members the categories of a collection comprise for them the natural facts of life and are oriented to as such, but for EM the interest is in members' use of such facts, how they are made out to be facts; culture does not exist independently of its production.

10. This lecture, dated February 16th 1966, was published in *Pragmatics Microfiche* 1976. There is no corresponding lecture in Sacks's *Lectures on Conversation*, though parts of it are contained in a lecture dated February 16th 1967.

11. We note here the relevance of the discussion by Zimmerman and Wieder (1971) of the 'occasioned corpus.' Other critiques of cognitive anthropology, both direct and indirect, include Eglin (1980), Sharrock and Anderson (1982), Wieder (1971), Wilson (1971), and Zimmerman (1974b).

Chapter Two

Acknowledgements: We are grateful to Jac Eke for her comments on an earlier version of this paper.

1. In this connection, Lynch speaks of the 'pre-interpretive intelligibility of conversation in action' and the 'prereflective way in which members hear utterances and act in accord with the 'heard' order of events in a conversation'. See Lynch (1993: 227).

2. These are discussed at length in Hester (forthcoming)

3. This extract is an edited version of a much longer transcript. The talk which is 'off topic' as far as this analysis is concerned has been omitted.

4. When confronted with the headline written up on the blackboard, students in Eglin's sociology of suicide classes report being quite confident about the above reading, with about ten percent taking it that 'officer' refers to a military man Moreover, many are inclined to think that the girlfriend's death was recent, probably within a few weeks, that the officer felt in some way responsible for it, and even that she herself might have committed suicide. Although it turns out from reading the article that these points are correct, we contend that they are distinct from the 'primary' reading The latter is more or less constitutive of

the good sense of the headline, whereas the former are merely probable. If the secondary points were not true we would not lose the sense of the headline. But if the primary reading were not true could we yet make sense of it? On the distinction between constitutive (or rule-based) and probabilistic features of human action see, from different disciplines, the similar accounts of Chomsky (1957), Goodenough (1969) and Searle (1969); see Eglin (1980: 19-22)

5. The matter of the interpretive basis for the 'male' reading is clearly of some interest given current concerns, but is something we would prefer to defer to another occasion.

6. It is at this point perhaps that the reader can also find some additional account of such an unusual event in the particulars provided in the headline. For him to have done that - he must have really loved her, this dead girlfriend; he must have felt responsible for her being in that grave; did she commit suicide too? That would explain it.

Chapter Three

1 One partial exception to this pattern is to be found in Atkinson (1978: 191-5); others are Benson and Hughes (1983: 132-9) and Hester and Eglin (1992b: 117-30).

2. Boden and Zimmerman (1991) contains a variety of papers on the agency-structure debate, though the issue of sociological description *per se* is often only indirectly addressed. See also Sharrock and Watson (1988), for a more direct treatment.

3. See, for an interesting overview and empirically-based discussion, Heritage and Roth (1995).

4. It is to be noted that I am not here alluding to any 'defects' in what are, in fact, two of the finest analyses of institutional talk: instead, I am addressing the methodological decisions that are rendered 'textually incarnate' in the making of such transcripts and that are made available as predisposing interpretative saliences for readers.

5. In one transcript (P239) Frankel provides the doctor and patient categorisations in the immediately preceding paragraph It is also to be noted that categorial identities may be furnished in the title of the article, as is the case in Frankel's paper: these too may be conceived as 'predisposing interpretative saliences'. I am not for a moment suggesting that the authors concerned are unaware of this aspect of their transcription and analytic practices, only that a) the methodological implications for conversation analysis have not been followed through, and b) the claims made in conversation analysis disattend these implications

6 On the chaining rule for ordinary (non-institutional) conversation, see Sacks (1974a: 230 -1) Of course, there are some sequential formats in 'institutional talk' that do not reduce to the chaining rule It might be added here that conversational analysts are, to highly varying degrees, explicitly cognisant of some of the issues concerning categorized identification in talk and transcript. However, to be cognisant of such issues does not guarantee that all the

available methodological options for addressing them will necessarily be entertained. For a thoughtful consideration of such matters, see Schegloff (1991). This paper attests to matters such as the mutability of what I have here termed salient categorial orientations and this, of course, renders categorial analysis a delicate and difficult operation. A difficulty is not an impossibility, however, as I hope to indicate below. It does, however, indicate an intractable difficulty for transcribers of 'institutional talk', i.e. that of stipulating categorial hearings in a constructivist manner We might agree with Schegloff that 'institutional' orientations in talk should be analytically focalized only if they appear in the detail of the talk - depending, that is, on how '(salient) details' is defined and analytically handled

7. I attempted ten years ago, in a preliminary and undeveloped way, to pursue the research protocol suggested (see Watson 1986).. The article attempts to explicate the categorial relevances of serial organisations such as disclosure-elicitation sequences.

8. Here, we do not necessarily have to agree, fully or at all, with the characterization of conversation-analytic work as 'mechanistic'/'positivistic'/ 'abstracted empiricism' in order to warrant the following analysis: the question is 'how do recent conversation analyses, on occasion, get to be seen that way?'

9. A variant version of this article was published in Schenkein, *op cit.*: 7-55. Their comments on recipient design occur on pp. 42-3 of the latter version

10. A case in point is preference organisation: see Sacks and Schegloff (1979)

11. Pronominal transformations across utterances in a sequence constitute but one case in point. See, for example, Sacks (1992a [1968, 1967]: 716-38; [1966]: 376 ff; [1965]: 157 ff), and also Speier (1973).

12. See their classic article (Schegloff and Sacks 1973), reprinted in slightly abridged form in Turner (1974) The characterization to which I am referring can be found on p. 238 of the latter reference.

13. For a development of this argument concerning MCDs, see the Editors' 'Introduction' to this volume and an application to data in Hester (1994). For an analytic application of the notion of 'assembled object', see Garfinkel (1967 [1984]: Ch. 5), and for some comments on this notion, see Messinger, Sampson and Towne (1962). For an earlier study of an MCD as an assembled object (in that case, 'parties to a rape'), see Lee (1984)

14. For an example of such work, note the artful use of the consistency rule and MCD organisation in the following in a move to achieve a shift in a reply whilst maintaining device relevances given in the question. Here, a police officer is being questioned by an attorney during a tribunal enquiring into a set of disturbances in Northern Ireland:

```
1      C:      So when you baton charged the Catholic
2              crowd for the second time you knew, because of
3              your previous experience, that the Protestant crowd
4              were likely to follow you
5      W:      I did
6      C:      How far did you drive the Catholic crowd
```

7		at that time?
8	W:	I stopped in Dover Street and nobody went
9		very far past me and no-one went on Divis Street
10		from the Protestant crowd
11	C:	No-one went very far past you, you say?
12	W:	No-one got more than a few yards past me.

(continues)

(NB: C = Attorney, W = Police Officer)

This data extract is taken from Atkinson and Drew (1979: 157) Again, this extract is offered in the present paper only for indicative purposes.

15. For more extended comments on analytic irony than can be offered here, see Anderson and Sharrock (1983), also Watson (1992) and Watson (forthcoming).

16. See, for instance, Sacks's oral declaration on pp. 12-14 of Hill and Crittenden (1968). This declaration may, in part, be seen as Sacks's distancing of his work from that of componential analysts.

17. On the advantages and pitfalls in the analytic use of such imagery, see Watson (forthcoming).

18. On 'caller'-'called' as turn-generated categories, see Sacks's*Lectures, op. cit.*, Lecture 19 (Spring 1971), Lecture 5, (Winter 1970) and Lecture 5 (Autumn 1971) Many of his 'caller'-'called' considerations derive from his New Year's Eve 1964' transcripts of calls to a 'suicide prevention center'.

19 On the notion of the unit 'a single conversation' as an 'overall structural organisation' see Schegloff and Sacks (1974).

20. This example, and the preceding and succeeding analysis of called-specific and caller-specific techniques is derived from Schegloff and Sacks (1974: 249), though I have chosen to focalize the categorial aspects of their analysis.

21. But not the first: *vide* Geoffrey Chaucer's *The Pardoner's Tale.* These 'practical reifications' of what is such a contextually-embedded categorial identity are worthy of serious examination on their own behalf.

22. A 'party' may refer to more than one person, e.g. two or more persons walking together.

23. For an initial formulation of this analysis, see Lee and Watson (1993a).

24 For a preliminary analysis of this, see Watson (1994) I should particularly like to thank my co-researcher John Lee and also our Plan Urbain research team colleagues Kenneth J. Brown, Michèle Jolé, Georges Knaebel and Isabelle Haumont for their contributions to the above analyses of locomotion and formations in public space in urban areas.

25. For the 'sequential' formulation of the context-freedom and context-sensitivity of natural conversation, see Sacks, Schegloff and Jefferson, in Schenkein (1978: 9-10 and *passim*)

26. Not to mention those of Sociolinguists, Pragmaticians, Ethnographers of Communication and social scientists who transcribe interviews in these ways, as conduits to 'social structures', 'institutional orders' etc.

27. An early, and most lucidly argued, formulation of such a policy concerning topic and resource is to be found in Zimmerman and Pollner (1971).

---

28. The authors treat 'the issue of' unaquainted persons as a kind of control in sampling terms (controlling for the effect of intimacy, friendship or aquaintance, p. 103) on interruptive activity. My argument is that 'unaquainted persons'/'strangers' are identities for-conversation too and as such may potentially form a basis for a range of recipient design features of the talk (including interruptive work) or some sequence in the talk. Either way, interlocutors' orientations to one or other identity (gender, 'stranger', etc) has to be analytically documented in more than a quasi-correlational way.

29. This study also manifests the way in which the very characterization of utterances by the analyst is influenced by categorial considerations

Chapter Four

Acknowledgements: I wish to thank the principal and staff for their support for this research, their agreement to tape-recording, and their time spent in talking about the school and welfare system The principal, deputy principal and chair of the welfare committee were particularly generous. Stephen Hester made valuable editorial suggestions.

Chapter Five

1. Bok's definition is corroborated in the more playful and nuanced treatment of lying in Barnes (1994: 11). Barnes also mentions that lies, lying and deception are 'slippery' concepts which defy tight definition.

2. For cogent arguments on the difference between academic concerns with 'epistemology' and 'motives' and ordinary concerns with knowing and knowledge, see Sharrock and Anderson (1991: 51-76); and Sharrock and Watson (1984: 435-451).

3. The relevant ethnomethodological policies toward work in the professions were developed by Harold Garfinkel See Garfinkel (1991); and Garfinkel and Wieder (1992). For a summary treatment, see Lynch (1993: Ch. 7)

4. Viewed from a more critical perspective, the encounter might be treated as evidence for the operation of the normalizing judgement deployed by an official in a carceral institution See Foucault (1979) and Goffman (1962). The point here, however, is that the doctor deploys a non-technical conception of what the patient can have known about his past

5. Analyses of the relations among membership categories, activities, and moral entitlements include Watson (1978) and Jayyusi (1984). For a study of police interrogations using membership category analysis see Watson (1990) A cogent review article on membership category analysis is Eglin and Hester (1992: 243-68)

6. Ekman's discussion of these examples focuses on salience or 'memorability' of the events in question, but he does not directly acknowledge the importance of the occupational categories and associated responsibilities for information.

7. Counterfactual conditionals often are used when persons speak of what they understood, intended, knew, or were disposed to do, under conditions where

such understandings, etc. did not concretely manifest. See Budd (1984 esp. 312).

8. Graham (1978: 162) asserts that, 'Feigned lack of recollection more frequently constitutes a tacit admission rather than a denial of the prior statement.' Whether or not this is so, interrogators rarely have the advantage of knowing whether or not a witness is 'feigning' particular disavowals of recall

9. Our descriptive interest in the situated use of counterfactual conditionals differs considerably from Hempel's and Goodman's formal analytic treatments

10. This is a variant of the 'witness's dilemma' discussed in Brannigan and Lynch (1987). Also see Drew (1992).

11. The idea that ordinary conversational usage exhibits a logic, even though it does not follow the straight and narrow path of formal logic, is discussed by Coulter (1991).

12. For a concise exhibit of how lawyers can demonstrably 'know' an expert witness's business, and expose apparent lapses of procedure, see Oteri, Weinberg, and Pinales (1982)

13. See Cuff (1994) for a similar criticism made about the tightness of the link Sacks draws between category and action, and the abstractness of the devices he formulates. Also see Eglin and Hester (1992: 261)

Chapter Six
Acknowledgments: The authors wish to thank Steve Hester for his extensive and valuable comments on earlier versions of this chapter

1. In relation to the analysis of texts, it is a commonplace of contemporary interpretive theory that texts are 'open' rather than 'closed', and that the meaning of any text is constituted in the act of reading (Iser 1978; Fish 1980). This view of textual meaning resonates with the perspective of ethnomethodology. Both emphasise the 'accomplished' character of understandings and reject any view of meaning as something *mapped onto* a pre-given or underlying 'reality'. Like the interpretive theorist, the ethnomethodologist conceives the meaning of a text as produced in and through the relationship between text and reader. However, notwithstanding this broad similarity, the differences between these two approaches are significant. Contemporary interpretive theory, especially in its 'post- or super-structuralist' manifestations (Derrida 1978; Harland 1988) tends towards an epistemological and moral stance on these matters. From the stand-point of post-structuralism, rooted as this approach is in the tradition of philosophical scepticism, it is argued that all meaning is 'groundless'. Since there can be no 'definitive' readings but only 'preferred' ones, then every act of reading is 'political'; each reading involves the implementation of some interpretive possibilities to the exclusion of others. By 'opting' for a given reading, the reader performs a political act, one which cannot have *empirical* justification. For the post-structuralist, then, the act of reading is an act of 'closure' or 'violence'. Ethnomethodology eschews such moral and epistemological theorising; from its stand-point the 'act of reading' (understood in either a

literal or a metaphorical sense) is simply one of an infinite variety of acts in and through which the *mundanely accountable* character of the world is accomplished

2. Sacks's question, 'how does it matter (to members) that something describable as a story is produced *so as to be recognisable as a story*' (Sacks 1992b: 222-3), directs analytic attention to the ways in which that some stretch of talk involves the telling of a story is *interactionally* consequential for conversational participants. Thus Sacks shows how conversational stories are built to be understood *as such* in their course, in and through the ways in which story-telling talk is fitted to its local interactional context. His studies of the sequential 'management' of storytelling in conversation exemplify his methodological commitment to investigating the activity of storytelling in terms of *participants' displayed orientations*. However, turn-by-turn organization constitutes only one context in which something is oriented to as a story can be 'something that matters'. Another is the *re-telling* of stories. Sacks, again, has examined some features of story re-telling in conversation, such as, for example, when a story recipient in one conversation 'passes on' the story to a third party in another conversation. What has not been studied, however, is the phenomenon of re-telling *across different* 'story vehicles'.

3. This is a methodological and practical question and raises no fundamental *epistemological* issues. It is no different *in principle* to the problem of representation confronting conversation analysts working with audio-recordings and transcriptions of talk (Bogen 1992; Psathas and Anderson 1990). Just as the conversation analyst's mundane *members' conversational competence* is constitutive of and provides the basis for their representations of some stretch of talk in the form of a transcript, so our members' mundane competence as 'everyday narrativists' provides for our ability to represent our phenomenon in the form of a story In line with the analytic orientation recommended by Sacks, we take it that the re-tellability of the story of the television commercial is one way in which *that* it is a story 'matters'.

4. Part of the Ph D project in the course of which the materials analysed in this chapter were gathered involved ethnographic study of the advertising agency which created it We make no further use of nor reference to this study for the purposes of this paper, but for those interested, see Hart (1993).

5. The concept 'affordance' derives from the work of the psychologist James J Gibson (1979). In borrowing the concept for our own (sociological) purposes, we stress that we would not endorse fully the uses to which Gibson puts it. For a critique of Gibson's work from an ethnomethodological point of view, see Sharrock & Coulter (1996).

6. In his discussion of the telling of a dirty joke in conversation (Sacks 1978), Sacks considers the 'designed economy' of stories. He notes that this phenomenon was a constitutive feature of the storytelling in the western cultural tradition until it was explicitly rejected by certain 20th century wrtiers. Sacks emphasises the historical significance of Gorky in breaking with

narrative tradition by having characters who 'simply appeared and disappeared' with no apparent relevance to the central action.

7. 'Motivational texture' therefore involves two elements of Kenneth Burke's 'key terms of dramatism' - namely 'agency' and 'purpose' (Burke 1962). 'Agency' Burke defines as the 'how he did it' of an agent's motivated course of conduct, while 'purpose' refers to the 'why' which informs and shapes that course. In Burkeian terms, then, the unfolding narrative makes available to the viewer a certain *'agent-agency-purpose ratio'*.

8. We are aware that, in speaking of the use of 'I' as 'referring' we are treading on philosophically sticky ground, and might be accused of taking up a controversial position within a debate over whether it is legitimate philosophically to conceive of 'I' as a term of 'reference'. (See, for example, Champlin 1988: ch 9). We simply assert that, in speaking this way, it is not our intention to endorse any particular position within that debate.

9. Following Wittgenstein's (1958) arguments about the public availability and accountability of 'subjective' emotional and mental states, it is clear that expressions of feelings are socially and normatively accountable, and that emotions and actions are linked in 'grammatical' ways. (See also Louch 1968).

10. The notion of a 'grammar' of socio-emotion is one which has been employed by others in relation to the contextualisation of motivated activities. For example, Eglin and Hester (1992) speak of a 'grammar of suicide' in emphasising the ways in which avowals of suicidalness by persons are commonsensically tied to anticipateable circumstances.

11. On the utility of the notion of a 'gestalt' linking motives, identities and predicates ascribed to persons and their situated actions, see Lynch (1995).

12. This understanding invokes commonsense knowledge about the nature of pubs, such as the one depicted, as 'locals'. A 'local' - in British culture - is a pub which is frequented by some collection of persons who not just use the pub regularly, but also use it for the purpose of sociability with others who may be anticipated to be found there. This set of persons are identifiable as 'the regulars'; typically they have patterns of use and levels of shared activity which mark them out from other kinds of users, such as those who use the pub 'occasionally' or those who are 'strangers'. The 'local', therefore, is defined as such by its distinctively *communal* character. To be a 'regular' is to be part of this community. As a collectivity, therefore, the regulars can come to acquire the characteristics of a *team* One such characteristic is the *accountability of absence;* any member of the group who 'fails to appear' can have this noticed, queried, commented upon, and so forth.

Chapter Seven

1. Hester (1992), for example, has analysed how the referral talk of teachers and educational psychologists can be recognized, through a course of membership categorization, as talk about 'deviance'

Bibliography

Abercrombie, N. (1974). Sociological indexicality. *Journal for the Theory of Social Behaviour* 4(1):89-95.

Albert, E. (1964). Rhetoric, logic and poetics in Burundi: culture patterning of speech and behaviour *American Anthropologist* 66(6-part 2):33-54.

Anderson, D. G. and Sharrock, W. W. (1979). Biasing the news: technical issues in 'media studies'. *Sociology* 13 (3): 367-385.

Anderson, D. G. and Sharrock, W. W. (1983). Irony as a methodological theory. *Poetics Today* 4(3):565-579.

Anderson, R. J. and Sharrock, W. W. (1993). Can organisations afford knowledge? *Computer Supported Cooperative Work (CSCW)* 1:143-161.

Atkinson, J. M. (1978). *Discovering Suicide: Studies in the Organisation of Sudden Death*. London: Macmillan.

Atkinson, J. M. and Drew, P. (1979). *Order in Court: The Organisation of Verbal Interaction in Judicial Settings*. London: Macmillan.

Atkinson, J. M. and Heritage, J. (Eds) (1984). *Structures of Social Action: Studies in Conversation Analysis*. Cambridge and Paris: Cambridge University Press and Maison des Sciences de l'Homme.

Atkinson, M. A. (1980). Some practical uses of a 'natural lifetime'. *Human Studies* 3(1):33-46.

Atkinson, M. A., Cuff, E. C. and Lee, J. R. E. (1978). The re-commencement of a meeting as a members' accomplishment. In J. N. Schenkein (Ed.), *Studies in the Organisation of Conversational Interaction*. New York: Academic.

Atkinson, P. (1985). Talk and identity: some convergences in micro-sociology. In H. J. Helle and S. N. Eisenstadt (Eds.), *Micro-Sociological Theory, vol 2* London: Sage, Studies in International Sociology, no 34 (Proceedings of the World Conference of Sociology at Mexico City, 1982).

Atkinson, P. (1988). Ethnomethodology: a critical review. *Annual Review of Sociology* 14: 117-32.

Baker, C. D. (1982). Adolescent-adult talk as a practical interpretive problem. In G. C. F Payne and E C. Cuff (Eds), *Doing Teaching: The Practical Management of Classrooms*. London: Batsford.

Baker, C D. (1984). The 'search for adultness:' membership in adolescent-adult talk *Human Studies* 7 (3/4):301-24.

Baker, C. D. and Freebody, P. (1987). 'Constituting the child' in beginning school reading books. *British Journal of Sociology of Education* 8(1):55-76.

Barnes, J. A. (1994). *A Pack of Lies: Towards a Sociology of Lying*. Cambridge, UK. Cambridge University Press.

Bennett, A. (1994). *Writing Home*. London: Faber and Faber.

Benson, D. (1974). Reply to Goldthorpe. *Sociology* 8:124-33.

Benson, D. and Drew, P. (1978) 'Was there firing in Sandy Row that night?'· some features of the organisation of disputes about recorded facts *Sociological Inquiry* 48:89-100.

Benson, D. and Hughes, J. A. (1983) *The Perspective of Ethnomethodology*. London and New York: Longman.

Bogen, D. (1992) The organisation of talk *Qualitative Sociology* 15(3):273-295.

Bok, S. (1979). *Lying: Moral Choice in Public and Private Life.* New York: Random House.

Brannigan, A. and Lynch, M (1987). On bearing false witness: perjury and credibility as interactional accomplishments. *Journal of Contemporary Ethnography* 16(2):115-46.

Budd, M. (1984). Wittgenstein on meaning, interpretation and rules. *Synthese* 58:303-323.

Burke, K. (1962[1945]). *A Grammar of Motives.* New York: Meridian Books.

Button, G. (1977). Comments on conversation analysis. *Analytic Sociology* 1(2): D09-E14.

Button, G. (Ed.) (1991). *Ethnomethodology and the Human Sciences* Cambridge, UK: Cambridge University Press.

Button, G and Lee, J R. E. (Eds.) (1987). *Talk and Social Organisation.* Clevedon: Multilingual Matters.

Caton, C. E. (Ed.) (1963). *Philosophy and Ordinary Language.* University of Illinois Press.

Champlin, T. S. (1988). *Reflexive Paradoxes.* London: Routledge.

Chomsky, N. (1968) *Language and Mind.* New York: Harcourt, Brace and World.

Cicourel, A. V. (1973). The acquisition of social structure: towards a developmental sociology of language and meaning. In A. V. Cicourel *Cognitive Sociology: Language and Meaning in Social Interaction.* Harmondsworth: Penguin Education Books.

Cicourel, A. V. and Kitsuse, J. (1971). The social organisation of the high school and deviant adolescent careers. In B. R. Cosin et al (Eds.), *School and Society: A Sociological Reader, Second edition.* London and Henley: Routledge and Kegan Paul / The Open University Press.

Coulter, J. (1971) Decontextualised meanings: current approaches to *Verstehende* investigations. *Sociological Review* 19(3):301-23.

Coulter, J (1973). Language and the conceptualisation of meaning *Sociology* 7(2):173-89.

Coulter, J. (1974). The ethnomethodological programme in contemporary sociology. *The Human Context* 6(1):103-122.

Coulter, J. (1975). Perceptual accounts and interpretive asymmetries *Sociology* 9:385-396.

Coulter, J. (1982). Remarks on the conceptualisation of social structure. *Philosophy of the Social Sciences* 12(1):33-46.

Coulter, J (1983a). Contingent and *a priori* structures in sequential analysis. *Human Studies* 6(4):361-376.

Coulter, J. (1983b). *Rethinking Cognitive Theory* New York: St. Martin's Press.

Coulter, J (1991). Logic: ethnomethodology and the logic of language. In G Button (Ed.), *Ethnomethodology and the Human Sciences* Cambridge, UK: Cambridge University Press.

Coulter, J (1992). *Mind in Action* Cambridge, UK: Polity Press.

Coulter, J. (Ed.) (1990). *Ethnomethodological Sociology* Brookfield, VT. Edward Elgar

Cuff, E. C. (1978). Some features of production accounting in the analysis of 'conversational materials' *Analytic Sociology* 1(4): A03-B02.

Cuff, E. C. (1994). *The Problem of Versions in Everyday Situations*. International Institute for Ethnomethodology and Conversation Analysis, and University Press of America. (Originally published in 1980 as Some Issues in Studying the Problem of Versions in Everyday Life *Occasional Papers in Sociology* No. 3, Manchester: University of Manchester, Department of Sociology.)

Cuff, E. C. and Francis, D. W (1978). Some features of 'invited stories' about marriage breakdown *International Journal for the Sociology of Language* Special issue on Conversational Analysis, 18: 111-133.

Cuff, E. C. and Payne, G. C. F. (Eds) (1984). *Perspectives in Sociology*, Second edition, London: George Allen and Unwin.

Cuff, E C. and Sharrock, W. W. (1985). Meetings. In T. A. van Dijk (Ed), *Handbook of Discourse Analysis: Volume 3, Discourse and Dialogue*. London: Academic.

Cuff, E. C., Sharrock W. W. and Francis, D. (1990). *Perspectives in Sociology*, Third edition. London: Unwin Hyman

Derrida, J. (1978). *Writing and Difference*. Chicago: University of Chicago Press.

Drew, P. (1978). Accusations: the occasioned use of members' knowledge of 'religious geography' in describing events *Sociology* 12(1):1-22 (Revised as Chapter Four in J. M. Atkinson and P. Drew (1979). *Order in Court: The Organisation of Verbal Interaction in Judicial Settings*. London: Macmillan)

Drew, P. (1992). Contested evidence in courtroom cross-examination: The case of a trial for rape. In P. Drew and J. Heritage (Eds), *Talk at Work: Interaction in Institutional Settings*. Cambridge, UK: Cambridge University Press

Eglin, P. (1976). Leaving out the interpreter's work: a methodological critique of ethnosemantics based on ethnomethodology. *Semiotica* 17(4):339-69.

Eglin, P (1980). *Talk and Taxonomy: A Methodological Comparison of Ethnosemantics and Ethnomethodology with Reference to Terms for Canadian Doctors (Pragmatics and Beyond No 8)*. Amsterdam: John Benjamins.

Eglin, P. and Hester, S. (1992). Category, predicate and task: the pragmatics of practical action. *Semiotica* 88:243-68.

Ekman, P (1985). *Telling Lies: Clues to Deceit in the Marketplace, Politics, and Marriage*. New York: Norton.

English, O. S , Hampe, W. W., Bacon, C. L. and Settlage, C. F. (1964). *Direct Analysis and Schizophrenia: Clinical Observations and Evolutions* New York.

Fish, S (1980). *Is There a Text in This Class?* Cambridge, Mass: Harvard University Press.

Fisher, S. and Todd, A. D. (Eds.) (1986) *Discourse and Institutional Authority: Medicine, Education and Law*. Norwood, NJ: Ablex Publishing Corporation (Advances in Discourse Processes, vol. XIX).

Foucault, M. (1979). *Discipline and Punish: The Birth of the Prison*. New York: Random House.

Frake, C. O. (1964). Notes on queries in ethnography *American Anthropologist* 66(3):132-45. (Reprinted in S. A. Tyler (1969) (Ed.), *Cognitive Anthropology.* New York: Holt, Rinehart and Winston.)

Francis, D. (1989). Game identities and activities: some ethnomethodological observations. In D. Crookall and D. Saunders (Eds.), *Communication and Simulation: From Two Fields to One Theme.* Clevedon: Multilingual Matters.

Frankel, R. (1990). Talking in interviews: a dispreference for patient-initiated questions in physician-patient encounters. In G. Psathas (Ed.), *Interaction Competence.* International Institute for Ethnomethodology and Conversation Analysis; Washington, D.C.: University Press of America.

Garfinkel, H (1956) Some sociological concepts and methods for psychiatrists *Psychiatric Research Reports* 6:181-95

Garfinkel, H (1963). A conception of, and experiments with, 'trust' as a condition of stable concerted actions. In O. J Harvey (Ed.), *Motivation and Social Interaction.* New York, NY: Ronald Press.

Garfinkel, H. (1967). *Studies in Ethnomethodology* Englewood Cliffs, NJ: Prentice-Hall. (2nd edition 1984, Cambridge: Polity Press)

Garfinkel, H (1991). Respecification: evidence for locally produced, naturally accountable phenomena of order, logic, reason, meaning, method, etc in and as of the essential haecceity of immortal ordinary society (I) — an announcement of studies. In G. Button (Ed.), *Ethnomethodology and the Human Sciences.* Cambridge, UK: Cambridge University Press.

Garfinkel, H and Sacks, H. (1970). On formal structures of practical actions. In J. C McKinney and E. A. Tiryakian (Eds.), *Theoretical Sociology: Perspectives and Developments.* New York, NY: Appleton-Century-Crofts. (Reprinted in H. Garfinkel (Ed.) (1986). *Ethnomethodological Studies of Work* London: Routledge and Kegan Paul.)

Garfinkel, H. and Wieder, D. L. (1992). Two incommensurable, asymmetrically alternate technologies of social analysis. In G. Watson and R. M Sieler (Eds.), *Text in Context: Contributions to Ethnomethodology.* Newbury Park, U S A, and London, UK: SAGE Focus Editions.

Gibson, J J. (1979). *The Ecological Approach to Visual Perception* Boston, Mass: Houghton Mifflin.

Goffman, E. (1962) *Asylums* Garden City, NY: Doubleday-Anchor.

Goldthorpe, J. (1973). A revolution in sociology? A review article *Sociology* 7:449-62.

Goodenough, W. H. (1957). Cultural anthropology and linguistics. In P. L. Garvin (Ed), *Georgetown Roundtable on Linguistics and Language Study* Washington, D C.: Georgetown University Press.

Goodenough, W H. (1969). Frontiers of cultural anthropology: social organisation *Proceeedings of the American Philosophical Society* 113:329-335

Goodman, N (1983). *Fact, Fiction, and Forecast,* 4th Edition. Cambridge, MA. Harvard University Press

Graham, M. H (1978). The confrontation clause, the hearsay rule, and the forgetful witness. *Texas Law Review* 56:152-205.

Gronn, P. C. (1983). Talk as the work: The accomplishment of school administration. *Administrative Science Quarterly* 28:1-21.

Gronn, P. C. (1984). 'I have a solution...': Administrative power in a school meeting, *Educational Administration Quarterly* 20(2):65-92.

Gumperz, J. J. and Hymes, D. (1972). *Directions in Sociolinguistics*. New York, NY: Free Press.

Hacking, I. (1995). *Rewriting the Soul: Multiple Personality and the Sciences of Memory*. Princeton: NJ: Princeton University Press.

Halkowski, T. (1990). 'Role' as an interactional device. *Social Problems* 37:564-577.

Harland, R. (1988). *Superstructuralism: The Philosophy of Structuralism and Post-Structuralism*. London: Methuen

Hart, C. M. (1993) *Work organisation in the production of an advertisement* Unpublished PhD thesis, Department of Social Science, Manchester Metropolitan University, Manchester, U K

Heap, J. L. (1979). Classroom talk: a critique of McHoul Unpublished manuscript, Deptartment of Sociology in Education, Ontario Institute for Studies in Education, Toronto, Canada.

Heap, J. L. (1990). Applied ethnomethodology: looking for the local rationality of reading activities. *Human Studies* 13(1):39-72.

Hempel, C. (1966). *Philosophy of Natural Science*. Englewood Cliffs, NJ: Prentice Hall.

Heritage, J. (1984). *Garfinkel and Ethnomethodology*. Cambridge: Polity Press

Heritage, J. (1985). Analysing news interviews: aspects of the production of talk for an overhearing audience. In T. A. van Dijk (Ed.), *Handbook of Discourse Analysis, Vol. 3: Discourse and Dialogue*. London: Academic Press

Heritage, J. and Roth, A. L. (1995) Grammar and institution: questions and questioning in the broadcast news interview. *Research and Social Interaction* 28(1):1-60.

Hester, S. (1981). Two tensions in ethnomethodology and conversation analysis *Sociology* 15:108-116.

Hester, S. (1985). Ethnomethodology and the study of deviance in schools. In R Burgess (Ed.), *Strategies of Educational Research: Qualitative Methods* London: Falmer.

Hester, S. (1990). Negotiating next moves in referral talk Paper presented at the World Congress of Sociology, Madrid, July.

Hester, S. (1992). Recognising references to deviance in referral talk. In G Watson and R. M. Sieler (Eds.), *Text in Context: Contributions to Ethnomethodology*. Newbury Park: Sage.

Hester, S. (1994). Les catégories en contexte. *Raisons Pratiques* 5:219-42 Special Issue title 'L'Enquête sur les Catégories: de Durkheim à Sacks', (Ed.), B. Fradin, L. Quéré and J. Widmer. Editions de l'Ecole des Hautes Etudes en Sciences Sociales, Paris.

Hester, S. (forthcoming). *Referral Talk:The Local Order of Deviance in Schools*. Falmer Press

Hester, S. and Eglin, P. (1992a). Natural and occasioned devices in membership categorization analysis. Paper presented at the International Conference of the International Institute for Ethnomethodology and Conversation Analysis, *Ethnomethodology: Twenty Five Years Later.* Bentley College, Waltham, Mass, August.

Hester, S. and Eglin, P. (1992b). *A Sociology of Crime.* London: Routledge.

Hester, S. and Francis, D. (1994). Doing data: the local organisation of a sociological interview. *British Journal of Sociology* 45(4):675-695

Hill, R. J and Crittenden, K. S. (Eds.) (1968). *Proceedings of the Purdue Symposium on Ethnomethodology.* Lafayette, Indiana: Institute for the Study of Social Change, Department of Sociology, Purdue University. Institute Monograph No 1.

Hustler, D. and Payne, G. C. F. (1983). Power in the classroom. *Research in Education* 28:49-64.

Hustler, D. and Payne, G. C. F. (1985). Ethnographic conversational analysis: An approach to classroom talk. In R G. Burgess (Ed.), *Strategies of Educational Research: Qualitative Methods.* London: Falmer.

Hymes, D. (1962). The ethnography of speaking. In T. Gladwin and W. C. Sturtevant (Eds.), *Anthropology and Human Behaviour.* Washington, D C.: Anthropological Society of Washington.

Hymes, D. (1964). A perspective for linguistic anthropology. In Sol Tax (Ed.), *Horizons of Anthropology.* Chicago: Aldine.

Iser, W. (1978). *The Act of Reading.* Baltimore: Johns Hopkins University Press.

Jalbert, P. (1989). Categorisation and beliefs: news accounts of Haitian and Cuban refugees. In D. T. Helm, W. T. Anderson, A J. Meehan and A. W. Rawls (Eds.), *The Interactional Order: New Directions in the Study of Social Order.* New York, NY: Irvington.

Jayyusi, L. (1984). *Categorisation and the Moral Order.* London: Routledge and Kegan Paul.

Jayyusi, L. (1988). Toward a socio-logic of the film text. *Semiotica* 68(3/4):271-96

Jayyusi, L. (1991a). The equivocal text and the objective world *Continuum* 5(1):166-190.

Jayyusi, L. (1991b). Values and moral judgements: communicative praxis as moral order. In G. Button (Ed.), *Ethnomethodology and the Human Sciences* Cambridge, UK: Cambridge: University Press

Jefferson, G. (1974). Error correction as an interactional resource. *Language in Society* 3:181-199.

Jefferson, G. and Lee, J. R. E. (1980). *The Analysis of Conversations in which 'Troubles' and 'Anxieties' are Expressed.* Final Report to the Social Science Council of Great Britain (now the Economic and Social Research Council of Great Britain), and Department of Sociology, University of Manchester, England M13 9PL.

Joint Senate-House Hearings on the Iran-contra affair, Afternoon Session, July 7, 1987, ML/DB Transcript.

Lee, J. R. E. (1984). Innocent victims and evil doers. *Women's Studies International Forum* 7:69-78.

Lee, J. R. E. (1991). Language and culture: the linguistic analysis of culture In G. Button (Ed.), *Ethnomethodology and the Human Sciences*. Cambridge, UK. Cambridge University Press.

Lee, J. R. E. and Watson, D. R. (1993a). Regards et habitudes des passants. *Les Annales de la Recherche Urbaine*, no. 57-8. Paris: Plan Urbain Pulications, 100-9.

Lee, J. R. E. and Watson, D. R. (1993b). *Final Report to the Plan Urbain: Public Space as an Interactional Order*, University of Manchester, Department of Sociology.

Leiter, K. C. W. (1974). Ad hocing in the schools: a study of placement practices in the kindergartens of two schools. In A. V Cicourel et al, *Language Use and School Performance*. New York: Academic Press

Livingston, E. (1987). *Making Sense of Ethnomethodology*. London: Routledge and Kegan Paul.

Louch, A. R. (1968). *Explanation and Human Action*. Oxford: Blackwell

Lynch, M, (1993) *Scientific Practice and Ordinary Action: Ethnomethodology and Social Studies of Science*. New York: Cambridge University Press.

Lynch, M. (1985). Discipline and the material form of images: an analysis of scientific visibility. *Social Studies of Science* 15(1):37-66.

Lynch, M. (1995). Springs of action or vocabularies of motive? In P. Gouk (Ed.), *Wellsprings of Achievement: Cultural and Economic Dynamics in Early Modern England and Japan*. Aldershot: Ashgate Publishing.

Lynch, M. and Bogen, D. (1994). Harvey Sacks's primitive natural science. *Theory, Culture and Society* 11(4):65-104

Lynch, M. and Bogen, D. (1996). *The Spectacle of History: Speech, Text, and Memory at the Iran-Contra Hearings* Durham, NC: Duke University Press.

Lynch, M. and Peyrot, M. (1992). Introduction: a reader's guide to ethnomethodology. *Qualitative Sociology* 15(2):113-22.

Marlaire, C. and Maynard, D. W. (1990). Standardized testing as an interactional phenomenon. *Sociology of Education* 63:83-101.

Maynard, D. W (1984). *Plea Bargaining: The Language of Negotiation*. New York: Plenum Press.

Maynard, D. W. and Clayman, S. (1991) The diversity of ethnomethodology. *Annual Review of Sociology* 385-420.

Maynard, D. W. and Zimmerman, D. H. (1984). Topical talk, ritual and the social organisation of relationships. *Social Psychology Quarterly* 47:301-16

McHoul, A. W. (1978). The organisation of turns at formal talk in the classroom *Language in Society* 7:183-213.

McHoul, A. W. and Watson, D. R. (1984). Two axes for the analysis of 'common sense' and 'formal' geographical knowledge in classroom talk *British Journal of Sociology of Education* 5: 281-302.

Mehan, H. (1983). The role of language and the language of role in institutional decision making. *Language in Society* 12:187-211.

Mehan, H. (1991). The school's work of sorting students. In D. Boden and D H Zimmerman (Eds), *Talk and Social Structure: Studies in Ethnomethodology and Conversation Analysis* Cambridge: Polity Press.

Messinger, S. E., Sampson, H. and Towne, R D. (1962). Life as theater: some notes on the dramaturgical approach to social reality. *Sociometry* 25:98-110.

Moerman, M. (1988). *Talking Culture: Ethnography and Conversation Analysis.* Philadelphia: University of Pennsylvania Press, and Cambridge: Cambridge University Press 1989.

Oteri, J S, Weinberg, M G. and Pinales, M S. (1982). Cross-examination in drug cases In B. Barnes and D. Edge (Eds), *Science in Context: Readings in the Sociology of Science.* Milton Keynes: Open University Press.

Payne, G. C. F. (1976). Making a lesson happen: an ethnomethodological analysis. In M. Hammersley and P Woods (Eds.), *The Process of Schooling.* London and Henley: Routledge and Kegan Paul and Open University Press.

Payne, G. C F. and Hustler, D (1980). Teaching the class: the practical management of a cohort. *British Journal of Sociology of Education* 1(1): 49-66.

Pollner, M. (1975). 'The very coinage of your brain': The anatomy of reality disjunctures *Philosophy of the Social Sciences* 5:411-430

Psathas, G. and Anderson, T. (1990) The 'practices' of transcription in conversation analysis *Semiotica* 78(1/2):75-99.

Reporter's transcript of proceedings (1995) *The People of the State of California v. Orenthal James Simpson.* Superior Court of the State of California for the County of Los Angeles, Case No BA097211, Volume 124, April 12

Sacks, H (1963). Sociological description *Berkeley Journal of Sociology* 8(1):1-16

Sacks, H. (1967). The search for help: No one to turn to. In E. S. Schneidman (Ed.), *Essays in Self-Destruction* New York: Science House.

Sacks, H (1968). Lecture, April 17, University of California, Irvine

Sacks, H (1972). An initial investigation of the usability of conversational data for doing sociology. In D Sudnow (Ed.), *Studies in Social Interaction.* New York: The Free Press.

Sacks, H (1974a). On the analysability of stories by children In R Turner (Ed), *Ethnomethodology: Selected Readings* Harmondsworth: Penguin Books.

Sacks, H. (1974b) An analysis of the course of a joke's telling in conversation In R Bauman and J. Sherzer (Eds), *Explorations in the Ethnography of Speaking* Cambridge: Cambridge University Press

Sacks, H. (1976). On formulating context *Pragmatics Microfiche* 1(7):F5-G8

Sacks, H (1978) Some technical considerations of a dirty joke In J. Schenkein (Ed), *Studies in the Organisation of Conversational Interaction* New York: The Academic Press.

Sacks, H. (1979). Hotrodder: a revolutionary category. In G. Psathas (Ed), *Everyday Language: Studies in Ethnomethodology.* New York, NY: Irvington.

Sacks, H. (1984). Notes on methodology In J. M. Atkinson and J. Heritage (Eds), *Structures of Social Action: Studies in Conversation Analysis.* Cambridge and Paris: Cambridge University Press and Maison des Sciences de l'Homme

Sacks, H. (1989). Harvey Sacks - Lectures 1964-65 In G. Jefferson (Ed), with an Introduction / Memoir by E A Schegloff, *Human Studies* 12(3-4)

Sacks, H (1992a) *Lectures on Conversation, Vol 1* G Jefferson (Ed), with introduction by E A Schegloff Oxford: Basil Blackwell.

Sacks, H. (1992b). *Lectures in Conversation, Vol. 2.* G. Jefferson (Ed), with introduction by E. A. Schegloff. Oxford: Basil Blackwell.

Sacks, H. and Schegloff, E. (1979). Two preferences in the organisation of reference to persons in conversation and their interaction. In G. Psathas (Ed.), *Everyday Language: Studies in Ethnomethodology.* New York: Invington Publishers, Inc.

Sacks, H. Schegloff, E. A and Jefferson, G. (1974). A simplest systematics for the organisation of turn taking for conversation *Language* 50:697-735. (A 'variant version' reprinted in J N. Schenkein (Ed.), (1978). *Studies in the Organisation of Conversational Interaction.* New York, NY: Academic.)

Schegloff, E. A. (1968). Sequencing in conversational openings. *American Anthropologist* 70(6):1075-95.

Schegloff, E. A. (1972). Notes on a conversational practice: formulating place. In D Sudnow (Ed.), *Studies in Social Interaction.* New York, NY: Free Press. (Excerpts reprinted in P. P. Giglioli (Ed.) (1972). *Language and Social Context: Selected Readings.* Harmondsworth: Penguin.).

Schegloff, E A. (1987). Between micro and macro: contexts and other connections In J. Alexander, B. Giesen, R. Munch and N. J. Smelser (Eds.), *The Micro-Macro Link.* Berkeley: University of California Press.

Schegloff, E. A. (1988). Description in the social sciences I : talk-in-interaction *Papers in Pragmatics* 2(1/2):1-24.

Schegloff, E. A. (1989). Harvey Sacks - Lectures 1964-65: An introduction/memoir. *Human Studies* 12 (3/4):185-209.

Schegloff, E A. (1991). Reflections on talk and social structure. In D. Boden and D. Zimmerman (Eds.), *Talk and Social Structure: Studies in Ethnomethodology and Conversation Analysis.* Cambridge: Polity Press.

Schegloff, E. A. (1992). Introduction. In H Sacks, *Lectures on Conversation: Volume One.* Oxford: Basil Blackwell.

Schenkein, J N. (Ed.) (1978). *Studies in the Organisation of Conversational Interaction.* New York, NY: Academic Press.

Schutz, A. (1962) Commonsense and scientific interpretations of human action. In A Schutz, *Collected Papers 1.* The Hague: Martinus Nijhoff

Schutz, A (1964). The stranger: an essay in social psychology. In A Schutz, *Collected Papers II: Studies in Social Theory.* The Hague: Martinus Nijhoff.

Sharrock, W. W. (1974). On owning knowledge. In R. Turner (Ed.), *Ethnomethodology: Selected Readings.* Harmondsworth: Penguin.

Sharrock, W. W. (1989). Ethnomethodology, *British Journal of Sociology* 40(4):657-77.

Sharrock, W. W. and Anderson, R. J. (1982). On the demise of the native: some observations on and a proposal for ethnography. *Human Studies* 5(2):119-35.

Sharrock, W. W. and Anderson, R. J (1986). *The Ethnomethodologists* London: Tavistock.

Sharrock, W. W. and Anderson, R. J. (1991) Epistemology: professional scepticism In G. Button (Ed.), *Ethnomethodology and the Human Sciences.* Cambridge, UK: Cambridge University Press.

Sharrock, W. W. and Button, G (1991). The social actor: social action in real time. In G. Button (Ed.), *Ethnomethodology and the Human Sciences.* Cambridge: Cambridge University Press

Sharrock, W. W. and Coulter, J. (1996). On what we can see. Forthcoming in *Ecological Psychology.*

Sharrock, W. W. and Watson, D. R. (1984). What's the point of 'rescuing motives'? *British Journal of Sociology* 34:435-451.

Sharrock, W. W. and Watson, D. R (1988). Autonomy among social theories: the incarnation of social structures. In N. G. Fielding (Ed), *Actions and Structure. Research Methods and Social Theory* London: SAGE Publications.

Sharrock, W. W. and Watson, D. R. (1989). Talk and police work: notes on the traffic in information. In H Coleman (Ed.), *Working with Language: A Multidisciplinary Consideration of Language Use in Work Contexts* Berlin and New York: Mouton de Gruyter.

Sharrock, W. W., Hughes, J. and Anderson, B. (1986). But a machine surely cannot think! Unpublished paper, University of Manchester, August.

Silverman, D. (1987). *Communication and Medical Practice: Social Relations in the Clinic* London: Sage.

Silverman, D. and Jones, J. (1976). *Organisational Work: The Language of Grading, the Grading of Language.* London: Collier Macmillan.

Smith, G. (Ed.) (forthcoming). *Goffman's Patrimony.* London: Routledge

Speier, M. (1971) The everyday world of the child. In J D. Douglas (Ed.), *Understanding Everyday Life: Towards the Reconstruction of Sociological Knowledge* London: Routledge and Kegan Paul

Speier, M. (1973). *How to Observe Face-to-Face Interaction: A Sociological Introduction.* Pacific Palisades, CA, U S A: The Goodyear Publishing Co

Stone, M. (1995[1988]). *Cross-Examination in Criminal Trials, Second Edition* London: Butterworths.

Times Books (1987). *Taking the Stand: The Testimony of Oliver North.* New York: Times Books.

Tully, J. (1989). Wittgenstein and political philosophy: understanding practices of critical reflection. *Political Theory* 17(2):172-204.

Tyler, S A. (1969b). Introduction In S. A. Tyler (Ed.), *Cognitive Anthropology* New York, NY: Holt, Rinehart and Winston

Tyler, S. A. (1969c). A formal science In S A. Tyler (Ed), *Concepts and Assumptions in Contemporary Anthropology.* Southern Anthropological Society Proceedings, No 3, Athens: University of Georgia Press

Tyler, S. A. (Ed.) (1969a). *Cognitive Anthropology.* New York, NY: Holt, Rinehart and Winston.

Watson, D. R. (1974). The language of race relations: making racial discriminations. *Journal of Comparative Sociology* 2:89-101.

Watson, D. R. (1976). Some conceptual issues in the social identification of 'victims' and 'offenders'. In E C. Viano (Ed), *Victims and Society.* Washington, DC: Visage.

Watson, D. R. (1978). Categorisation, authorisation and blame-negotiation in conversation. *Sociology* 12(1):105-13

Watson, D. R. (1983). The presentation of 'victim' and 'motive' in discourse: the case of police interrogations and interviews. *Victimology: An International Journal* 8(1/2):31-52.

Watson, D R. (1986). Doing the organisation's work: an examination of aspects of the operation of a crisis intervention centre. In S Fisher and A D Todd (Eds.), *Discourse and Institutional Authority: Medicine, Education, and Law.* Advances in Discourse Processes, XIX. Norwood, NJ: Ablex.

Watson, D. R. (1987). Interdisciplinary considerations in the analysis of pro-terms. In G. Button and J. R. E. Lee (Eds.), *Talk and Social Organisation* Clevedon: Multilingual Matters.

Watson, D R (1990). Some features of the elicitation of confessions in murder interrogations. In G. Psathas (Ed.), *Interaction Competence: Studies in Ethnomethodology and Conversation Analysis*, No 1, Washington, DC: International Institute of Ethnomethodology and Conversation Analysis and University Press of America.

Watson, D. R. (1992). The Textual Representation of Nacirema Culture. *Occasional Paper no 35.* Department of Sociology, University of Manchester, Manchester, England M13 9PL

Watson, D. R. (1994). Catégories, séquentialité et ordre social. *Raisons Pratiques* 5: 151-185. Special Issue, December. 'L'Enquête sur les Catégories: de Durkheim à Sacks', (Ed), B. Fradin, L Quéré and J. Widmer. Editions de l'Ecole des Hautes Etudes en Sciences Sociales, Paris.

Watson, D. R. (1995). Some potentialities and pitfalls in the analysis of 'process' and 'personal' change in counselling and therapeutic interaction. In J. Siegfried (Ed.), *Therapeutic and Everyday Discourse as Behavior Change* Norwood, NJ: Ablex Publishing Corporation

Watson, D. R. (forthcoming). Reading Goffman on interaction. In G. W. H. Smith (Ed.), *Goffman's Patrimony.* London: Routledge

Watson, D. R. and Sharrock, W. (1991). Conversational actions and organisational actions. In B Conein, M de Fornel and L Quéré (Eds), *Les Formes de la Conversation* 2. Paris: C N E T Publications, a special issue of the journal *Reseaux*, February.

Watson, D. R. and Weinberg, T. S. (1982). Interviews and the interactional construction of accounts of homosexual identity *Social Analysis* 11: 56-78.

West, C. (1990). Not just doctors' orders: directive-response sequences in patients' visits to women and men physicians *Discourse and Society* 1:85-112

West, C. and Zimmerman, D. H. (1983). Small insults: a study of interrruptions in cross-sex conversations between unaquainted persons. In B. Thorne, C Kramarae and N. Henley (Eds), *Language, Gender and Society.* Rowley, Mass: Newbury House Publishers.

Wieder, D. L. (1971). On meaning by rule. In J. D Douglas (Ed.), *Understanding Everyday Life: Towards the Reconstruction of Sociological Knowledge* London: Routledge and Kegan Paul.

Wieder, D. L. (1974). *Language and Social Reality: The Case of Telling the Convict Code* The Hague: Mouton

Wilson, T P. (1971). Normative and interpretive paradigms in sociology In J. D
    Douglas (Ed.), *Understanding Everyday Life: Towards the Reconstruction of
    Sociological Knowledge*. London: Routledge and Kegan Paul.

Wittgenstein, L. (1968 [1958]). *Philosophical Investigations* Oxford: Blackwell.

Wittgenstein, L. (1969). *On Certainty.* Oxford: Blackwell.

Wong, J. (1996). You're nothin' in this town. *Globe and Mail.* Saturday May 25 1996,
    p C1

Wowk, M T. (1984). Blame allocation, sex and gender in a murder interrogation.
    Women's Studies International Forum 7:75-82.

Zimmerman, D. H. (1974a). The practicalities of rule use. In R Turner (Ed.)
    Ethnomethodology: Selected Readings. Harmondsworth: Penguin Books.

Zimmerman, D. H. (1974b). Preface. In D. L. Wieder, *Language and Social Reality:
    The Case of Telling the Convict Code*. The Hague: Mouton.

Zimmerman, D. H and Pollner, M. (1971). The everyday world as a phenomenon.
    In J. D. Douglas (Ed), *Understanding Everyday Life: Towards the
    Reconstruction of Sociological Knowledge*. London: Routledge and Kegan
    Paul.

Index